OUR OCEAN'S BROKEN HEART

DOINA CORNELL

Ὠκεανός

He who with his sleepless current encircles the whole earth

Aeschylus, Prometheus Bound

Dyma gariad fel y moroedd

Here is love, vast as the ocean

Traditional Welsh hymn

Enjoy the journey!
Doina
19.9.24

CORNELL
SAILING

DEDICATION

To the people of the places we visited in the Arctic and the Pacific, who are on the front-line of climate change. It is not too late for us to humbly learn from their hospitality and their self-sufficiency, and to stand in solidarity with them for climate justice. But I especially dedicate this book to the Tinilaus of Nukulaelae, for the warm welcome you gave us, family to family, love across the ocean.

Doina Cornell

First published 2024

Cornell Sailing, Epsilon House, The Square, Gloucester Business Park, Brockworth, GL3 4AD, U.K.

www.cornellsailing.com
www.doinacornell.com

British Library Cataloguing in Publication Data.

A catalogue record for this book is available from the British Library.

ISBN 978 1 7391889 5 5

Typesetting and origination by Megan Sheer

Printed by Tipografia Everest, Blvd Timisoara 121-137, 061327 Bucuresti, Romania

OTHER CORNELL TITLES:

978-1-4081785-9-1

978-1-4081738-5-5

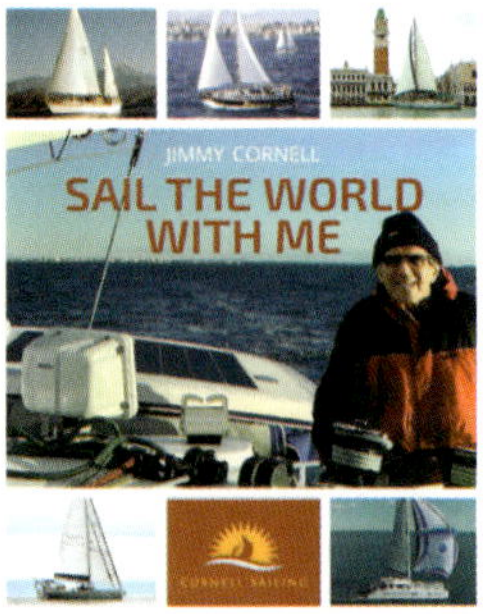

978-1-9160910-5-4

CONTENTS

PREFACE

In 2014 and 2015 I made two sea voyages with my teenage children, Nera and Dan, sailing to parts of the world then on the frontline of climate change. Our personal experiences changed us for good, but were they worth sharing? For a long time after I wondered about shaping my diaries and notes into a book. Busy with other things, I tried many times to abandon the idea of telling these stories, but time and again they returned, and would not let me go, even as the years passed by. It took me thirty years to start writing the story of my sailing childhood, after all, so perhaps it is not so much of a delay.

It is impossible to capture in a few pages all that has happened since 2012 when our idea of sailing to those parts of the world came about: the increasing amounts of data and evidence, expanding our understanding of climate and ecological change, the global political movements pressing for change, the endless negotiations and grand speeches, and the let downs, disappointments, and profound lack of progress. What was urgent in 2012 is even more so today, and we are still nowhere near as far forward on the path to controlling our excess carbon emissions as we need to be, for the comfort of our future human lives. We've now seen what efforts can be made when a virus threatens us, but can we do the same for a far greater threat?

In this book I write about land that is not my land, about places and people who must tell their own stories, as they, and not I, are at the centre of them. I am a white European. One, granted, who has experienced racist taunts and othering as a person of dark hair and brown skin, but I am part of that continent. I cannot erase the centuries of exploitation, cruelty, slavery, oppression, infection and debt that has not been atoned for, nor reparation paid for, and continues right to this day.

All I can say, humbly, is I see it, I know it, I acknowledge it.

Every person of European descent, every citizen of the global North, we must all acknowledge this truth, before we have the audacity to put pen to paper.

All I can offer here are some fragments, imperfect and incomplete that they are, which may give you pause for reflection, or open your eyes to something you did not know.

After all these years, I send this book, like a child, into the world, with a mother's pride. You may take it or leave it, but these fragments, this story, I give to you humbly, with love and hope.

Doina

Wall on Priory Road, Dartford, Kent, embedded with pieces of Arctic rock.

BY WAY OF INTRODUCTION

WINTER 2019

'There it is!'

I jumped out of the car, ran across the road, and laid my hand on one of the black rocks embedded into the wall. Nera joined me. She touched a rock with her finger.

Dan was waiting in the car. It had taken us a while to find this place. Five years earlier, in the course of reading one of the books we took with us on our travels, somewhere very far away from here, in stormy northern seas, seasick and bunk bound, I'd read about this rock and determined one day to track it down back in England.

The old wall, made up of grey stones, with black rocks added here and there in no particular pattern, seemed rather out of place beside the modest terraced houses on this ordinary road in Dartford, Kent, on the eastern outskirts of London. A car passed and the young men in it turned their heads to us and stared. I doubt few passers-by noticed this wall, and yet the fate of our planet – or at least, our human life upon it – might be symbolised by those forgotten bits of black stone.

Four hundred years ago the black rocks were dug out of the icy ground of the Arctic by freeminers from the Forest of Dean (only a few miles from where I am now writing this in my Gloucestershire home), and also men from Cornwall, my birthplace. Laden into ships' holds to sail back across the stormy north Atlantic to England, a cargo that carried men's hopes and desires, to make untold riches from old things torn out of the earth. Martin Frobisher had found the black rock, having led the first English expedition to the north in 1574. The desire to discover a new route through the northern icy seas across the top of the world, all the way to the riches of India, burned bright in the hearts of those early modern explorers. Frobisher set off down the River Thames and Queen Elizabeth I waved him off from a window of

Greenwich Palace, which lies on the southern bank of the river. The expedition returned some months later, having found a cold land, bound by ice, but no way through to the East. A black rock 'as great as a half-penny loaf' was brought back and lay forgotten for a long while. Until an Italian alchemist claimed he'd extracted gold from it.

The prospect of gold caused great excitement: those were feverish times in Elizabethan London, when the modern and the medieval worlds, science and superstition, melded into one heady mix. With support from the Virgin Queen, funding was raised for two more expeditions to the north, or, as the Queen named the new land, *Meta Incognita*. Two hundred tons of ore were extracted by the labour of the Forest of Dean and Cornish miners. A smelting plant was constructed near the river Thames in Dartford and for five years they tried to get gold out the tons of ore that were brought there.

But there was no gold and the rock was worthless. Today, all that is left of those broken dreams are a few specimens forgotten in the wall on the Priory Road and the local museum.

The lands of the north, of course, were not 'Incognita'. They were already known, intimately, to the people whose ancestors had made them home for thousands of years. Three Inuit people, a man, woman and child, were forcibly taken from their land by the expedition, and brought back along with the rocks. The Inuit man, Kalicho, was made to show his kayaking skills on the river at Bristol. I've often stared at those brown still waters framed by the green slopes of the Avon gorge and wondered how it was for him, taken so far from his home, to this alien, mild place of trees and white-skinned people. He, and the woman, Arnaq, died soon after their arrival and were buried in a Bristol graveyard, while the child perished not long after in London. They were not the first nor would be the last victims of European first contact.

And, in other places, other times, men did find a way to extract riches from the earth – the fossil remains of ancient forests, compressed into a thick black oil. And even today, they still cast their eyes to the Arctic, for oil and the earth's treasures that they covet.

A short distance upriver from Dartford, is the place where my own sea life began some forty years ago. The Thames winds past Greenwich from where the Queen waved farewell to Frobisher, up to the Royal Albert Docks, once a bustling part of the port of London, helping build a world empire of trade, sugar and enslaved people. But when I first became acquainted with the docks as a small child, the empire was threadbare, and the docklands were a broken wasteland of empty warehouses and mountainous tips of rubbish. A place of dreams too,

Launch of Aventura, 1974

in the warehouses where small sailing boats were fitted out for long voyages, to escape from the trials and confines of grim 1970s Britain. From here my parents launched our own boat into the muddy waters of the Thames and started to make their own dreams a reality. I was seven then, and for seven years we sailed around the world.

Years later, I wrote about this in my book, *A Child of the Sea* and when I finished writing it, at the end of 2011, I thought I had come to the end of that story.

I was wrong.

THE ODYSSEY BEGINS

In 2012 my father Jimmy asked me to accompany him to a US boat show where he was signing books and giving talks. After we returned from our circumnavigation he'd built a reputation as a best-selling author of weather and routing reference books, helping thousands of sailors decipher the patterns of weather around the world, especially as regards the predictable nature of hurricane and cyclone seasons and trade winds that for centuries have allowed sailors to circumnavigate the world. His knowledge was not book-based as he had sailed twice more around the world after our own voyage, thousands of miles under the keel, and interviewed hundreds of sailors to gather data.

The fourth Aventura, carrying her message

'I've had an idea,' he said when we were flying high above the Atlantic. I wondered what might be coming next. He'd had a lot of ideas in his life, and made many of them a reality.

'I want to organise a round the world sailing rally to raise awareness of climate change,' he told me. 'I've been reflecting on what's going on – there are too many still denying climate change, despite the scientific evidence. And places that you and I sailed to all those years ago, like Tuvalu in the Pacific, where we were warmly welcomed as a family, are now under threat from changing weather patterns and rising sea levels. I want to give something back. We sailors need to show them solidarity.'

He paused.

'Would you like to help me organise this event?' he asked.

(The irony of thinking about climate change on a transatlantic flight is not lost on me now).

He and I had worked together on and off over the years, on books and sailing events. He was 72 and supposed to be retired from event organising, although he remained busy with his writing and lectures. He had launched the Atlantic Rally for Cruisers in 1986 which was the largest ever rally for amateur sailing yachts and made it into the Guinness Book of Records. From that had followed many other rallies, across the Atlantic and around the world.

Meanwhile, I'd been living in a Gloucestershire village far from the sea for the last ten years and I'd just been elected that year to serve a four-year term as a local district councillor. Small town politics, being a mother of two young children, and working at part-time jobs I didn't much care for, just to pay the bills, seemed to anchor me to the land. I'd taken no more long ocean passages since my children were born. The ocean and the island nations of the Pacific felt a long way from my life. And yet – at times, the ebb and flow of the river tides, the wide-open skies of the Severn estuary a few miles across the flat lands from my house, and the salty odour of a warm westerly wind rushing over from Wales, sometimes made me yearn for the sea I'd left behind. So I answered without any hesitation.

'Yes,' I said.

A few months later, early in 2013, we launched the Blue Planet Odyssey. Jimmy devised a Northern and a Southern route around the world, to the Northwest Passage in the Arctic, and to remote islands in the Pacific and Indian Oceans. Hundreds of sailors all over the world expressed an interest in taking part, although as the time came to make a firm decision to take two years off to sail around the world, this dwindled down to a dedicated handful.

The icy wonder of Antarctica

We had no plans to take part ourselves in the Odyssey. But Nera, who was thirteen, changed that. My father told her about the Northern Route that would attempt the Northwest Passage.

'I want to do that,' she said straight away. Ever since she was tiny she'd had an affinity for animals, and as she grew older this became more specifically, wolves, and Arctic foxes, and anything to do with the coldest and wildest places on the earth.

'But I haven't got a boat anymore,' my father said.

'So why don't you get one?' she asked.

So he did. He designed a boat, *Aventura*, specifically for high latitude sailing in the tough seas of the extreme north and south of our planet, and partnered with a French boatyard to have her built. You can read about the concept of the Expedition yacht that became a prototype for more boats, and all the technical stuff in his own writings.

The north tempted me too. In 1996, in my child-free days, I sailed with him and my brother Ivan from Chile and Argentina, across the Drake Passage to Antarctica. The wonders of that trip never left me. Not all sailors yearn for the warmth of the tropics: any sailor who has visited the high latitudes of the ocean, north or south, the great waves of the Southern Ocean, the fantastical icescapes of frozen seas

Off Cape Horn

and broken glaciers, and the wild dark lands of Cape Horn, will tell you how addictive it is – and I believe a sliver of ancient blue ice had burrowed its way into my soul and left me with some sort of yearning. So the prospect of a trip to the icy north, of which I knew almost nothing, was very appealing.

All of this meant a great deal more preparation, on top of all the other work, as now we had our own expedition to organize as well as the rally.

And I promised my son Dan, who was then eleven, that I'd sail with him somewhere warm, on the second part of the Odyssey, into the Pacific.

❄ ❄ ❄

A key part of the Blue Planet Odyssey event was an educational and citizen science programme that was my responsibility to develop. We encouraged our sailor participants to build links with their local schools and reach out to schools along the route so children around the world could link up. As I undertook the research for the educational and scientific pages for our website, I found I was taking a deep dive into what was currently understood about climate change in 2013, and more specifically, the threat it posed to the ocean and the island nations that border and depend upon the seas. I was aware of climate change, but to be quite truthful, it was not much more than a concern which I accepted, niggling somewhere vaguely at my conscience, but little more than that. Most of what I knew related to land-based concerns and I didn't know much of the ocean's part in all this.

One of the common themes of ocean science is that despite the ocean's health being so vital to the planet's wellbeing, scientists admit that there is still much they do not know about the state of the seas. The ocean (there is technically only one ocean, even though it goes by different names in different parts of the planet) is vast and mostly unknown by humans: the last wild frontier of our planet. It's a costly business to fund a scientific expedition to head off and study just one tiny and remote portion of the sea. The scarcity of data from much of the ocean was a major problem for scientists and meteorologists; data was largely concentrated around the major commercial shipping routes of the North Atlantic and North Pacific. There are enormous 'data sparse areas', such as the Southern and Arctic Ocean, and remote parts of the South Pacific.

This is where we sailors came in and the Odyssey could play its part. Small yachts travel off the beaten track, well away from the shipping channels, to the remotest parts of the ocean. We could be of some use. Onboard ship observations have been at the heart of marine science and weather throughout history, and even now, with the advent of satellite observations, the data that ships and other vessels can provide remains of great importance.

Our Odyssey formed a partnership with NOAA (the US National Oceanic and Atmospheric Administration) and JCOMMOPS (the Joint Technical Commission of the World Meteorological Organization and Intergovernmental Oceanographic Commission of UNESCO), joining their scheme of getting volunteer ships and boats to deploy autonomous scientific floats in remote parts of the ocean that were hard for scientists to reach. We also connected with citizen science projects on sea bird sightings and the Secchi disk project taking readings to check on the state of plankton in the seas.

Of which more later.

The Ocean is under the most unprecedented threat in human history... and is critical to enabling life to exist on Earth. Yet ... the Ocean and the life within it are the least understood components of our planet.

2013 State of the Ocean Report
(IPSO, International Programme on the State of the Ocean)

I immersed myself in the science of the day, especially in relation to the places we were to visit, and the ocean we'd sail on to get there: new studies and data were coming out thick and fast. I learnt of the threat of warming waters to the polar ice caps and coral reefs, of rising sea levels for those Pacific island communities where I'd spent my sailing childhood, and what was a relatively new field of study, how the absorption of excess CO_2 was making the ocean more acidic and impacting on those organisms that constructed their carapaces and skeletons from the carbon in the water, and needed the fine chemical balance of the sea to stay as it was.

WHERE IS GLOBAL WARMING GOING?

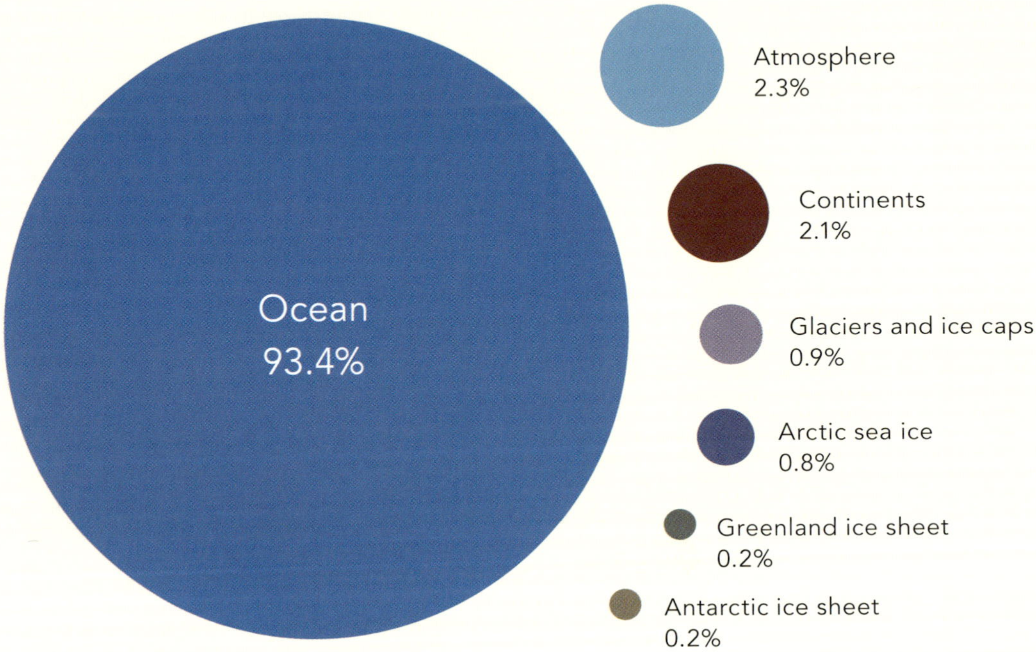

The reports were devastating. There was a heap of data out there that was being gathered together, and all of it stacked up to one undeniable fact. The health of our lives upon the planet depended on the health of our ocean.

And our sea was getting sick.

The ocean was absorbing more than 90% of the heat added to the climate by increasing temperatures, and one third of carbon dioxide emissions. Warming and acidification combined might see the end of tropical coral reefs and threaten the formation of the delicate carbon shells of the tiniest but most essential of creatures like phytoplankton, on whose photosynthesis we depend for some 50% of the oxygen we breathe. Pollution, overfishing and extractive industries added to the impact and all of this together was having a greater impact that previously understood. But as most humans are firmly land-based, most give little thought to the ocean and its role in keeping us alive and healthy.

Turns out for some forty years I'd been living in ignorance. Blown out of the water. It was a revelation.

And it hit me very hard. Because this was my sea, my ocean.

I'm sure we all have a favoured childhood place: a house, a yard, or a scrap of green somewhere where we hung out and played as kids. For me, that place was the sea, my home for seven formative years as I moved from childhood to adolescence. There was no special place on land of warm childhood memories, sweet and soft, like a Proustian madeleine dipped in tea, to sustain me. My place was blue and salty, immense and yet as familiar to me as the back of my hand.

And in all the years since, I'd always thought the sea was doing ok. It was ageless, and aside from a bit too much plastic, I believed all our blood and our human crimes eventually would wash away, and the sea would go on forever.

So it was terrible, what I learnt. So terrible I wished I could unlearn it. Wish I could stick my head right down into the sand, know nothing, block my ears, and be blithe and uncaring. Because when you know, and you care, how can you not despair?

I am a mother and my children will live in a world – well, what sort of world will it be? A less ignorant one, that is for sure.

And the sea will be saltier then, for all the mothers' tears.

Me and my brother Ivan playing as we cross the Pacific, 1978

ARCTIC DIARY: SEEKING THE NORTHWEST PASSAGE

MAY – SEPTEMBER 2014

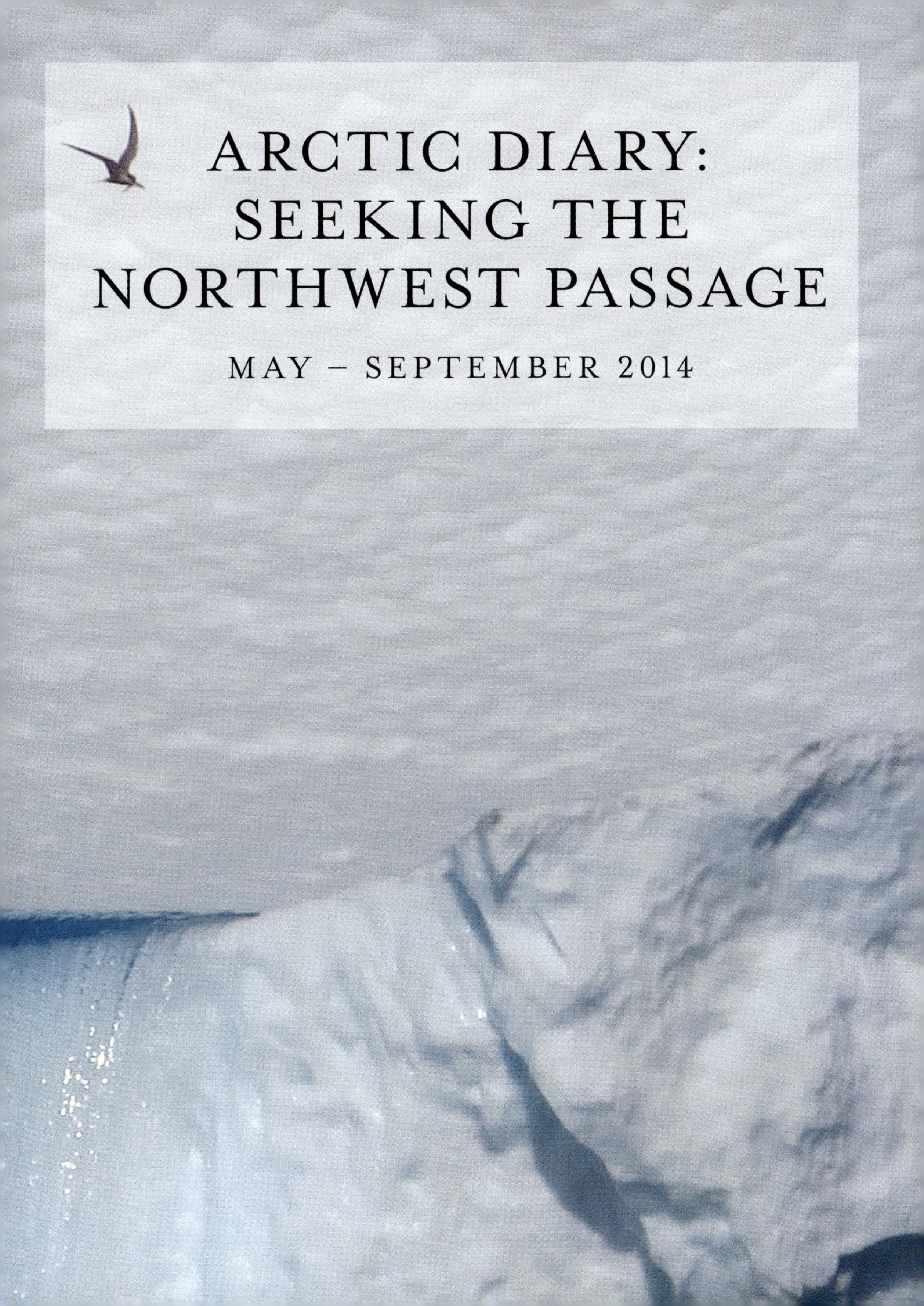

LONDON LAUNCH

The new boat *Aventura IV* was launched in France, where she had been built, and then sailed up the Thames to Limehouse Basin in east London, not so far from where our very first *Aventura* was launched in 1974. Forty years ago. Friends and family gather by the dockside, many of whom were also present all those years ago, when my cousin Marianne and I had performed the naming ceremony as small girls. Marianne, who is a filmmaker, is going to join us on the expedition north. This time it is our firstborn daughters, Lina and Nera, who crack the bottle of bubbly on the grey sleek bow and make a little speech:

We name this ship Aventura and God bless all those who sail in her.

Aventura looks like a serious boat for the north, with a strong aluminium hull. She is well-insulated against cold weather, and has solar panels, as well as a wind turbine and hydrogenerator, to make her more self-sufficient. *The Ocean, our Future*, the Blue Planet Odyssey motto, is written in bold letters on the boom of the main mast.

My brother Ivan and I, now both in our forties, have a mad impulse to climb the main mast to the spreaders some twenty feet above the deck. We balance there on one leg, recreating a family photo from many years ago. My father laughs, and grabs his camera, just as he did when we were kids.

Ivan will join my father, and new crewmember Nick, to sail *Aventura* north, to Nuuk, the capital of Greenland. We will join the boat there once Nera's school holidays begin, along with the rest of the crew. I'm sorry Ivan's work means he can only take time off for the maiden voyage, and not join us for the rest of the summer as I would have enjoyed sailing with him again.

Nera and I visit the National Maritime Museum near Ivan's house in Greenwich. The museum has a huge floor map of the world where the many islands and passages of the northern part of the American continent, Canada to Alaska, are clearly marked. Nera walks the floor, stepping carefully on the sea, past the islands, from east to west, Atlantic to Pacific, which is our intended route.

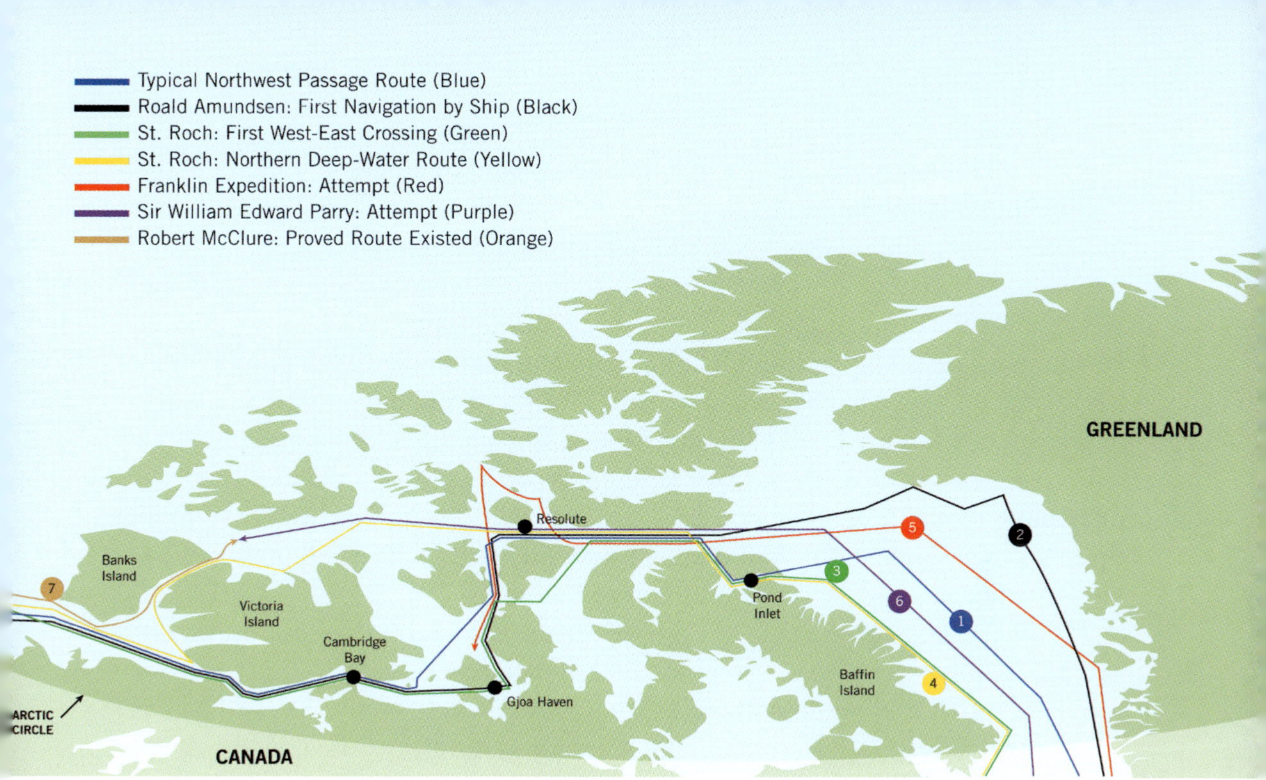

'The easiest way to do it,' I say. There is a long and difficult journey ahead of us, and many sailors have gone before us and failed. The museum has a small exhibition about the efforts by sailors to explore the Northwest Passage through the 19th century. The so-called 'Northwest Passage' is in fact not one single passage, but names the sea route that winds its way through the maze of islands at the top of the North American continent, from the Davis Strait in the east to the Bering Strait in the west, connecting the Atlantic to the Pacific Ocean. For most of the year the Arctic Sea is frozen solid, and although the sea ice melts somewhat in the short summer seasons, it has never been enough to let a boat get all the way through. Only in 1904 did Norwegian explorer Roald Amundsen finally manage this feat, but even he could only do this by overwintering twice. A few specially reinforced ships made the transit subsequently, but it was in the summer of 2007 when the warming climate, increasing the summer melt of the ice, meant that the Northwest Passage became first open to ships without the need of an icebreaker. And then smaller vessels such as sailing yachts decided to try.

To date, even now, very few had made it through. A transit remained one of the great sailing challenges, and more people have climbed Everest.

In preparation for the trip, I read as many historical accounts as I could of the first European attempts to find a passage; more recent stories by modern sailors trying to make it through the ice; and writing from those peoples whose forebears had lived in the Arctic long before Europeans arrived.

Reading modern-day accounts and testimony, such as *Arctic Voices: Resistance at the tipping point*, which brings together voices from indigenous leaders, activists, scientists and writers, it would appear that even now, many outside view the North as just a blank space 'up there', empty and clean – a white page to be written on. The people with pens, drills, hard hats, money, political power – they have much the same, unchanged attitude as the explorers, colonisers, missionaries of the past five hundred years, and the Queen who called the land *incognita*.

If we cannot break with our tradition, of the attitude that runs like a straight dirty black thread from Frobisher and his rock right through to the New Arctic Prospectors – we are in trouble – and yet, how on earth to change human nature? How to build a completely different way of living?

The black, black oil is still lying beneath the cold seabed of the north and calling, calling with its siren voice to those who want to extract and sell it. Siren voice – if you don't stop up your ears, like Ulysses, if you listen to the call, you'll send your ship crashing onto the rocks. The ship is our dear planet, and then we all will be lost at sea.

OUR OCEAN BLOG: INTRODUCING NERA

My name is Nera Cornell. I am a 15-year-old British teenager, and I go to Rednock School in a small town called Dursley in the UK.

My hobbies are horse-riding, art, and Explorer Scouts mainly. I also happen to be a fan of music, sing, and play guitar. Other than that, I love all kinds of animals, but especially Arctic foxes, and wolves.

So, when I was told I would be sailing through the Northwest Passage, who wouldn't get excited?

I mean icebergs, animals, the sea, a nice boat, and exciting new communities. That was just a few of the things I was thinking about, but I'm also really interested in science, and the animals especially thrilled me.

I can't exactly put into words how much this means to be doing this, with climate change affecting Earth, the Arctic has begun to melt, which is the main reason we believe we can accomplish this hard voyage through the ice.

So, either way, my name's Nera and I will be blogging about the exciting things we'll be getting up to in the Arctic! Hopefully, you'll learn things as well.

HEADING NORTH

The plane flies high above the Greenland ice sheet. Gigantic masses of white cover the land, and there are lakes of melt water shimmering on top of the ice, a startling bright blue. At the edges, the ice melts and spreads, white tongues pressing down into valleys and feeding pale rivers. Where the land is exposed, the mountains are dark brown, almost black. There are no roads, no humans, nothing is scratched onto this earth, and the land looks ancient and inscrutable.

I read *Greenland Today* and the inflight magazine *Suluk* to pass the time. There are articles about climate change and polar bears. But the adverts are all for prospectors, exploration, and mining:

> *Greenland remains one of the least explored frontiers and hosts an impressive array of mineral deposits and geological environments... Your strongest partner in support and logistics for oil and gas exploration in Greenland.*

This contradiction bugs me as I gaze out the plane window at the ice and the dark land. After eighteen months of preparation, this is it.

Mountains of paperwork and emails, hundreds of potential sailors wanting to join the Blue Planet Odyssey, months of preparing an event that spans all the ocean and continents of the world, weeks of getting a household ready to run without me, as I have taken Nera and left the other half of the family, husband and son, to cope for a summer on their own. At the end of it all, it comes down to this: only two small yachts have committed to the Odyssey attempt at the Northwest Passage – *Aventura*, now waiting for us in Nuuk, where we are headed, and the British yacht *Suilven* that is making its own way north.

All the worry and stress, preparing for this journey, I imagine now dropping off me, smashing on the ice below.

The plane lands at Kangerlussuaq airport where we must wait for a connection south down to Nuuk. Nera and I step outside into the sun. There is a fierce northern bite in the wind and not a bird or any other living thing moves in the landscape, not even an insect. Dark hills surround us on all sides. I imagine that if you walked away from here, you'd go for days never meeting a living soul or seeing anything but the bare and inscrutable land.

The airport building is small, modest, and crowded. Besides a few tourists, the people waiting are blond Danes and dark Inuit. These people, living on opposite sides of the Atlantic for centuries, in very similar northern, cold climates: why so dark, so fair? The fault-line of humanity, into which so much pain, hatred and misunderstanding has fallen over the centuries, between the pale and dark peoples of our world, seems to be physically represented here amongst the passengers patiently waiting together. These Arctic lands were populated thousands of years before the Europeans arrived, as people crossed over the Bering Strait land bridge from Siberia to America. Their descendants, who inhabit the Arctic region stretching from Canada across to Greenland, survived for centuries in this harsh climate of extreme cold. First contact with Europeans was probably with the Vikings who arrived in Greenland in the 10th century BCE, but by the early 15th century the Viking settlements were abandoned, and Europeans forgot about the Arctic regions for a while.

❄ ❄ ❄

Our connecting flight takes us to Nuuk where *Aventura* is waiting for us, in a port full of rusty fishing boats. For the first time, all eight of us crew are together. As well as my cousin Marianne, Nera, Jimmy and myself, we are joined by French sailing journalist Luc, Emily, ocean campaigner, and as extra crew, English couple Nick and Nikki who are experienced in sailing high latitudes. We are going to be spending six to eight weeks together on this small 45-foot yacht. You might consider this number of people too much, but my father was not very good at saying no to people who asked to come along. We shall see. For the moment, we are all excited to begin our adventure.

FROM NERA'S OCEAN BLOG

When we finally arrived at Nuuk, as you step off the plane you get hit by this wonderful feeling – I seriously hope it wasn't just me – as the air is so much fresher reminding me of cold water. Then you get hit by the sudden change of environment...

No trees.

You think about the small fact that the landscape would look different, but the reality is surreal.

Nera and I take a walk into the town. There is a feeling of temporariness, as if Nuuk barely makes an impact on the land and there are no names on the white crosses of the graveyard. The colourful houses have no foundations and perch on top of the grey rocks. Buildings turn blank faces outwards, without large windows, so when we step into the busy and bright mall it feels like the Tardis, bigger on the inside.

Beyond the old town, the sea is sparkling blue and there is no ice in sight. We pick a few sorrel leaves to nibble, wondering if we will find these up north when we are low on fresh produce and might need a boost of vitamin C. Along the shore the sand and stones look like a typical English beach, although the canoes lined up in the racks are too thin and sharp for England. At the water's edge there is an impressive pink granite statue of a sea goddess, surrounded by sea creatures. A man combs her long and beautiful hair and she rests her hand on the head of a bear. She is Sedna, Mother of the Sea, and she has other names also. In many of the myths about her, she loses her fingers from cold, or her father chops them off, and they turn into seals and sea creatures. She is angry and vengeful, and a shaman must comb her hair to placate her rage so the hunters can have a good hunt. As the tide comes in, the water covers her. But I wonder – why is her back to the sea?

Another statue, of a man in European clothes, stands tall on the headland above her, looking out to sea. Hans Egede came here in the 18th century from Norway in a vain hope to find the Norse people who hadn't been heard from for some five hundred years. He founded the town, and proceeded to convert the Inuit Greenlanders to the Christian faith, though many succumbed to European viruses and disease.

It is time for us to return. On the grassy slope above the dock, a black crow watches us and caws. Nera wonders if it is an omen.

❄ ❄ ❄

The crew gathers in the main cabin to discuss the plan. It would appear that our chances of getting through the Passage, despite the warmer summers, are still slim. The summer season is very short when the sea ice which formed over the long winter, adding to the ice left from previous winters, melts to a greater or lesser extent. A passage through the many islands and channels of the archipelago may at this short moment be possible, although each year the ice melts differently in different places, so the route is never quite the same. There are about seven possible routes, though the most commonly used is that which runs from the Barrow Strait into Peel Sound and Victoria Strait, and from there to Alaska and the Bering Strait.

What is predictable is that the ice usually retreats from west to east, so most years the eastern approaches are the last to become free of ice, which makes it more challenging for us.

'So,' says my father, 'In order to have a realistic chance of getting through, we can't spend too long in Greenland, by about the 25th July we need to be on station, at the easternmost point of the Northwest Passage.'

'And then what?' someone asks.

'Beyond that, we just don't know, how long it'll take, or even if the ice will melt enough for us to get through. We will just have to get there, and then be prepared to wait for the right conditions.'

Our time was very limited: the transit had to be completed in the late part of the summer, before the days got shorter and nights longer again. Sailing, or motoring, in the dark, through the ice, was not advisable, and in the northern part of the Pacific the weather would rapidly deteriorate as the short summer ended. We had to get through quickly, before the window of opportunity snapped shut. Nera has been given extra time off school, but I wonder how far we can stretch our time beyond the school summer holidays. By early September we will need to be heading home. At present, however, this seems far enough away, and doesn't concern us.

The crew talks on into the evening. The night never comes; here, the summer daylight is never-ending which lightens our spirits. Despite the obstacles ahead, and the uncertainty, we all feel hopeful, and ready for the adventure ahead.

NERA'S OCEAN BLOG, WILDLIFE IN NUUK

Oddly enough, when you arrive at a harbour, you expect it to be filled with squawking gulls. There really aren't many: a few gulls and some huge and loud crows. This may be because of the cold climate, but seagulls do live in Greenland.

To be honest, I kind of wanted to see my first seals alive rather than being tugged behind a boat and then hung from a crane by the tail flippers, draining blood into the water through their oozing eyeballs.

Enough of the gore, that's Inuit traditional lifestyles. They had to survive on hunting their own meat and that same tradition has lasted through the ages.

One piece of wildlife which seems to be abundant is unfortunately the insects and mosquitoes.

A few chores left to do. We are required by the authorities to have a gun, to guard against polar bears. Jimmy visits the nearby fuel station that doubles as a hardware and hunting store and discovers they have a stash of old Soviet rifles. The man in the store is a bit vague as to where they've come from, but Jimmy buys one, with some bullets. Helpfully, Nick and Nikki are ex-military, so know what to do with it, as none of the rest of us have a clue.

We gather in the cockpit and Nick runs through the crew's safety briefing – lifejackets and man overboard drill. A rota is set up to share out cooking and cleaning as well as watches for when we are at sea. We've a few last fresh items to buy although the boat was loaded with most of its provisions before leaving London. The supermarket cashier stares in disbelief at the eighty oranges we pile onto the check out. Every available space on the boat is crammed with supplies. I've been put in charge of overseeing the provisioning; how much are eight people likely to eat over six to eight weeks? Bread and cake mixes, canned food, special vegetarian meals for Nera were loaded on board before *Aventura* left London. There are sacks of potatoes and onions picked up in the Orkneys on the way here, stored below the floorboards, and trays of Orkney eggs kept cool in one of the lockers out in the cockpit.

Nera and I occupy the forward cabin in the bow of the boat which will be our home for the rest of the summer. Netting is fixed to the ceiling above our double bunk and there are apples and oranges and about 200 cereal bars swinging above us as we fall asleep. Nera is excited – tomorrow she begins her first major ocean voyage.

AT LAST TO SEA

A grey fog settles over the sea as we leave Nuuk. There is no wind, but the sea is not calm – a swell left from long gone winds makes the boat pitch up and down. Nera gets seasick.

'Fresh air will help,' I tell her. She curls herself up in a miserable ball in a corner of the cockpit.

NERA'S BLOG – FIRST OCEAN VOYAGE

I knew in the back of my mind that I would get seasick, but the reality is a lot less appetising than the thought. I threw up twice in about 1 hour, but not again after that and I now feel a lot better.

Your body has to get used to the constant movement of the boat: this can take up to 3 days.

The day passes slowly. Watches come and go. Off watch we eat, read or sleep in our bunks. Nera doesn't have to take watches, as the youngest one onboard, and I share my shift with my father and Marianne. Our first night watch begins at 2am. There is still no wind, and the fog means the visibility extends no more than half a mile around. The daylight does not end: grey seas and grey skies are close about us. We've yet to see any ice.

Six long, cold hours. All the clothing which seemed far too ungainly when tried on at home is now not so at all. I'm wearing so many layers: thermals, fleece trousers, cashmere jumper, two fleece jackets, ocean waterproof jacket and trousers, hat and neck warmer and yet I cannot get warm, and my feet are freezing despite extra warm socks and seaboots.

So. So...

After all these months of imagining it all in bright colours – books I have read, websites studied, stories and accounts peopled with characters, adventures, history, tragedy, oil, climate change, heartfelt words, passion to defend one's traditional life, one's unspoilt wilderness – a fiery cauldron of facts and beliefs about the North swirling in my head – the reality turns out to be no more than a little grey boat pushing through grey seas. Nothing at all to be seen except a solitary sea bird, a fulmar, wheeling around us and taking a curious look before flying off into the grey.

Is this all it has come to? I feel utterly disconnected.

TRAWLING FOR PLASTIC

Coming off watch at 8am and crawling into my sleeping bag is very welcome. And Nera feels a little better today.

Emily has brought with her an ocean trawl that can capture the tiniest of plastic fragments from the ocean. Long before it came to the attention of the world, she has been campaigning and spreading the message about how bad plastic pollution is. The trawl we have now is borrowed from Five Gyres, the organisation that raised awareness of the Great Garbage Patch, that floating dump of plastic and garbage the size of Texas swirled into one place by ocean currents in the remotest part of the Pacific Ocean. Now we know there are five gyres – one for each ocean.

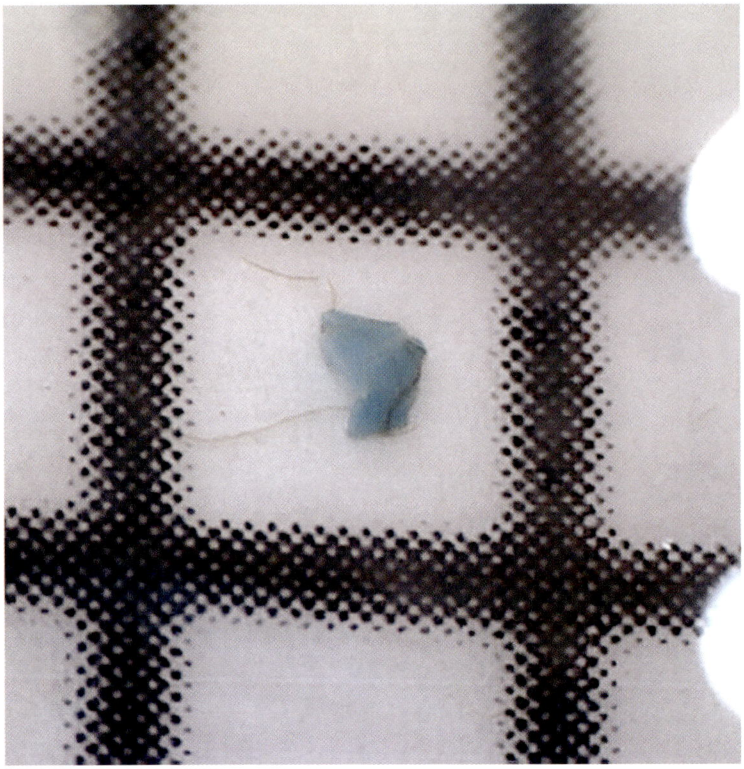

The trawl is an ingenious device with an aluminium frame and a very fine nylon mesh that is dragged through the water beside the boat as we sail. Seabirds come to take a look, perhaps hoping it is a net. After an hour or so it is hauled in and Emily and Nera tip out what has been caught in the mesh and inspect the findings. There is a tiny fish and plenty of seaweed. Nera examines some of the tiniest particles with a handheld microscope that plugs into our laptop. The most outlandish and unnatural specks of colour turn out to be some miniscule bits of plastic and fibre. Emily lays them onto paper marked out with gridlines to show their dimensions.

This was a tiny sample of water in one of the remotest parts of the vast ocean – and so you can be pretty sure there is now plastic everywhere.

'Can we know how old this plastic is, or where it came from?' I ask. No, we can't know that, Emily explains. It could have come out of the melting ice, a fifty-year-old fibre from someone's 1960s rayon mini-dress that has drifted here in the air or water. Or more mundane, the more modern thread of a Greenlandic fishing boat's mooring line.

NERA'S BLOG

We deployed the trawl into the water and jotted down the time and the GPS coordinates to show how long the trawl was in the water and how far it went. We found quite a few very small fragments which were unfortunately clearly plastic.

Nera: What is the use of trawling for plastic?

Emily: It's so we can understand how much plastic is in the ocean, where it's accumulating, whether or not it's breaking down, if it's harming marine life, where it's coming from, and how to stop more plastic getting into the ocean.

Nera: Why is it so important to complete trawls in the Arctic?

Emily: We have very little understanding on how much plastic is in Arctic waters so the samples we collect will build on that knowledge. We will be able to see how far into this remote region just how far our plastic has managed to reach.

Nera: How can anyone get involved?

Emily: You can get involved by going to your nearest waterway (the sea or any river) and look at any plastics you find there. You can use an app called Marine debris tracker which allows you to log how much plastic you find and the types. You could also set up a plastic clean up with your local school. You can also reduce your personal plastic consumption by thinking about single use plastic like plastic bags or drinks bottles which are designed to only be used once.

Jimmy explains the Arctic circle to Nera with the aid of an orange

By afternoon we cross the Arctic Circle, considered to be the true start of the Northwest Passage, and as we do, the clouds clear away to reveal the Greenland coast in all its glory. High dark hills in places topped by white ice. In the calm water black heads of seals pop up to examine us, like curious dark-haired swimmers, but before any of us can grab a camera, they are gone again. The sun paints silver and gold upon the smooth waves, pools of light gathering and sliding over the sea.

It is a restful picture to gaze upon – to port the sun, to starboard the land, and in between the grey-blue ocean. Her face is one that I have looked upon for most of my life, and yet only now I've learnt what is a terrible secret, slowly being unpicked and revealed to the world. She shows us her blue and beautiful face which looks as ageless as ever, but she is sick – hidden like the portrait of Dorian Gray – the secret picture is one of rot. Too much plastic, too much heat, too much CO_2.

These things can be measured.

You throw down a net and up comes a piece of blue plastic less than two mm long.

That's all.

TOWARDS AASIAAT

Our first iceberg appears, sailing south, a bright shape against the grey. Sea birds are sprinkled black upon its white surface. A deep fissure has opened up into its heart, where I see that ancient blue I remember from Antarctica.

The wind continues to elude us and we have yet to sail, the engine has been on continually. Jimmy had anticipated, in the planning of this expedition, that weather conditions were likely to be unfavourable, with either contrary winds, or light winds and calms, when we would have to motor not sail. This meant taking a good reserve of fuel and, although there are fuel depots along the way, we cannot take for granted being able to refuel, as some locations might not be accessible due to the ice or weather, or the depot may be out of supplies. As a sailing boat, this unfortunately means relying on ship's diesel, fossil fuel, for this voyage. In the design stages, Jimmy had investigated more environmental options but a reliable form of electric regeneration for the engine, or hydrogen fuel, was a technology not yet available for boats sailing far from land. We did at least have the capacity to generate much of the power we needed for day-to-day consumption from the boat's solar panels, wind turbine and hydrogenerator. *Aventura* had been specifically designed with extra capacity for generating her own clean power.

Marianne with her first iceberg

Even so, I was forced to accept that for so much of our so-called 'environmental voyage', we'd be coughing out black diesel particles that settle on the ice and make it dark, so it melts even more. This fancy new boat was laden with electronics, laptops, cameras, i-pads and mobile phones, not to mention our spanking new waterproof clothing and our flights to Greenland. We cannot make one step in this world without ourselves contributing to the mess.

We enter a maze of islands southeast of Disko Island, from where many of the old-time explorers set off west on their quest for the Northwest Passage. Two humpback whales spout and raise their sleek black backs, lazily rolling through the water before they dive.

Nera's first whales.

Icebergs are grounded in the narrow channels between the islands. The bright colours of our destination appear, the town of Aasiaat, houses painted red, yellow, blue and green, sprinkled like a child's colourful painting across the slopes. A few people gather to watch as we tie up alongside the rusty quay in front of a French yacht called *Manevai* that we later find is owned by a retired French admiral. Moored nearby is a Norwegian tugboat. Its crew are heading into the Northwest Passage to Cambridge Bay with a plan to raise the *Maud*, the ship built for Amundsen's second attempt on the Passage; she sank there in 1930 and has been abandoned all these years. The Norwegians tell us they want to 'take *Maud* home'. I wonder if she wants to go…

For all of us sailors, there is a strong sense of anticipation, at what lies ahead, and an awareness our time is short here in Greenland and we cannot linger. Instant camaraderie grows up amongst the crews, hanging out at the Seamans' Mission to do laundry, get showers and check emails – while the captains are more aloof, solemn, and serious with their responsibility.

Nera and I walk through the town, finding cute husky puppies for her to photograph, but also the market where they are cutting up seal meat and porpoises. Great red slabs of meat that vegetarian Nera struggles to look at. On a slope above the port is a bleached white arch of whale bones tall as a house, and an old stone and peat house which was the traditional Inuit winter home before they adopted (or were forced to adopt) the bright Scandinavian wooden houses. The peat house, built with layers of stone and soil, flowers and grass growing from its walls and roof, looks very snug. In summer in days gone by there were sealskin tents for mobile living, and families travelled by *umiak*, larger canoes, that the women rowed. Kayaks were for hunters, swift and slim, and there is a beautiful one in the museum, stitched carefully and skin-watertight. *Qajaq*: a perfect piece of technology.

NERA'S BLOG

In Aasiaat the local people were quite interested in a yacht like us coming into the port. The rest of the boats were a mixture of fishing boats and little dinghies with outboard motors so us and the yacht next to us caught people's attention.

I actually made friends with a young couple, 16yr old girl Kurlungua and 19yr old boy Aatam (I think those were the spellings) who were very interested in our boat. Kurlungua's family owned the fishing boat opposite which caught shrimp to be immediately shipped out in huge containers to places like Scotland. They took me to their house and her whole family was very welcoming. The houses in Aasiaat – in fact Nuuk as well – were very bright and colourful which were brought in when the Danish settlers came to Greenland.

We went to the local museum and found out some interesting facts. The Inuit traditionally had two forms of shelter: in winter a peat and stone house which included a few families and in summer each family had their own seal skin tent. The Inuit invented the Annoraaq (anorak!) and the kayak which are made of this completely waterproof sealskin which the hunters would use.

Throughout the village you could see the sledge dogs; we think of our huskies when you think of the cold, but really, these sled dogs look about three quarters wolf and quarter dog they have such a wild look about them. These dogs are chained up and are fed fish like Arctic char.

The only minor problem was the language barrier, my new friends knew a few words of English from school, but I knew absolutely nothing. It just gives you a wider view of how reliant we are that we can understand each other...

Suddenly when that's taken away from us, we're kinda left like a fish out of water.

Nera returns very late, having met most of the town on the long walk to her friend's house. The sun never sets, and at midnight the town is still busy with people, kids, all out and about – enjoying summer to the full. They will have months of darkness. What a darkness that must be!

Boys clamber over shipping containers and later come and look at the boat, daring each other to touch her. About half past midnight they climb on board, Nick and Jimmy chase them away. In the morning I see their dusty footprints on the coach roof.

Their ancestors must have watched so many foolish people arrive and sail off westwards and never return. Not so different today.

THE MOTHER OF BERGS

'The weather forecast looks good for the next few days,' Jimmy tells us. 'So we're going to push on. Peter says we must get ourselves across the Davis Strait as soon as we can so we'll be ready and waiting when the ice melts in the central part of the passage.'

Peter Semotiuk is a local ham radio operator who has been advising sailors about the Northwest Passage for decades and Jimmy has been in regular email contact with him.

We leave the town behind, and head up the coast towards the Sermeq Kujalleq glacier, the most productive mother of icebergs in the northern hemisphere. Greenland holds 10% of the world's ice, and has the second largest ice sheet in the world, after Antarctica. The ice locked into glaciers and ice sheets on the land has been formed by snow and rain accumulating over thousands of years. As the glacier moves by gravity slowly towards the edge of the land, pieces break off, or calve, on the coastline and these float off as icebergs. The ice in a berg might be hundreds or thousands of years old, and the older it is the bluer it becomes.

The sky stays clear all day, and the sun illuminates the ice. So much ice. It begins with a slow procession in the distance, far away, white shapes of ever more fantastic proportions, all of them vast and stately, shimmering in the blue haze of summer. And now bergs are everywhere. Some have sea-smooth round tops where they have capsized, sea grooves sparkling in the sun, some have tabular surfaces and sea birds' tracks across their flat tops, others, improbable vast pinnacles and towering cathedral-blue spires. Each type of shape has an official name in the Canadian Ice Service manual (MANICE): tabular, blocky, wedged, domed, drydock, pinnacle, but in fact each is unique. We see bergs the same size and shape as the Arc de Triomphe, or an enormous giant's chair, or a doomed Arctic convoy parading slowly through the islands. Three huge ones slowly head out to sea together like three white misshapen sisters, the witches of Macbeth.

Except for a handful of fishermen scooting past in tiny motorboats, we are on our own, and this nature's parade of extravagance, the ultimate in temporary art, is ours alone to witness.

We never get too close. Icebergs are beautiful, but also dangerous, because only about one seventh of their mass can be seen above water, and melting can make them very unstable and liable to capsize without warning. The glacier is a long white line in the distance, visible from a long way off, the shore cracked and pressurized into peaks; as we creep closer, the bergs and smaller pieces crowd ever more thickly round us, like creatures from a mythical stable.

All of these creations, broken off from their mother-glacier, each one is a calf sent out into the sea but not to grow, to melt and finally disappear, thousands of blue ice years dissolving back into the sea. Before this end, though, one may make its imprint upon the world, a terrible child sowing death to 200-odd souls on a dark Atlantic night. *Titanic* and iceberg, *twin halves of one august event*, as Thomas Hardy wrote.

Titanic's berg melted long ago, but for these past hundred years humans have wreaked, and are still wreaking, their long, slow, hot revenge upon the ice.

We sail along the edge of the glacier, at a respectful distance. Getting too close would be dangerous if a building-sized piece of ice broke away while we passed. A pod of four or five humpbacks browse nearby. We are finally sailing so there is no engine noise to disturb them.

Wrapped up in our tourist delight, oohing and aahing all day, snapping away at photos, I realise that the idea of highlighting climate change by sailing the Arctic has been lost. Has this glacier retreated more in recent decades, were those bare hills once white, is there less ice, is the sea warmer? *I don't know.* All I can see is a sparkling stream of water running off the end of a berg like a snout, a baroque Viennese fountain – the ice is melting – I can see that.

And then, as we sail, quietly slipping through the water, with tiny floating fragments of ice, bobbing alongside the boat, and swirling in our wake, I hear a faint crackling noise.

What is that sound, and where is it coming from? I listen again – it is coming from the water. It is the ice.

It fizzes in the water as it melts, after a thousand, thousand years of being locked in, the ancient air is being released, a gentle noise, almost musical.

Yes, the ice is singing.

An orchestra of ice – singing its swan song as the summer sea dissolves it. The ice has a voice, and at its expiration it will not be silent, if we listen, if we are quiet.

If we listen, if we are quiet.

Evening comes, the midnight sun pouring liquid gold upon the waters, gilding the beautiful ice shapes floating all around us. I persuade Nera out of her warm bunk to come out into the cold. However long a cold night watch seems to last, these are just fleeting moments and this experience and wonder will never come again.

We sail through the narrow channel between Greenland and Disko Island. White-blue shapes of bergs set off the darkness of the land behind. Brown tall ranges, sharp peaks, the land grooved deep by ice, vast calderas scooped out of the earth, sliding down to rocky dark beaches, a coating of green on the lower slopes. Vestiges of thick ice cling to the mountain tops compressing the rock down like flat white hands, pushing and squeezing with a giant power – until pieces break off into the sea and dwindle before our very eyes, all the power, thousands of years gone in the melting blink of an eye. The land is brown, the sea slate grey, the ice white, the birds grey and white – the only colours are the blue heart of a berg and the golden wake of the sun upon the waves.

Beyond the channel is the open sea.

DAVIS STRAIT, BAFFIN BAY

In the open straits, the wind rises to 40 knots, the seas are grey and lumpy, and seasickness hits me hard in my stomach. The electronic compass races back and forth and will not settle, so the autopilot stops working and we cannot hold the course, so we must steer by hand. After hours of this, the crew is miserable, tired, wet and cold.

Yesterday the Arctic lulled us into a false sense of security with all the sun and brightness. Now she laughs a cold laugh, at our expense.

The sea temperature drops to less than 2°C. Small pieces of hard ice, remnants of sea ice, or fragments of bergs, lurk low in the waters. As I had learnt years before in the Antarctic, there are also names for these smaller pieces: bergy bits, which are about one to five metres above the sea surface and some five to fifteen metres long, and growlers, smaller than a bergy bit. Growlers are hard to spot amongst the waves, so give us the most concern. We must keep a fierce lookout at all times.

Huge icebergs hem us in, moving slowly with the sea currents up the west coast of Greenland. Later they'll drift on the other current, down the further side of the Straits. Some travel right into Lancaster Sound, which is the stretch of water regarded as the mouth of the Northwest Passage, before drifting with the currents back out again into the open sea, eventually heading south into the Atlantic. Their slow journey of some 1800 miles may take two to three years before they melt to nothing.

A wet and exhausting night steering by hand as the autopilot continues to flip flop and the waves break over the boat. I am let off steering duty because by now I'm sick as a dog and keep throwing up. Nera burrows herself in the cabin and sleeps, surfacing only for meals.

By morning the wind lightens, the sea is gentler, the sun comes out, and everyone is in a better mood after some rest. So far we eight people are surviving each other's company and rubbing along reasonably well in the small confines of the boat. Emily and Marianne share a cabin and both have stashes of sweets and chocolates they dole out now and then to keep up morale. We have renamed their cabin Lidl. Jimmy has given up his cabin for Nick and Nikki; perhaps not a good idea as he now sleeps in the main cabin beside the galley so is often woken by people clanking around making cuppas on their night watch. This causes a bit of tension as he struggles to get a decent rest when off watch.

I persuade Nera up into the cockpit for an hour of sunshine and fresh air. I'm on cleaning duty today and spend my watch cutting up plastic rubbish into tiny pieces so it takes up as little space as possible, before stuffing it into a used milk bottle. We need to store all our waste compactly onboard until we find a place to recycle it, which may be weeks away. We've dispensed with as much packaging as we could before we set off. Sanitary products, toiletries – all carefully chosen to take up as little space as possible and environmentally friendly, although all waste has to be stored onboard until suitable places for disposal can be found.

Sea birds keep us company. Sociable dovekies, *alle alle* or little Auk, with their distinctive black head and backs, and white bellies, group together and gossip floating on the waves, or fly away very, very fast like hurried little groups of busy commuters. Fulmars are more solitary, they glide around the boat, skimming low on the waters, encircling us for a good look before moving on. Their dark eyes and brow, their slightly hooked beak, gives them an intense expression. They are welcome companions, though; at least another living creature that is curious as to who or what we are. The skuas are less frequent but fierce when they come – 'parasitic buccaneers', is how the bird book we have onboard describes them. One attacks a fulmar, and another spends an hour trying in vain to land on top of the mast. I get the camera and try photographing them – but on a moving boat, with moving birds, it is almost impossible to get anything other than shots of blank sky or sea without a bird in sight.

Short-tailed skua

Birds are the only wildlife we see on this whole sea passage. I'm diligent in recording them, as one of the citizen science projects we are participating in is the 'SeaBC Seabird Count', inspired by the land-based citizen counts in the UK and the USA. Seabirds are the last frontier of birding, being poorly documented and in dire need of conservation data, as few people venture to the remote parts of the ocean where they live – other than sailing yachts. Sailors are therefore the 'eyes on the water' for reporting sightings. For example, land birds sometimes take a rest on boats crossing the ocean or broad stretches of water: a sailor logging this and reporting it back can provide a clue to over-the-ocean migration patterns. Participation in the scheme was easy, all we needed to do was log our sightings of birds, take lots of photographs and note the exact position where we saw them. We didn't need to worry about identification, as when we had internet access we would email them to the SeaBC team, and volunteers would help identify the birds. Our reports would contribute to the Cornell University eBird database, so sailors' sightings become a resource for scientists and conservationists worldwide. To quote one of the SeaBC volunteers, 'A handful of organized pelagic birding trips out of a few select ports can't compete with the potential coverage of thousands of coast-running and ocean-crossing private boats.'

So I persevere with my photographs, and in each case take a photo of the electronic display of longitude and latitude at that moment of the sighting, as *Aventura* slowly creeps north.

A helpful email arrives from the company that makes our instruments to tell us the reason our autopilot is flipping about is because we are getting close to the magnetic north. Their advice to switch to the GPS system seems to work and the autopilot starts working again, which makes watches less tiring as we don't have to steer by hand all the time.

My sickness slowly ebbs as I get my sealegs. I share my watches with Marianne and we talk and talk about the past, present and future. Off watch I curl up beside Nera in a warm sleeping bag. *Aventura* pitches hard into the sea as she sails to windward. Our forward cabin takes the worst of it, bouncing up and slamming down with every wave.

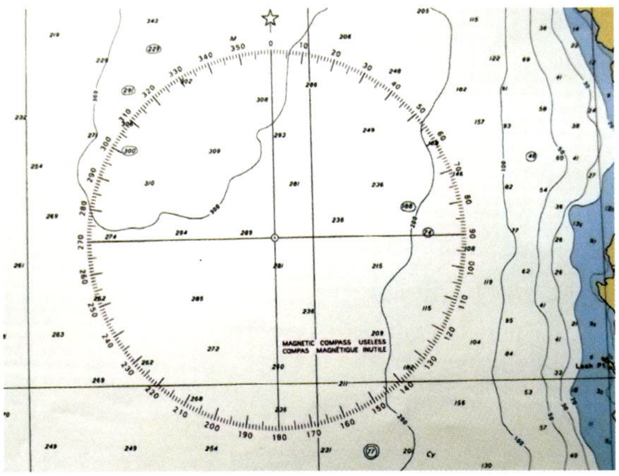

'Right now I'd rather be walking through a field or riding a horse,' she declares miserably. I'm not a sailor at all.'

'But you'll be a scientist,' I respond encouragingly. The BBC website has just posted a report on our citizen science projects, stating Nera could be the youngest Briton to sail the Northwest Passage, if we get through.

Yet I wonder, in my seasick muddled head, how much of a sailor am I myself, these days? Do I really enjoy these sick days and nights broken by watches? Each day I step away from my younger days, away from the thirteen-year-old would-be poet dreaming and scribbling poetry about the ocean as her boat rolled its way across the Indian Ocean some 30 years ago. And with each step away from my childhood it feels as if the poetry and intensity are leaching out of me, drop by drop, like the salt that leaches out of the sea ice, the older it gets and the longer it survives each summer melt, and I am marching relentlessly on towards a pedestrian, dull old age.

But then again, I do know this sealife so well, so intimately, and feel at home out of sight of land. I still love the blue rolling to the horizon to meet the sky, and there is never a speck of fear there, ever.

Even so, I'll probably be quite happy when this is done, to head home to my house, and my routine, even though I know that for a while everything there will seem very small and crowded, so long as the blue and vast horizon remains imprinted on my soul like the sun's imprint upon a closed eye. The sea and the cold dark land and the ice – all that enormous beauty and space goes inside and expands the soul until the soul is as huge as what it sees – I'll never go back to what I was, even when this passage has become a years-old memory. The only Tardis that truly exists, that is us – we are really bigger on the inside.

So on this question of my relationship to the sea, I haven't yet made up my mind. Stuck in my bunk, I read a lot – accounts of sailors fighting this same stretch of ocean at the same time of year, but some two hundred years ago. In the 19th century a frenzy of exploration arose as the idea of a passage northwest or northeast across the top of the world, became something of an obsession. When the modern age of exploration and empire-building took off, and the Pope split the 'discovered' world in two between Spain and Portugal, the other maritime nations, England, France and the Netherlands, felt put out, being now denied a sea route to the trade of Asia either around Africa or America. The British Navy was particularly gripped by this quest. In the early 19th century, with peace in Europe following the defeat of Napoleon on land and sea, the British Navy now dominated the seas, which meant these experienced officers and their disciplined crews had little purpose, with no great sea battles left to fight. The idea of finding a way north through the ice to the Pacific, and the trade and riches of China and India, which had smouldered in the imagination for some two hundred years since Frobisher made the first expedition in 1577, sparked into flame now. Expedition after expedition was sent on its way to the ice, to find a way through the inhospitable frozen waters of the north. In those days, even during the brief

summer, the sea was thick with ice, old tough ice, pushed into pressure ridges, humps and other crazy wild shapes, described in graphic detail by sailors' first-hand accounts and depicted in prints and engravings of square-rigged tall ships stuck in a frozen sea.

In Captain William Parry's 1819 account of their endeavours to get through the ice of Baffin Bay and the Davis Strait, where we are sailing now, the pack of ice was 80 miles wide. For three weeks they warped and towed the ships through the channels. One day they hauled for eleven hours to make four miles progress. On another they sawed for 7 hours to free *Hecla* only to find her frozen again by nightfall. And Parry's voyage was considered one of the most productive as after overwintering, in 1820 they had reached further west than many other expeditions.

A more common experience was that of Sir John Ross who, the year before, in July 1818, wrote the following, off Greenland,

> *We endeavoured by every exertion to work towards the entrance of the channel, but no sooner had obtained our object than the ice closed in upon us, and nothing was to be done unless by setting the crews to saw through the floes.*

Every expedition failed. The ice defeated them every time.

Two hundred years on, in this same place and time of year, the sea is clear. We see no ice at all today.

July: no ice in the Davis Strait

ILIGLIUK

Iligliuk takes a pencil in her hand for the first time in her life. The naval officers crowd round the chart table and watch her start to draw.

She has lived her whole life in the frozen north, and these are the first Englishmen she has met, the first sailing ships seen, and the first time she has come across pens and paper.

It is 1823. Parry is leading his second expedition to the Arctic. Their mission is to find the northern extremity of the North American continent. They overwinter in Hudson Bay from October on the *Fury* and the *Hecla*. In February they meet the Inuit for the first time, a group of families wintering in their igloos nearby, who become regular visitors to the ships.

A woman named Iligliuk stands out from the rest, with her intelligence and love of music, even taking part herself in the curiously British habit of putting on elaborate entertainments and musical concerts to while away the dark winter months.

The officers become hopeful that the Inuit could help solve the puzzle as to whether there was a sea to the west of this place. They learn Iligliuk's words for north, south, east and west, show her the charts and ask her to help.

She begins to sketch, drawing the missing coastline, as skilful as any cartographer, continuing the line of the land and making the unknown known. The map is beautiful in its fine and precise detail. Marked onto the shore are captured moments of life: Iligliuk's birthplace, Iligliuk's son born here.

This was still in the early days of the new empires, before the world had been totally carved up between European states, when vast riches were just starting to be built on the backs of slave labour, land grabs and resource appropriation. And perhaps, therefore, here with this woman, and the English sailors, was a moment when a different history could have been realised from the one we ended up with … an understanding, that there is no such thing as 'primitive' or 'savage', 'civilised' or 'developed'. An understanding that we are the same people as our ancestors who stepped on the long road out of Africa, who crossed the narrow straits from Asia to America, and if we could bend time to meet them, we would find that we were just alike. Any one of us could pick up a pen and put down marks of the places we know so well. There is only one human race, and we are all long lost cousins.

This so-called 'savage', and a woman to boot, could draw you the most beautiful and accurate of charts.

Parry's experiences, including the mention of Iligliuk (which is how we know her name), were recorded at that time and published. I'd read of her in *The Search for the North West Passage* which we had on board.

But there was another record of life then, which of course the Europeans did not note in their histories. Stories of Parry's visit had been handed down orally from Inuit elder to elder and I came across them in the book *Encounters On The Passage: Inuit Meet The Explorers*; a living link back to that time. It was told, for example, that a local shaman, imprisoned during Parry's visit for the theft of a shovel and subsequently tortured, cursed the white men, not only for his own treatment but for their threat to take his wife. Indeed, after Parry left, no white men returned to that place for a hundred years.

Like these tales, the map has survived for these two centuries, although the moment, and the knowledge Iligliuk held, has been lost, like so many others.

Iligliuk never had the chance to tell her own story; but at least some fragments of who she was remain, living with us down through the years.

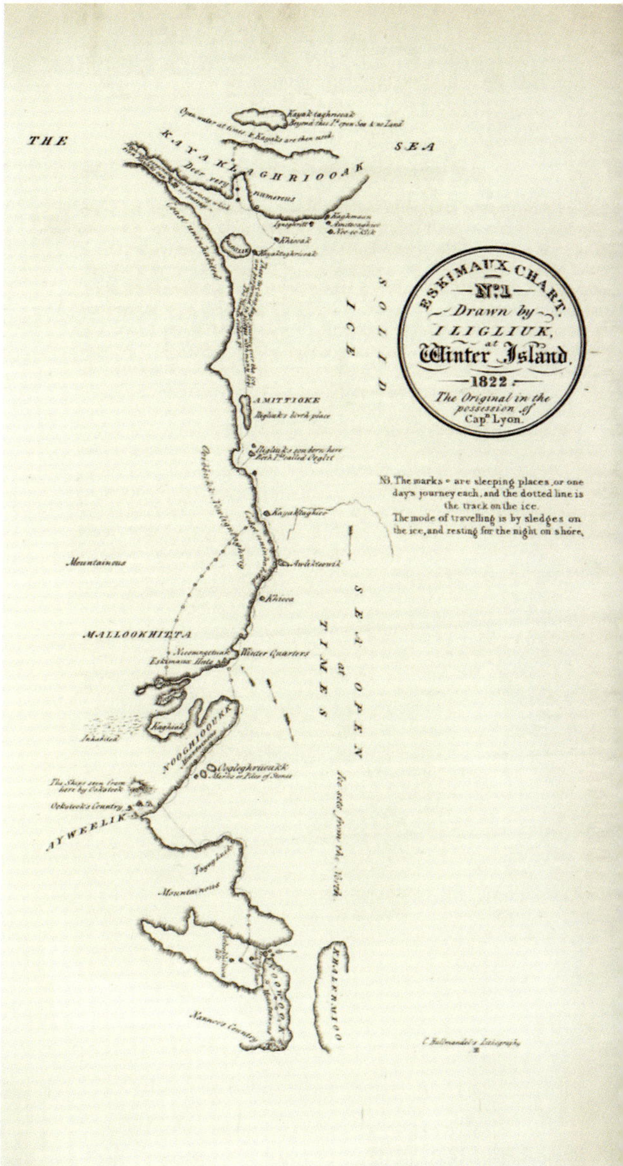

INTO THE PASSAGE

A dark shape is spotted on the distant horizon early in the morning of 24th July. Land! Bylot Island, gatekeeper of the southern side of the entrance to the Northwest Passage. A few miles ahead of us, we spot the yacht *Suilven*, the only other official participant in the northern leg of the Blue Planet Odyssey. We've been chasing them ever since we arrived in Greenland, always one step behind, as they left Nuuk and Aasiaat before us. We gain on them now, creeping across the sea, until they are barely a mile away across the water. Then fog settles over us and they vanish into the grey.

When the fog eventually lifts, Bylot appears again, some sixty miles away, and beyond, Devon Island, on the northern border of the Passage. Between these two lies Lancaster Sound, the long stretch of water that marks the eastern entrance to the Northwest Passage.

We have one clear advantage over the earlier explorers: the daily ice charts sent to us by email, a coloured depiction of the current state of the sea ice. There are two types of ice to consider, fresh water from glaciers, and salt from the frozen sea. As the amount of sea ice present at any one time impacts so significantly on the Arctic, for both humans and animal habitats, the Canadian Ice Service invest much time into providing detailed information. Daily ice charts are published, indicating the position and concentration of ice, as well as explanations on how to interpret the charts, using the so-called 'Egg Code' which shows ice concentrations, age and floe size in a simple oval form (that looks a bit like an egg). The figures used in the code, alongside the colours, show whether the sea is navigable or not – areas marked red, with a 9/10 or 10/10 ice coverage, are quite impassable where the ice is consolidated or compact. Green, and perhaps yellow, have less ice, from 1/10 to 6/10. Ice charts are invaluable as wind and currents move the ice around as it breaks up, making it impossible to plan which way to go until the final moment.

The melting and freezing of sea ice is a natural part of life in the Arctic. At the end of the short summer season, September marks the minimum extent of the sea ice, and through the long winter the sea ice builds up again, reaching its maximum in March. There is the first-year ice, which forms and melts each summer, and the 'multi-year' ice which remains all year round. In the past, the winter ice pack in the Arctic was mainly composed of multi-year, very thick ice, as can be read in the descriptions of historic expeditions. Today, very little old multi-year ice remains. The amount of summer sea ice has declined year on year through my lifetime, with the lowest level to date occurring in 2012. It does vary year on year, but the trend is always downward. As yet, of course, we don't know what the full extent of the 2014 melt will be.

The accelerated melting of the Arctic ice cap due to warmer air and sea temperatures in recent years, is a simple fact. The consequences, though, are complex and far-reaching – not only for the Arctic itself, but for the entire planet. White snow and ice reflect the sun's heat away from the planet, in what is known as the albedo effect. As the area of land and sea in the Arctic covered by snow and ice diminishes over the years, the darker sea and land absorbs more heat. Forest fires, another side effect from global warming, send soot into the atmosphere, much of it landing on Greenland snow, further darkening it.

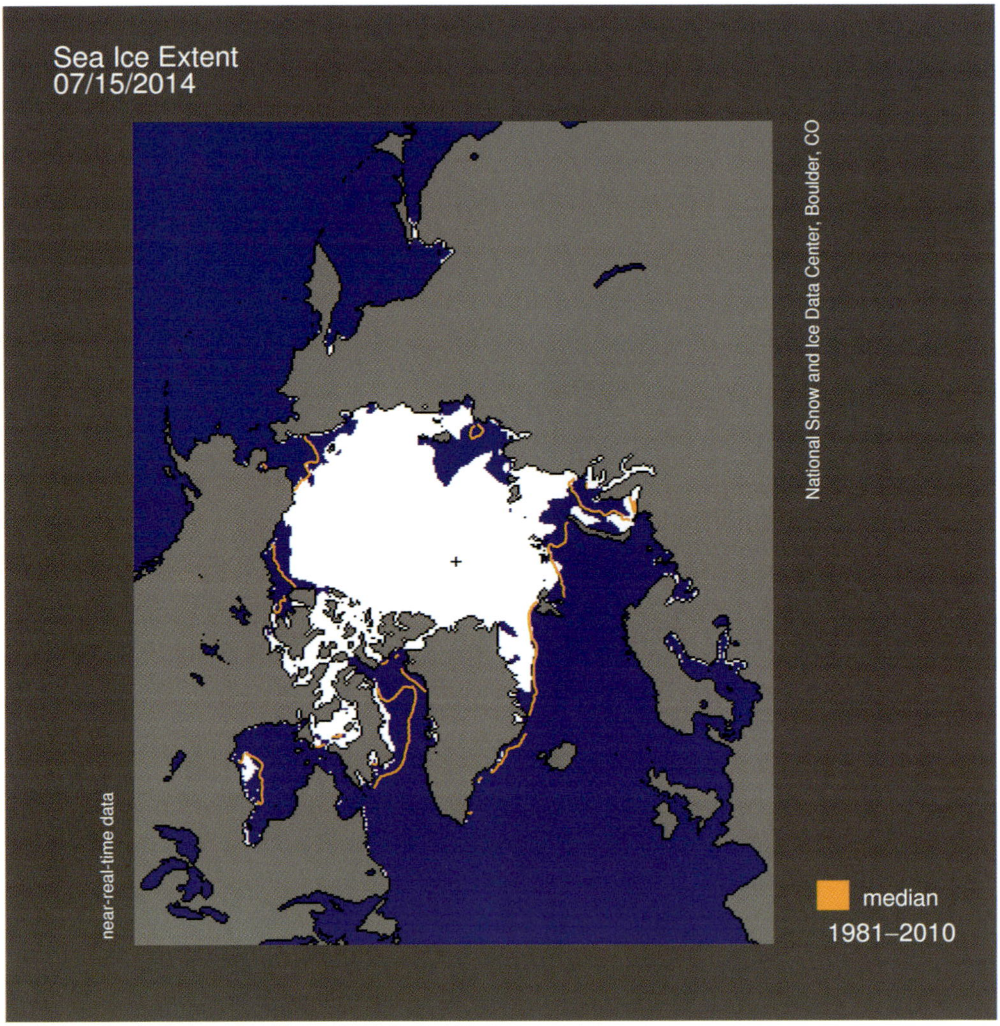

All of this contributes even more to the warming of the planet, in a process scientists had by now begun to call Arctic Amplification.

Onboard, we study the ice charts avidly. At present it seems the sea ice is breaking up and moving in our direction at a speed of about two knots out of Lancaster Sound. Floating low in the dark sea water are bluish slabs, transparent, almost impossible to spot, as if the pure heart of an iceberg is all that is left, clinging to the waves. These are older pieces of sea ice, more than a year old, having survived more summers; with each year the salt leaches out into the sea and the ice becomes harder and more transparent. And therefore the most dangerous to hit, even with our strong metal hull. We keep our eyes peeled while on watch.

Our destination is Dundas Harbour, a protected anchorage on the southern coast of Devon Island. The coast slowly unrolls before us, looking seriously inhospitable. Mountains topped by ice, glaciers descending to the sea. Not much like its namesake, the green county of southwest England, but rather a cold desert of an alien planet, the sort of place that NASA pick as a training ground for astronauts that'll one day head for Mars. (They have such a base, on the north of the island).

We start a quick rotation to all take showers and profit from the engine which is now running, giving us power and hot water. We've a watermaker that produces fresh water from the sea. Showers are rationed – a rare luxury. By late evening, the crew are all clean and fed, and we turn into the entrance to the harbour with *Suilven* just ahead. To starboard, fat brown walruses cram onto an islet. An iceberg is grounded not far from the entrance, shaped like an immense wedge of white cheese, and pieces have broken off from it.

The VHF radio crackles to life. It is *Suilven's* crew.

'Polar bear swimming to port.'

A piece of the broken berg is moving low through the dark water, a small white smudge barely visible.

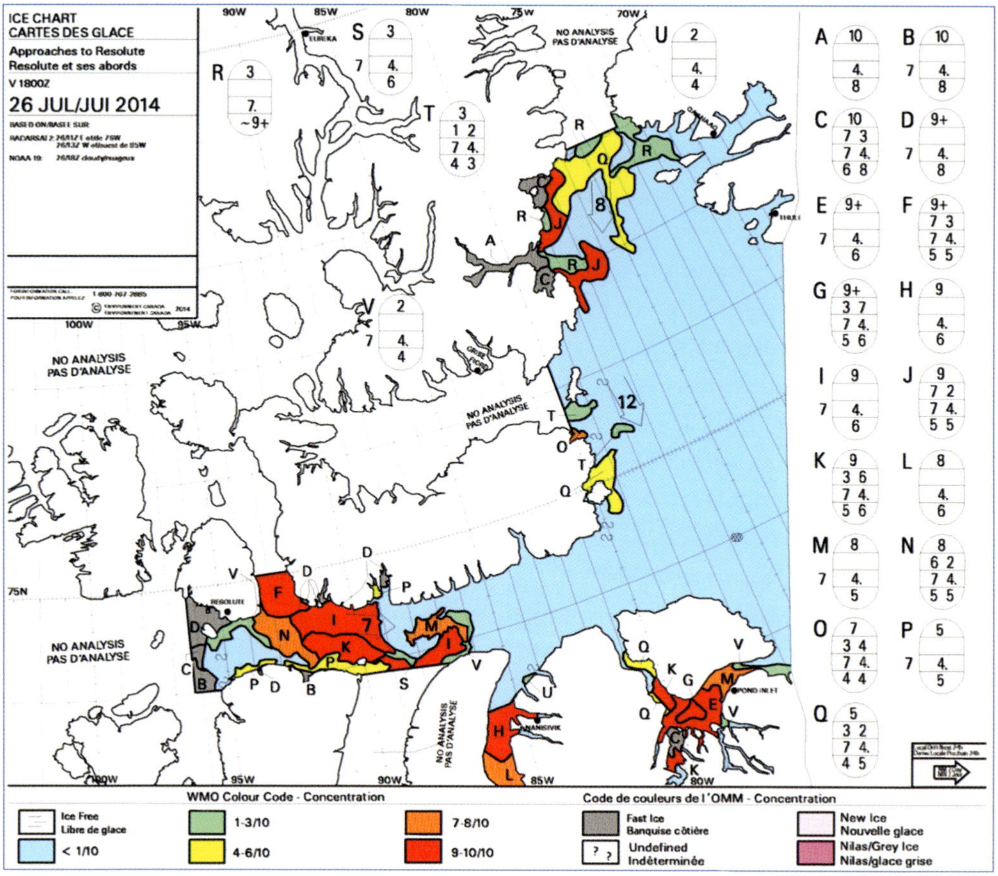

Nera, who had been lolling below decks reading, gets dressed in her foulies (foulweather gear) and up on deck in a flash.

We can see the bear now. She swims fast and sure in the water, and as we get closer, she looks at us once or twice, no doubt irritated by our alien, unwelcome presence and the thud of the motor. She makes for the land, hauls herself ashore dripping wet and slowly climbs up the steep rocky slope, stopping for a moment to shake herself dry like a huge shaggy dog, and glance back at us with look that is curious, but also aloof, and faintly hostile. At last she disappears behind a rock where she lays down to rest, just out of sight of cameras and loud human exclamations of delight.

You can imagine the pleasure of the two crews, on this, our first proper day in the Northwest Passage, after the long haul of many days at sea, and the cold passage to arrive here. Nera, of course, is joyful. Her long-time fascination for all white wild beasts of the north is finally leaping from the pages of books into reality.

NERA'S BLOG: POLAR BEAR SIGHTING

Did he raise his shaggy head in defiance and in his mind scream his annoyance at us humans bringing our metal craft to disturb his cold domain?

The name 'Arctic' is derived from arctos, *Greek for 'bear'. The heavenly constellation of the Great Bear – Ursa major – points the way to the Pole Star, Polaris.*

(from *The Arctic: A guide to coastal wildlife* by Tony Soper)

For we have seen one of the mightiest creatures Earth has yet to show us and to put it bluntly, it was rather awe-inspiring. This marine mammal, the Polar Bear (Latin – Ursus maritimus) was spotted as we were sailing into Dundas Harbour. He very kindly chose to swim about in the water awhile before dragging his bulk out of the freezing water with the sopping wet guard hairs forming a watertight overcoat and leaving his skin happily drip free. We watched him lumber slowly up the side of the brown mountain nearby while sending us what probably could be translated only as a look of annoyance or simple fright at what things were oogling at him from across the water. Either way, he was an incredible sight.

No matter how wonderful seeing a Polar Bear is I know there is a nagging feeling of how dangerous they really are. I know this because immediately when we saw him, the rifle was brought out and sat there like a stewing toad ready for the next unfortunate insect to fly into its range before it shoots and gulps the remnants of the meal.

For my part, I reflect that the fierce solitary bear, white as the ice, looked lean in her hungry summer robes. She of course doesn't give a damn about being a symbol of the Arctic. She would like there to be no humans, no oil, no chemicals filtering up through the planet and concentrating in her blood so she cannot breed, or her cubs are sickly – why can't we just leave her alone? She just wants a rest and a sleep now, and will then go look for lean summer pickings of birds' eggs and berries, desperate for the winter to return, for the ice to be thick, so she can hunt the fat seals once again.

Elated by our ice bear, we round a headland and drop anchor. Our first target, to be on station on the 25th July, is achieved. How deep we sleep that night, the boat not moving at all, tucked into the calm, protected bay.

THE LAND IS NOT WHAT IT SEEMS

I'm woken by a loud 'huffing' sound that appears to be coming from the water just outside the portholes of our cabin. It is the walruses, feeding noisily in pairs out in the bay. Before you see them, you hear their strong outbreath and a spray of air mists above the water, out come their brown snouts and they dive, round brown bottoms followed by tails, searching for tasty greens on the seafloor below.

The water is full of silt, a milky green colour which is pushed here and there depending on the wind. There is a deep valley at the head of the bay, where a glacier feeds into the water. To the west and east we are enclosed by tall peaks of rock, ice folded into indents on their sides, plunging down to broken shorelines. White gulls circle over the hills, and nest high up on the cliffs where white droppings mark out a ledge, and here and there surprising green patches colour the rock face. Occasionally the solitary bear can be seen, slowly moving across the slopes, a distant yellowish-white dot visible against the dry land. Eventually she curls up by a big rock, far off on the other side of the bay, and spends the day sleeping.

Waiting, as we had anticipated, for the right moment to move on, we end up spending some days here in Dundas Harbour, named by those long-ago explorers after one member of the influential Dundas family, who held positions in the British navy, military and parliament. This alien name has stuck, and is what the chart tells you, but it has another, in the Inuktitut language: *Talluruti*, which means 'a woman's chin with tattoos on it'.

You may take your pick as to which you prefer – or perhaps they are both valid, each name expresses a layer of human experience and history overlaid one upon the other, from the first visitors some three thousand years ago right up to modern day explorers – was any human who ever spent time here anything other than a visitor to a land not made for us to live? All past settlements here have been abandoned. The Royal Canadian Mounted Police (RCMP) post across the headland was given up fifty years ago; and even an attempt to re-settle an Inuit community here didn't last.

In the afternoon a few of us take the dinghy and venture ashore. The beach is rocky and steep and the rocks are shattered, tumbling down to the shoreline. The stones are square and right-angled; they have not been rounded by years of sea waves rubbing and smoothing them over, nor broken down into coloured sand, as would be the case on other beaches. They enjoy a brief ice-free moment before they will be frozen into place again. I've never seen a beach like it, and its strangeness disturbs me.

Our French journalist Jean Luc has taken the rifle that Jimmy bought in Nuuk though I wish I felt more confident in his ability to fire it. He walks fast on ahead with it slung over his shoulder when I'm sure the whole point is to stay close together. Nera and I grumble and try to keep up, constantly looking over our shoulders for a moving white threat, the ice bear, lurking behind each hill and rock. Our destination is the walrus islet. They are there in the water, a boiling brown mass of family love, large adults and tiny babies with ugly wrinkled faces, not yet grown into their skin. The photographers snap away, but I keep a sharp eye to the land. My nerves are on edge all through this excursion. Fear is on the land not the sea. Where is the bear?

We pick our way over the spongy, peaty soil, batting off the fierce mosquitos that cling in black hordes to our heads and hats. Nera quotes a favourite line of ours from the *Lord of the Rings* film as the hobbits wade through the swamps: 'What did they eat before they had hobbit?'

There is much to see and exclaim at. Here is a freshwater pond, not quite grand enough for a lake, where little shrimp-like creatures swim about. The ruins of ancient Inuit stone winter houses, circular walls of peat and stone not so different from that in Greenland. Huge whale bones and solid walrus skulls are scattered or placed beside the ruins, alongside rusty tin cans, hunters' or explorers' relics. Various types of animal droppings are thick on the ground: small round ones, just larger than a rabbit's, which might be Arctic hare, and larger ones that could be muskox, walrus, or bear. The occasional muskox hoofprint marks the soft soil, and in places the grass is as green and lush as any English lawn. According to the *Naturalists Guide to the Arctic* these are distinctive peat lands and the peat is 5-10,000 years old. Whorls of black and yellow lattices of lichens decorate the rocks, pattern the bones red, and the black ground is encrusted with white lichen that looks like salt. The brown flutes and yellow rounds of mushrooms. And many wildflowers, yellow, pink, red and white: moss and bladder campions, scurvy grass and mountain sorrel – the last two, good sources of Vitamin C.

And look, there is a butterfly! A butterfly. In the High Arctic.

From afar at sea, I had seen those dark forbidding slopes and thought of Mars, but once we come treading ashore it is like an Alpine meadow bright with flowers. It is as if spring, summer and autumn came at once in all their intensity, one colourful sharp burst of all the seasons before the long winter sets in.

This land is astonishing.

NERA'S BLOG: ARCTIC TUNDRA

When you picture the Arctic terrain, you imagine rolling ice sheets and sky-high glaciers, right?

Well, ever thought about what happens in the summer when all that begins to melt and some of the ground is left bare?

Of course, there are no trees up here because it is frozen for half the year. This is because the period where the temperatures are warm enough to allow photosynthesis to be strong enough to produce plants is very short. This means plants can't afford to grow tall, but have to concentrate on growing out roots and leaves for storage and producing energy.

The tundra of the Arctic includes shrubs, herbs, mosses and lichens. These plants have many difficulties to survive, one of the main being the cold. They have to be able to lay dormant under the deep cold of Winter, and survive the periods of freezing spells in the Summer when the plants are growing rather than lying dormant.

For animals such as Polar bears, Summer is a dreadful time of the year, when the sea ice has broken up they have to come inland to the meadows and snooze the Summer away, eating eider ducks and any ripe berries they can come across. That sounds a little like luxury, doesn't it? You have to remember that Polar bears are adapted to harsh Winter conditions and don't turn brown like Arctic foxes in the Summer and so become very lean, and are at the peak of their hunger. This makes them very dangerous as they will attack if provoked. Now you can understand why we were particularly cautious at our sight of the bear the other day.

A SAILOR'S LIFE

Some eighty small yachts have passed through the passage successfully since the first in 1977. We do not know yet if we shall too but the Blue Planet Odyssey Northern Route has finally become a reality. The *Suilven* crew row over in their dinghy to pay us a visit and we crowd round the table in the main cabin and pore over the latest ice chart that Ivan has emailed to us, deciphering the runes using the Egg Code. There is still a block of red-coloured, 9/10 ice between us and Resolute to the west. Impassable.

On the following evening it is our turn to visit. *Suilven* is very cosy down below, a more lived-in boat than ours. We drink wine and whiskey, and the snacks and nibbles on offer go down very well for our crew on rations. They tell us tales of their trip to Iceland, and Jean Luc, who typically likes to begin a story with 'When I was on the *Calypso* with Cousteau…' recounts a long salty tale of running out of food crossing the Indian Ocean and trying to shoot down seabirds like a modern day Ancient Mariner.

But for the most part the talk is all about the ice. The latest ice charts show there is a thick mass at the west end of Lancaster Sound heading our way, but it seems to be breaking up. As yet there is no daily analysis of the crucial mid-points of the passage, like Peel Sound to our west, but beyond that, by King William Island and Cambridge Bay, the ice does seem to be getting thinner.

Where shall we go while we wait for the ice to melt? One option would be to visit a settlement to get some extra fuel – but there is still a lot of thick ice between here and the settlement at Resolute, and if we did head west, we might get blocked in by ice, exposed to southwesterly winds, or just too far west to get back quickly if a suitable opening occurs.

It feels just the same as the sailors before us, in all the history books we have onboard. Seafarers hoping for a way through, waiting, waiting; and the end of the voyage is always a question.

In fact, the middle is a question too. All we are sure of at present, is where we have begun.

It is like a great game of chess, all strategy and decision, and our opponent is – the Arctic herself, the white Queen, her courtiers amassed around her – the air temperature, the sunlight, the pack ice and the icebergs. She is neither an evil Queen nor good. She is supremely indifferent to her opponents, a handful of small ships scattered across the sea. If they win, and pass, or if they lose, and remain and must turn back – she does not care.

❄ ❄ ❄

Cleaning and cooking duty today for me: bread to bake, cabbage to grate for salad, beef stew to prepare, as well as fruit salad with some fruit that's on the turn. Nera and I check the oranges which hang above our heads in the nets in our cabin as now and then one suddenly goes mouldy-green. The Orkney eggs stored out in a locker in the cockpit, and potatoes below the floorboards, are still good and fresh.

Nera poses for a photo on deck with the gun to send to Dan at his request.

I spent an afternoon reorganising provisioning, working out a 7-day meal plan, and moving all 37 French milk bottles out of starboard bilge locker as well as two soggy boxes of wine. I recount all the tins, and shift twenty cartons of milk from Nuuk into the bilges.

Nick and Jimmy fix the terminals on the dinghy outboard motor. Emily snips and stuffs rubbish. Jean Luc cleans the heads (a sailor's term for the bathroom and toilet), as I get stuck headfirst in the dark bilge locker. 'It's hard to work out how to clean the floor grate,' he says. 'I had to use all of my brain, all two and a half neurons.' His wry French humour does amuse us.

Dan emails back to ask what we're eating and to exclaim how big the gun is of course.

In the evening we settle down with popcorn and watch a DVD. Yes, we have emails and DVDs – our expedition isn't based on suffering. The film is *Passage*, the docu-drama about the Orkney-born explorer John Rae and English naval officer John Franklin whose 1845 Arctic expedition famously disappeared and was never found despite many efforts.

In the film a Russian historian comments on Franklin, 'Ok, he was old and fat, but that doesn't matter when you're on a boat as you don't have to do anything.'

We laugh, remembering all the chores we had today.

After the film I go out on deck for a breath of midnight air. The glaucous gulls and kittiwakes are plunging into the water, catching what seem to be fish, but turn out to be butterfly snails, one of the rich bank of invertebrates that nourish much life up here in the High Arctic. *Clione limacina*, or copepods, travel on the North Atlantic drift up into high latitudes, 'grazing' on the phytoplankton. I learn that copepods, of which I knew nothing until this point, are the most important link in the marine food chain, eaten by almost everything, fish, birds, walrus and whales. The hidden web of food that nourishes and sustains life, of which most of us are largely ignorant.

❄ ❄ ❄

Other yachts arrive, French *Manevai* we'd met in Aasiaat, and American *Revenge*. We and *Suilven* are leaving this morning, and will try for the Arctic Bay settlement (also known as *Ikpiarjuk* 'the pocket') across the sound.

Jimmy phones various Canadian police offices bemused by receiving a call from a yacht in the middle of nowhere until he finally gets through to an officer at Arctic Bay.

'This is James Cornell, captain of the British yacht *Aventura.* Is it ice free there? Can we get fuel?'

The voice at the other end sounds young, innocent, and reassuringly Canadian. I swear he says he hasn't been outside and doesn't know the conditions; though the port is ice-free. And he will 'consult the hamlet' about fuel availability and we must call back in half an hour. We wonder what asking the hamlet involves.

As we weigh anchor – a great green abominable snowman of weeds attached – everyone is happy to be moving again. No sign of the bear, just one lone walrus on the rock. Once offshore, Emily does a trawl again, and we find two possible bits of plastic which we'll check tomorrow under the microscope as the laptop has run out of power, and some living creatures, krill perhaps, that spin around in the jam jar that Nera puts them in to study, before letting them go.

Soon after supper, sea ice is spotted. We shall now find out if the ice charts and reality match, and whether we can continue or will be forced back. The chess pieces played – one grey yacht, and across the blue game board, the floating white pawns. For the moment, we are sailing steady, and the noise of water beneath the hull is the most wonderful music you could imagine.

The engine has just started. End of music! I write my diary as we head south, and then read in my bunk until my night watch begins. Meanwhile the ice is gathering ever more thickly around us.

BESET

Like a ghost ship we glide through the silent white seascape, no noise other than the thrum of the engine. It is the dead middle of the night. Nothing living moves except for one black seal in the distance, resting on the ice, that raises its head in alarm, and slips away into the water.

There is ice in all directions. We seek out clear leads, stretches of clear water, dodging the larger pieces floating low in the water. Once or twice the ice touches the hull and scrapings of green antifouling paint are left on the white.

'This was what this boat was designed for,' Jimmy says with relish as the metal hull withstands the knocks.

Nera keeps the ship's log, noting down key facts each hour throughout our night watch. The sea temperature drops down to 0.1°C and the air 0°C.

The leads grow ever narrower and now ahead nothing is to be seen but white, with no clear way through.

'We must turn back,' Jimmy decides at last.

But going back is not so easy.

Suilven has taken a slightly different route to us, and are a little way off, where it is clearer water, but as we try to reach them the ice grows closer together and we are forced to bear towards the land. Then we hit a dead end. Here there are no leads, no way out.

For some moments we are stuck there, unable to go on, but then a way is spotted, a little to the north, and after much winding, we come out into clear sea. Our night watch ends. My warm bunk is very welcome.

At 5am I'm woken by the hull thudding into ice, crashing against the bow and sides. I feel the boat manoeuvre, twisting this and that way through the water.

'What's happening?' Nera whispers.

I peek out to see everyone is out in the cockpit – there is nothing much I can do to help so I doze until our next watch begins at 8am.

By which time we are stuck fast.

Suilven can barely be seen less than half a mile away, a ghostly silhouette in the fog. Their electrical instruments have stopped functioning. We share our woes via VHF radio and send them messages about their position.

As there is nothing we can do for the time being, Jimmy and Nick, who have been up most of the night, get some rest, leaving Marianne and I alone in the cockpit to keep watch. Away to the north and south seems to be clearer water, but between here and there, the ice stretches in an impenetrable patchwork of white. It is hard to differentiate sea from ice, those faint silver lines that could be open lines of water – looking with our eyes or binoculars, the lines of white, ridges, mounds, circles and squares of ice, could be anything at all.

Some of the floes are flat and white, and in places melt ponds have formed on top, coloured a stunningly intense blue. In other places, the pressure of the ice pushing and colliding together has pushed it up into crooked humps, broken ridges and smoother hummocks. These are likely to be formed from old ice, which has survived at least two summers' melt. As with the icebergs, there are many names in the MANICE manual if precise descriptions are required, floeberg, ice breccia, brash ice and so on.

While we watch through the hours, I observe how the ice has its own dynamic and never ceases to move: larger pieces come together and apart, and smaller pieces bob and rush through the channels that open momentarily. There's no pattern to this slow and random dance, and our fate is in its cold white hands.

Calm and utter silence engulfs us. Like being trapped in a white place of death and ghosts. Beautiful but deadly. The hours pass and there is nothing we can do except stare at the ice hoping it'll move apart. We are fixed, caught in the white trap.

Perhaps the most remarkable thing is that its only frozen water, and a few sunny days can obliterate it. Unlike a mountain, it is soon gone, temporary. Perhaps it is better to liken it to a force of nature like a hurricane – which can destroy landscapes and change lives – but leaves no trace of itself as it is only moving air. Only air! As the massive berg ripped down the side of *Titanic's* hull, think, only water!

The cold sea, glimpsed between cracks in the ice, is the deepest black I've ever seen.

I scoop up a little piece of ice with the bucket on a rope. It is clear all the way through, bubbles of air trapped inside it, shaped like a great misshapen glacier mint, or a tiny Hammer of Thor. Rather appropriate in view of all the ice in those Viking creation myths, gods born out of the ice, cows licking it away.

A rope tied around my middle for safety, I venture onto the flattest floe beside me. (I fail to persuade Nera to sing *Let it go*, the song from the film *Frozen*, on the ice, though she has a beautiful singing voice and the words mean a lot to both of us.)

Nera takes a Secchi disk reading. As well as the sea birds, this is another of our citizen science projects.

CITIZEN SCIENCE: SECCHI STUDIES

Phytoplankton, living at the sunlit sea surface, are the ocean's primary producers – the 'plants' of the sea. Despite their small size they are so numerous that they account for approximately 50% of all photosynthesis on Earth. From their position at the bottom of the marine food web phytoplankton determine the abundance of all creatures at every step in the web.

A study recently reported that phytoplankton might have declined globally by 40% since the 1950s. This was controversial – could it really be so? Corroborating this faced the same problem as other ocean studies; the ocean is vast, there are not that many scientists to study it and so the data is sparse. There are a lot of sailors however. A group of Plymouth scientists led by Dr Richard Kirby, had created a project to enable sailors to contribute to the largest global study of marine phytoplankton with the aim of establishing an extensive, long-term dataset to help address the debate surrounding changes in the ocean's phytoplankton. Sailors could sign up to help with a mobile phone app to record data and a Secchi disk, easy enough to make onboard. The Secchi disk was invented in 1865 by Pietro Angelo Secchi who described the method of lowering a white disk into the water until it disappeared from sight, in order to measure the clarity of the water, which can also suggest the amount of phytoplankton in the sea.

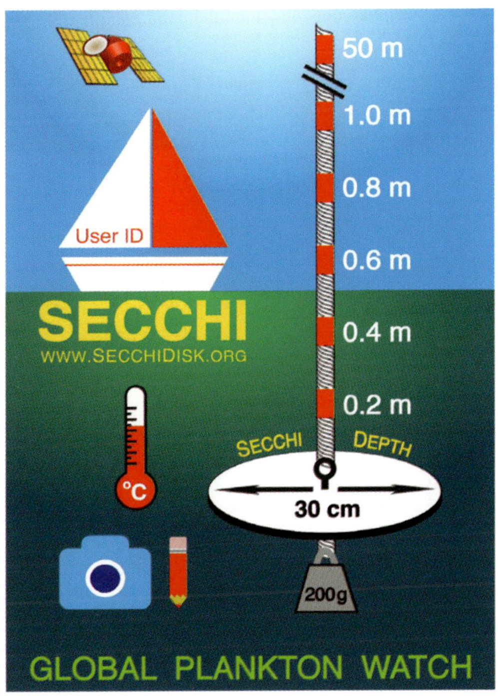

We're happy to be able to contribute in our small way, and before leaving for the expedition, we liaised with Dr Kirby about how best to take Arctic readings. He is hopeful we might beat the existing depth record, and we have a 100m measuring tape just in case.

NERA'S BLOG

Our Secchi disk is a 30cm white round disk made out of plastic using the laser cutter in the tech department of my school: Rednock School. It is attached to a weight and tape measure.

We drop the Secchi disk into the water and if everything goes accordingly, it will go straight down until it has disappeared. This is called the Secchi depth.

I've done two readings so far, one in Dundas Harbour and one in the middle of the ice in Admiralty Inlet. Dundas Harbour has lots of silt in its waters as many streams and a glacier run into it. That first reading we got 6.9m. We use an app to record the readings and sea temperature and any photographs of the area. The second reading was done in the ice and also a relatively large channel so the waters were constantly moving. That reading was 11m which suggested that water was a lot clearer.

A THANK YOU NOTE

For my part, I want to write a thank you note to these tiny creatures. I suppose there may be millions, billions of them. They are not even creatures... they are simple plant-like organisms, too small to see with our eyes, floating through the seas.

When we are little we are told to write thank you notes to those who have given us presents. For the most part we do this grudgingly.

Those tiny *coccolithophores*, one single cell, phytoplankton – right at the bottom of the food chain, the plants of the ocean.

Out of light, out of the CO_2, they grow their white armour.

They lock up CO_2 in their bodies, building cages of calcium carbonate to protect themselves. They look like tiny Christmas baubles, their outer parts made up of overlapping circles patterned like fine lacy crochet.

After their lives are done they still play a part, forming a layer at the bottom of the ocean locking in carbon. Creatures such as these make up the chalk of the white cliffs of England.

While living, their waste product is oxygen, and at least half, and perhaps more, of the oxygen we need to breathe, comes from them.

So I am thanking them for my breath, for the first and last thing I shall do on this earth.

And yet they are at risk now as the ocean turns to acid, soaking up our excess carbon like a mighty and over-efficient sponge. Our breath and our life now hangs in a delicate balance – will all we oxygen dependent creatures be tipped over the edge into a place where we can no longer breathe?

Like naughty children, we left it too late to send the thank you note.

STILL BESET

After lunch, when people are rested, one thing has become clear – we must do something to get out. The ice is not opening up, and we are drifting with the current, slowly but surely, towards the shore, only a few miles away. *Suilven* manages to extricate themselves and head back to Dundas. We are on our own. If we don't move soon, the boat will be crushed between the ice and the land.

It is time for an attempt to escape by brute force. With the engine on, the boat is edged slowly forward, to nudge through a small gap, but when we yell 'astern' to go backwards and Jimmy flicks the gears, they don't work and we charge headlong forward. With an almighty crunch, the bow embeds itself in the ice, leaving more scrapings of green paint. There is no panic onboard, but nerves are highly strung. Nick and Jimmy work on the engine, trying to diagnose what is wrong, replacing something broken with a new split pin. Jimmy must charm the gear lever which has become quite whimsical as to how it responds.

All hands on deck! It is a team effort, Jimmy at the wheel, the rest of us spread out – up the mast keeping a lookout, calling out directions, relaying these back to Jimmy at the wheel. Nick and Jean Luc use two long carbon fibre ice poles called *tuks* to push at the ice from the foredeck, sides and stern.

Slowly we edge through the ice, this way, that way, forwards, backwards, pushing with the weight of the boat at the large flat floes until they spin away across the water. The underwater shelves of ice are the most treacherous, solid ledges that jut out below the surface, – but the worst are the completely transparent ones, hard as rock and almost impossible to see. The flat ones are also deceptive, looking easy and thin to push from the top but below water they carry a good 30 cm keel of ice which makes them heavy and unyielding. But the blue ones go down much, much deeper. The underwater ice is pocked in crazy patterns from the melt, full of mini-caves and holes and tunnels. Ice scrapes mercilessly against the hull. All we can hope is we don't back into a shelf and damage the propeller or one of the two rudders.

At least the crew feel better for doing something, a sense of purpose and energy shot through us, we are attempting to control our destiny, and not just wait passively for our fate.

It is hard, bitter, intense work. Pushing, shouting, the same over and over. No sense of time. No time to rest. We live only in the moment, utter concentration on the task. Zero degrees air, zero degrees sea.

Progress is painstakingly slow, and in the early evening, after hours of slog, we stop for a breather and some food by a 'landmark', a huge blue berg-fragment we'd been pushing towards for what seemed like hours.

The latest ice chart has arrived by email and shows that the edge of the ice is not so far, to the north and east. We start again, determined to get out, whatever it takes.

A low point comes when Nick loses his grip on his *tuk* – everyone lunges to grab it in vain as it slowly, tantalisingly sinks, lower, lower, then suddenly in a gush of bubbles the hollow core fills up with water and shoots down into the black depths like a stone. After a moment a white bung pops up like a sad little goodbye. Those black cold depths look horrible.

I have to give up my boathook to Nick, so grab an oar out of the dinghy. It is rather piddly and I try to help by pushing away at the sides.

Push, push, push. Port, starboard. On and on. Still so far to go. But less thick now, less close packed. So focussed on what is immediately around the hull, I don't look further.

'We are close,' someone says but I don't believe it and don't even look up. Then I pause, look forward – suddenly where there was nothing but white lines to the horizon, is a grey line of sea. It takes a moment for my eyes to register and see that in fact we are very close. But I won't dare to believe or hope until we actually get there.

'Phew,' I breathe, for all the hard work so far, and the last push to come.

'Not yet,' says Jimmy.

The work isn't done until it is done – the ice is further apart but no clear line yet. Hours pass. A swell starts to lift the floes, gently up and down – before, all of the waves were quite flattened by the ice. As it compresses and moulds the land, so too the water.

Our last efforts, and then we are out. It is ten o'clock in the evening and we are finally free, after sixteen hours beset. Throttle on full to get away, north, away from the land, away from the ice.

Relief all round. The ice chart shows much ice to the west plus strong winds forecast in the next two days. The decision is made to return to Dundas. It's our watch now, a cold business until midnight. The rest of the crew sleeps, exhausted.

Ice can be seen away in the distance and a long low fog bank rolls along the horizon. But nothing comes our way, and sleeping at watch's end is very sweet.

The pages of the history books had come to life, and we'd completed our first rite of passage as all those sailors before us. Pick any one of the history books we have onboard and the accounts are full of fighting the summer ice, written in dramatic Victorian prose. For John Barrow, the Admiralty secretary who for some forty years promoted the Arctic voyages of discovery relentlessly: *ice was the enemy, to be brushed aside, smashed, defeated... as closely and unremittingly watched as an enemy in a state of blockade.* (Arctic Labyrinth)

I prefer to see this as a game not a war. I'm not fighting nature here. The chess pieces are spread across the board: on one side, frozen white pieces. On the other, warm red-blooded creatures of breath and bone. Who won this particular match? Who knows? The game continues.

NERA'S BLOG

Well, since the last of my logs, we have acquired a new experience to tick off our bucket-lists. By our decision to sail to Arctic Bay, we were unfortunately waylaid by ice floes. As the ice thickened about us, and leads became less frequent, we decided to turn back to Lancaster Sound. While making our way back through Admiralty Inlet, we soon found that the ice was packing us in with no clear leads ahead.

Sea water, due to the salt it contains, freezes at a lower temperature than fresh water. The air and sea temperature were very low while we were in the ice: around 0°C.

The ice which was around us ranged from bergy bits to ice islands which are very deep. It also ranged from very blue ice which sat on the surface and ice that was practically see through which made it difficult to discern from the water around.

The ice surrounding us was multi-year ice and pockets of first year ice which was still frozen. Multi-year ice stays frozen for the whole year and in summer, breaks up and drifts on top of the sea. During summer, multi-year ice loses its top layer, while in the winter, the water beneath it cools and freezes on the bottom of the ice. As the ice melts, meltwater pools form on the pieces of ice.

We eventually, through various punting techniques, made our way out of the ice into clear waters. Overall, we've decided to look upon the event as a very good team building exercise.

DOUBLE DUNDAS

We are back in Dundas Harbour. *Manevai* and *Revenge* have left, heading west, and a new yacht *Lillian B* has arrived. The cheese wedge berg is still grounded in the bay, the walrus are still on the rock, but there is no sign of the bear.

Ashore, the ground is sodden from recent rain and scattered with ribbons of bleached white seaweed. Cotton grass and Arctic poppies are blooming beside a desiccated body of a muskox. A black spider, heavy with an egg sac, runs over the ground.

Humans have tried and failed to settle in Dundas – it is a place of ghosts. In the abandoned huts of the Royal Canadian Mounted Police post we find rusty relics of their supplies and 1940s posters and magazines in perfect condition, as if the original inhabitants had left in a hurry.

Some never left. On the hill above the huts, a neat white picket fence and the clean gravestones of two young Mounties, in their twenties. Two sad stories – one who shot himself by accident, and the other took his own life. Here, in one of the most northern cemeteries in the world.

The abandoned huts are huddled into the corner of a bay which opens out to the sea, bergy bits and small bergs scattered artfully across the shallows. A dark-hulled sailing boat is making her way towards the entrance to the anchorage. This is the Australian yacht *Drina* – and at this point I don't yet know how significantly she is going to figure in this story. But more of that later.

That evening everyone gathers once again on *Suilven*. Michael, owner of *Drina*, has come along with his lively young crew. He is a true old salt, and has sailed his green-hulled yacht for some forty years across all the oceans of the world. Twenty years ago we met him first when he was part way through a round the world voyage with his wife and young family – my brother Ivan, on his gap year out of uni, shipped as crew across the Atlantic.

Michael's family are grown and it is just him now. Last year he turned up out of the blue and joined our Atlantic Odyssey, a transatlantic rally we had organised off the back of the BPO. His intention was to head south and into the Pacific but Jimmy mentioned his plan to attempt the Northwest Passage.

'I'll do that too,' he said, with a wry smile. I suppose I didn't quite believe him, but then, here he is.

Someone gets out a guitar, and Nera and Nikki give us a rendition of the old song 'Northwest Passage':

Ah, for just one time I would take the Northwest Passage
To find the hand of Franklin reaching for the Beaufort Sea;
Tracing one warm line through a land so wild and savage
And make a Northwest Passage to the sea.

Conversation then returns to everyone's favourite topic: the ice. The ice forecast for August has arrived. At present the west all looks blocked, and might only open much later in August. If the ice that beset us clears out of Admiralty Inlet we could go down to Arctic Bay for fuel. We still have provisions until the start of September. One thing alone is clear, we are going to be waiting for a good while longer. Patience, for the moment, must be our virtue.

So we wait – reading, drawing, mending things, writing emails to the outside world.

The light and the wind change throughout the day. Fog comes down, then lifts. Strands of low cloud drift in ribbons past the hills. The sky is grey and uniform, and then bursts asunder in a flash of stunning midnight sun, the sunlight floods the bay and even the rocks of the cliffs and beach seem to be shining. The sunlight stays all evening and at least we get some power from the solar panel which has been rather useless these last grey days. At 1 am the sun is still shining bright above the hilltops.

On a Sunday outing we climb the granite outcrop which dominates the headland, and at the top have a beautiful vista of the distant peaks of Bylot, illuminated in yellow and pink, foregrounded by a large iceberg, building-size, as stately as an opera house. I've brought the Naturalist's book with me, and crouch and identify a small plant with a woody stem that creeps across the ground as Arctic willow – the fluff around the flowers acts as a 'greenhouse' to raise its temperature. So there are trees in the Arctic, only very tiny ones.

Crawling slowly along nearby is a big black fluffy caterpillar, an Arctic 'woolly bear' that can survive being frozen for years at a time; they spend years as a larvae and only a few brief weeks as a moth. I wonder if this will be the summer when it transforms and flies.

You walk across the earth and spot things, once you can give them an identity, a name, the world is a little more focussed.

We clamber down the hill towards the pond with a plan to look for those 'tadpoles' we thought we had seen on our first visit. Nera has brought a cleaned-out jar and a sieve and she scoops up two strange swimming creatures that are not tadpoles at all. Back at the boat we examine them, one is like a little shrimp with many legs, that ripple under its body as it swims around the jar. The other is a more formidable brown beast with a carapace and a long forked tail (about one cm long head to tail). It decides to go for the other little creature and locks onto it in mortal combat, a deathly struggle around the bottom of the jar. Like a miniature version of Predator v. Alien. We sieve them out, put a drop of water on them in the petri dish and separate the fighters, but the poor thing is dead, crippled, drained of colour. We identify them as a tadpole shrimp and a fairy shrimp, two hardy little Arctic crustaceans. Sadly, the fairy came off worst in this fight.

Jimmy has been fishing off the aft deck with a hook baited with cheese. He's caught three wide-mouthed fish, spotted brown with spiny dorsal fins and wide pectoral fins.

'I saw a girl fishing them off the dock in Greenland,' says John from *Suilven* who is passing by in their dinghy. 'But she threw them back – her grandmother said they were too bony to eat.'

Jimmy guts them anyway and cuts off their spine and fins with scissors while they squirm. Nera watches and I wonder if some thousand years ago an Inuit girl watched her grandfather in much the same way.

The next day the fog drifts in and it pours with rain. Rain – this is supposed to be a desert! One of the driest places on earth, the books say. But things are changing so fast, the books are already out of date, and only serve for us to contrast with the present day.

When the rain eases and the fog lifts, waterfalls have sprung from nowhere, white streams are rushing off the bare slopes. Some of the yachts harvest fresh water from running streams but we head out to sea to make some fresh water as the bay's water is too silty and clogs up the filters of the water maker.

A polar bear has been spotted on the eastern shore, the crazy young guys from *Drina* scoop up Emily and dinghy towards it. I do worry that really they ought to steer clear of a hungry bear which can swim at 6 knots when they are only in a poky rubber dinghy. But I get some great photos from afar and they come back unscathed.

New arrivals come by to say hello: Hungarians from *Maia*, Canadian *Moloda*, and the Welsh on *Katrin*. I find out that ice in Welsh is – *ia*.

Katrin has come from Pond Inlet on Baffin Island. The settlement there has a population of about 1500 and the average age is about twenty. Jobs are few, which just leaves people reliant on subsidy and welfare. Three young people had already killed themselves this year. Pond is a dry town due to the alcohol problems but the locals make their own. This, of course, I know only from what the crew from *Katrin* tell us. I haven't seen it for myself, but I can guess that people are stuck in a soul-destroying halfway house: too much of their traditional culture has been lost for them to be able to survive on it any longer, and modern life cannot sustain them meaningfully up here in their ancestral land.

The days pass.

Waiting waiting waiting… Mornings I lie in my bunk watching my breath, not wanting to leave the warmth of my sleeping bag; all the rest of my life, and the world, seems to have receded and it has narrowed to a point, this harbour and the boats anchored here, nothing but the Arctic, and silly fretting about rations, and whether people are eating too much bread or drinking all the tea, filling my head. I wonder – when I return home will I be quite sick of the Arctic and never want to think of it? or will it fade to a rosy glow of memory, all the pettiness forgotten?

When I imagined this journey, before it began, it was a complete whole, July-September, something to be prepared for, done, and then back, with beginning, middle and end, as self-contained and finite as an egg. But now I am in it, it is messy, days-long, with ends as yet to be tied up, and the middle hasn't even begun yet. Moments of beauty and irritation lie cheek by jowl – inconvenience, privation, cold – we are presently stuck in one very long prelude, and it gnaws at people's nerves.

I ask myself – how is this story going to turn into one of climate change? How will we transform it in the face of critics – when our most pressing need right now is to find a place where we can buy fuel – the oil that is causing much of the problem. We're just a bunch of wretched contradictions.

The end of the game, still, is just a question – a massive black question mark ahead, dangling metaphorically over the ice to the west.

The ice charts have finally been released for the central part of the passage – Prince Regent, Peel Sound. We all gather round the laptop, the highlight of our day. There is still a lot of ice there and it would be hard to push through – but we might manage to get down to the narrow Bellot Strait which is one of the most likely ways to pass through the crucial central part of the passage, although there is still too much on the western side beyond. Admiralty Inlet looks much more ice free. If we want fuel at some point it is our only option as there is a lot of ice between us and Resolute, it seems a band of 10/10 sea ice has bunged up the western end of the Sound. News comes in via email, 140-character text messages from *Drina* who left a few days ago, *Suilven's* regular radio chat with *Manevai*, of conditions further west. They've encountered much ice, at times they have been blocked in bays or not able to get out. What is found in reality and what's indicated on the chart doesn't seem to quite tally.

'We'll wait until the next ice chart tomorrow,' decides Jimmy, 'and then go straight away if it looks alright.'

The bear appears again, walking alone across the slopes.

'Maybe,' I say to Nera, 'this is one of the last wild polar bears we'll see, if the ice goes perhaps the only ones to survive will be in zoos or those that have learnt to live off human rubbish outside settlements.'

The bear ought to be on the ice. There should be ice here now. We shouldn't be here. It is a tragedy and we profit from it.

STORM

We do not leave the next day. At 4.30 in the morning a north-easterly gale comes howling over the mountains.

Jimmy lets out more anchor chain to hold us firm. The chain is stretched taut and rumbles ominously above our heads on the foredeck, and where it plunges into the sea over the bow.

Then a gust of wind over 44 knots seizes hold of the boat and the brake on the anchor chain goes. The chain rushes out, a furious metal snake that can't be stopped. There is a rush of people onto deck, starting up the engine and checking the chain in the forward locker. Jimmy tightens the clutch on the windlass and lets out almost all the chain – some 100 metres of it.

By now the storm wind has whipped the waves into a grey-green fury and lifts a white cloud of spray out of the water, sending it whirling across the bay. Everyone on all the boats is awake and all we can do is hope our anchors hold, and the boats aren't dashed onto the rocky shore.

The Arctic is bearing down on us from the north and has no mercy.

By late morning the gale is lessening and Talluruti, the tattooed lady whose name should be on the chart, not Dundas, graces us with a rainbow at the head of the bay. See, she says, I can throw this wind at you but I am gracious also and I understand what beauty is. Her fulmars wheel above us in the wind – they look like they are enjoying the storm. I catch a brief glimpse of a bird of prey, with hooked wings and a yellow belly, winging high in the air. Perhaps it was the falcon that *Katrin's* crew had been looking for up in the cliffs the other day. By the time I fetch my camera it was gone and I wondered if I had quite imagined it.

The lull is brief but in that time I bake three loaves of Galeforce bread, help Jimmy make cabbage salad, prepare soup and lunch, read a few pages, clean the fore bathroom, watch boats re-anchor around us. *Maia* comes very close at one point.

And then it starts again. We take a fierce beating for the rest of the day. No pleasantries now, no rowing between boats on social trips. Messages over the VHF are cheerful but terse, and crews hunker down below except for those souls pinned on deck in full foul weather gear, wrestling with anchors or keeping watch as the rain and spray drenches them.

Earlier the barometer rose a hopeful few points but now it is down again – a howling wind catches the boat and pushes her violently so she is almost on her side. Those on watch, watch. Watch and wait.

The wind takes the blank canvas of the sky and sea, and transforms it like an artist. One moment calm and golden, then grey-green and spitting white fury. Last night we raised our faces to the warm sun. Now we're on deck wiping the salt from our skin.

For a time I like the storm, it blows away our cobwebs. *Nuannaarpoq* the Inuit say: *taking an inordinate pleasure in being alive.* Joy in the moment and nature before us.

Weather – that's all that counts to sailors. What really matters other than the wind – its direction and its strength? Once you push off from the shore and are floating on the waters, you place your destiny in the hands of the fickle moving airs of the world. The right wind will grant you a dream of a voyage, the wrong one will give you the fight of your life.

Although the forecast says the storm should relent, by evening there is still no sign of that. We watch the witch's knitting of our black tracks on the electronic chart plotter, swinging back and forth in a raggedy tangle, hoping we won't drag out of the pattern. The anchor chain, despite the clutch, has slammed right out of the locker until we've barely a metre left. Nick improvises a shackle and strop, to hold it on, then eventually Jimmy ties a great big knot in the chain. We are lucky not to lose the anchor. Thankfully our anchor holds, dug firmly into the sea

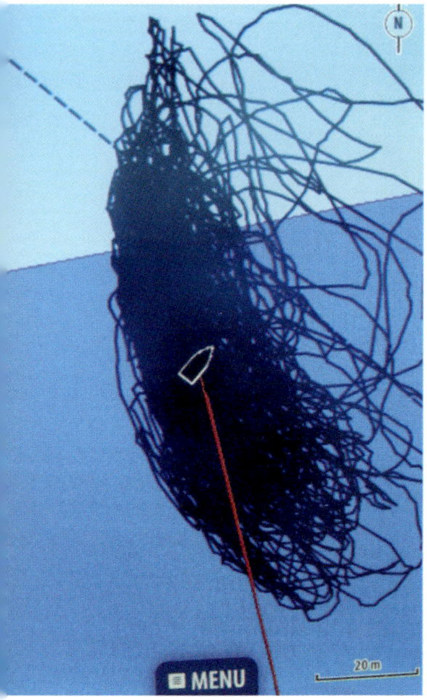

bed. Otherwise our worst danger is other boats coming too close – there is a hair-raising moment as *Gjoa's* foresail unravels and drives them towards us. At least the others moved and re-anchored during the afternoon lull.

I spend the three hours of our night watch staring at the other boats, and the shore behind us while Jean Luc and Jimmy share steering into the wind with the engine on, easing pressure on the chain. The gusts are relentless, forewarned by white smoky walls of foam curling up from the sea and whipping furiously towards us, darkening the waves beneath. Gusts are often a strong gale strength of 40 knots or force 9, and one is over 50 which is force 10, a full-on storm. For a short while around 1 am, I have a turn at the wheel, getting a salty wet slap from the sea spray for my effort.

Now I feel quite beaten down and want it to end. My brain is too tired to do anything more than call upon Talluruti, and all the spirits of the sea and sky and earth that the Inuit believed inhabited all places and all things animate and inanimate – making this desolate land alive. Mostly I called on Talluruti, that we were only visitors but here to help if we could, and had we been chastised enough? I watched her fulmars glide and wheel low over the waves, flicking them with their wing tips, and silently beseeched them also.

The weather forecast predicts that it will ease between 1 and 3 am which would seem to be the case when we go off watch. My feet are so cold it takes about two hours to warm them in my sleeping bag.

Only it pretty much kicks off again straight away. Same again, all over, with *Gjoa* coming too close, Emily trapping her finger in the door, Jean Luc claiming he saw a black animal walking along the shore (fox? Although we are not sure), Marianne feeding Jimmy pieces of Toblerone to keep his energy up.

My prayers probably didn't work, as all storms do pass, but perhaps they helped: now it is a calm and beautiful morning and I'm sitting in the cockpit in ten knots of soft wind and balmy sunshine, the only one awake as everyone sleeps, exhausted after the battering of the last 24 hours.

The other yachts start to leave and after lunch when everyone is rested we do also. The ice charts show the Channel west of Pond is blocked, Resolute blocked too, but Admiralty Inlet is clear of ice. We are heading there now.

'I do hope,' I say to Nera as we stand on deck watching the land pass by us, our cold wild home for these few intense days, 'that this is adieu to Dundas, not au revoir.'

IKPIARJUK

A rainbow greets us as we round the headland, colouring the little settlement at the head of the bay and the white name picked out in stones on the hill above: *Arctic Bay, Nunavut*. Nunavut is the largest, most northern territory of Canada, established in 1999, and its name means 'our land' in Inuktitut.

We didn't see one hint of ice all the way here and the sea is clear, smooth as a mirror. Where did it all go, in just one week? The boat slips easily through the calm water. So strange that this was thick with ice only a few days ago. I am glad now it happened, otherwise we would never have believed that it could.

The bay's name is *Ikpiarjuk*, meaning 'pocket' but it is no more than an indentation into the coast up here on the northern tip of Baffin Island. Baffin, the largest island of the Canadian archipelago, stretches south all the way to the Hudson Strait, the very first land 'discovered' by Frobisher and the Elizabethans' misnamed *meta incognita*.

Some 150 or so coloured houses are spread in a thin line along the shoreline. Today, the Inuit traditional nomadic ways have been locked down into small remote settlements like these. The beach is cluttered with small boats and shacks, a traditional stone and sod house, small tent-shaped structures of metal, large sleds with small boxes on top, like a rough and ready sedan-chair vehicle for the ice. Used for winter hunting – combining shelter and transport in one simple design.

Suilven is already here, taking fuel on with jerrycans from a bowser truck that has parked up on the beach. Another truck rushes along the coast road from the airstrip in the south of the bay; it is strange to see actual cars, actual traffic again. Pickups and quadbikes race along the dirt roads: there isn't really anywhere much to go, as you could walk the settlement one end to the other in half an hour, but I guess it is a form of entertainment.

Jimmy and Nick dinghy ashore to complete formalities. We wait in anticipation: it takes longer than expected as there are two relief police officers on duty and the formalities somewhat throw them, especially trying to ID the Russian rifle for the necessary gun licence. When Jimmy and Nick return at last, they bring a bounty of cigarettes for the smokers, fresh strawberries and raisin and cinnamon bread for the rest of us all. It seems the local supermarkets are full of flown-in goodies, contrary to what the guidebooks led us to believe.

In the afternoon we finally get ashore ourselves. Cheeky, bored boys try to help pull the dinghy ashore. They tell us they have four days left of holidays before they go back to school. We wander in the direction of the one hotel. There aren't many people out and about. A young woman passes us pushing an empty buggy. She is wearing a traditional coat, longer at the front, and a chubby-faced baby is snugly tucked into the huge pouch-like hood at the back.

'Welcome to Arctic Bay,' she says cheerily. 'Where are you from?'

We point to silver *Aventura* swinging on her anchor in the bay.

The hotel allows us to use their washing machine for the afternoon, while we visit both supermarkets, the Coop and Northern, absolutely full of food, even fresh asparagus and melon. As we walk into the Coop a young man stands by the door and shakes our hands. It is fair to say, they don't get many visitors here. The boys from the beach pile in with us and finger the overripe bananas. A scribbled sign is taped to the fridge: *Don't let children buy energy drinks.*

We get tea, sugar, coffee and hot chocolate. Nera craves chocolate and chewing gum. She studies the dyed fox furs disapprovingly.

'That's expensive!' laughs a woman before me at the checkout, pointing at Nera's Hershey bar.

'Yes,' says the young check out girl. 'Everything is expensive. Welcome to Arctic Bay!'

Back at the hotel, Nera, desperate for some younger company, makes friends with Tina (11) and Kristina (13). The two girls are skinny and shivering in their cropped leggings. 'It's cold,' they say, and I wonder what cold means to them as I thought it was warmer and had taken off my hat and gloves, though I am wearing thermal leggings under my jeans.

The girls take a photo of Nera on their i-pod. There is no mobile phone coverage here.

A young woman joins us, Roselin, a cheery chatty twenty-year-old who had laughed at the expensive chocolate in the Northern supermarket. She has just finished her shift there.

'You look familiar, do I know you?' she asks Nera. With her dark hair and sallow skin, it is true Nera doesn't look so far removed from her Inuit sisters.

NERA'S BLOG: PEOPLE OF ARCTIC BAY

Immediately when we jumped off our orange dinghy and into the frigid waters of Arctic Bay we were met with a sea of expectant faces who all clamoured and hollered for our attention. All boys, they pulled at the dinghy handles and made faces while we stepped into the waters and pulled the dinghy up onto the shingled beach.

The people of Arctic Bay don't set eyes on many sailing boats much each year, only 7 in 2013, and yet, now 4 had sailed right into their midst and 2 others were potentially following in our wake.

Wherever our obviously foreign feet took us, we weren't shunned by the community as outsiders, coming to use up their fuel and buy their food. No: we were welcomed by all. From the young boys splashing boisterously on the beach, to the checkout women of the two local supermarkets. I quickly made friends with some of the local youth who must have been as interested in a pale, blue-eyed girl with a strange accent as I was in them. Either way, we were able to connect in seconds and they were able to delight me in their stories of life in the bay.

Nera and I stand outside on the hotel steps overlooking the Bay and chat with Tina and Kristina for a long time. We learn that the Inuktitut words on the hill as we entered say 'welcome'. That the hamlet has a school, a college, a clinic, a heritage centre and a community building. That the kids often sleep all day and stay up at night in summer. That the only time Tina and Kristina have left Arctic Bay is for medical emergencies, a broken leg, a cut lip – to Ottawa. 'We saw trees there,' they say.

There isn't much wildlife round here, though once a hungry polar bear came scratching at the door of their home. Sometimes killer whales came into the bay, but that is rare, and now the hunters must go far out to hunt for seal and narwhal. There are yearly hunting quotas for wild meat and all the community goes out to hunt. In the supermarket we'd seen public information posters that show the benefits of the traditional diet over the processed sugar and carbs of modern food. But it is a problematic comparison, I think, as studies have shown the wild meat to be full of modern toxins, heavy metals and all the rest. Nature – no longer pure.

Hunting – at least it gives the men and boys something meaningful to do. If you take it away, what do you put in its place? But fuel for outboard engines is expensive. As is an airplane ticket out of here. I guess you can only leave when you have a medical emergency.

Tina tells us that her father and uncle were drowned out in the bay in strong winds when their boat capsized a couple years ago. She points to the large white cross on the hill which another of her uncle's raised in memorial.

'I had to go out of the house,' she says 'to my friends. There was too much crying.'

It is not an earth-shattering conversation, in a sense there is no weight to it at all, but all the small details and facts are like little drops, one by one, filling up the glass. It isn't always clear how knowledge will come. In a light and friendly conversation on the steps of the inn. It may be there. You may only realise later on – much later – what was significant, which words exchanged will remain with you for always.

Like an eleven-year-old fatherless girl saying: there was too much crying.

❄ ❄ ❄

Sunday comes, and it pours with rain – rain which falls as snow on the mountain tops. I don't go ashore at all except to deposit some of the crew desperate for the hotel's internet access. The hotel runs out of water today, no doubt from all our washing – the other guests aren't best pleased.

Marianne wanders around on her own and meets two women both with babies tucked behind them in their traditional hooded parkers. They stand on the street corner and sing her their traditional songs. Marianne takes her camera everywhere and films everything. She has a knack of being in the right place at the right time, and her natural warmth of character draws the best out of people so she can capture these moments on film. She has had a passion for photography all her life, and I recall being in awe of her when she visited us years ago in London as a cool eighteen-year-old and I felt like a lumpy, uncool fourteen-year-old at odds with the world. She went on to make a career for herself as an editor in TV and film. She sailed to Tuvalu with Jimmy years ago, when I was too pregnant with Nera to travel, and subsequently got a commission to return and complete a full-length documentary.

On Monday we accompany Jimmy ashore so he can arrange fuel delivery with Ruth, who runs the hotel. A woman with a week-old husky puppy, eyes still closed, comes in with her three young daughters. The puppy is named 'Little Boy' and that cheers Nera up who is bored.

I listen to the women speaking their language and wish I could reproduce the resonant q and k sounds, and the u that comes from the back of the throat. It sounds like a language that has absorbed thousands of years of ice.

Marianne and I interview Ruth on film. When we mention climate change, she shrugs her shoulders. We get the same reaction from other people we speak to in the settlement. Because they'd rather not say? because they don't know? because the winters are still cold and the ice melts in summer, mostly, and life is still hard?

The trouble is, it is all invisible to the naked eye. Airborne and ocean borne pollutants from the rest of the world seep upwards and accumulate in Arctic animals and humans. Studies have found heavy metals accumulating in the milk of Arctic mothers. But – I can't see into the blood and fat of the polar bear, into the bones of the cheery, healthy-looking young girls that chat to us on the hotel steps.

What am I supposed to write, what am I supposed to see?

❄ ❄ ❄

Outside the hamlet office, the settlement's administrative centre, a bulldozer shifts earth here and there and yesterday's rain has turned the dirt streets to mud. It is hard to find the doors in these places as in Greenland, they are often at the back, the buildings have no windows and are blank and uninviting except for stern signs saying *Tobacco has no place in our community* and *Don't smoke within three metres of the entrance.*

We'd hoped to talk to some of the hamlet officials, but they are away at another meeting. I wonder who reads the English-Inuktitut Climate Change glossary, many copies of which are piled in a cardboard box by the door.

Hilaup Aalannguqt irninga : Climate Change.

We head on to the cultural centre, along the muddy streets. Nera perks up when she spots a cute puppy who wants to play. It is accompanied by a wiry suspicious looking dog that keeps its distance and barks when it has decided that playtime is finished.

The heritage centre is modest, a place to buy souvenir stone carvings, walrus and sealskin earrings, watch a jolly tourist video and look at a display of traditional clothing. The young girl on the desk helps Nera get onto the internet. Just before they close at noon her boss turns up. He is a white Canadian who left the police and settled here, married a local woman and had a family. The first thing we discover in talking to him is that the fact it is now raining is significant – as it didn't before.

'This was a desert,' he says. 'Precipitation is new. People notice the melt is earlier and the freeze is later these years, but they try to keep their traditions going.'

So few yachts visit as it is off the route, and most prefer to stop in Resolute, if they can get there through the ice. He wishes more would come, as it would help the hamlet's economy.

I rush to meet Jimmy and help with the provisioning. It is busy on the beach, refuelling from the lorry, the boys helping. Jimmy does a crazy lot of shopping, buying everything on offer that is going out of date and I guess no one locally can afford or want to buy. As a result, we now have a couple of hundred chocolate spoons.

Nera hangs out with Tina, Kristina and the other young people gathered on the beach, to chat and chat, enjoying herself after weeks of only adult company.

'I don't want to leave Arctic Bay,' she says when she comes back.

… but we do, as we must.

WILDERNESS

Slowly the dark coast of Devon Island appears again. A few miles west of Dundas, the coast is already a little different as we approach Cuming Inlet. The cliffs are steep, black forbidding fortresses of stone somewhat like you'd imagine the mythical land of Mordor. Glaciers coming down to the sea are the only pale respite in the landscape of gloom. Arctic Bay now seems like an oasis. Buttresses of yellow sandstone bulge along the headlands, while below the jutting cliffs swell the yellow bellies of crumbled fallen soil, rubble and shattered stone, tapering away to low headlands and beaches – a curiously hermaphrodite landscape from the masculine fortification above, to the feminine, soft, falling away to the water. Each groove and valley in this rock represents a tongue of ice rubbing its way through – and all that might is almost gone, only scraps remain on the hill tops, and cling to the valleys, remnants of once huge glaciers. A soft drizzle falls. The dry, cold, Martian desert is turning soft, wet and green.

We motor up the inlet, *Suilven* behind us. The green on the lower slopes and the spits of land running along the shoreline, colouring the rocks – this may be the green that comes each and every brief summer, so perhaps nothing unusual. I see a speck of moving white on the shore, far away, and with my camera's zoom spot a ghost-white caribou family cropping plants along the shore. Two adults, two young ones, who skip up the bank, happily unaware of human eyes watching. These creatures have been here a long time, and the vegetation, their summer bounty, must have always been here too, to sustain them.

These are Peary Caribou, of the High Arctic islands, not found amongst the vast herds of caribou in other parts, and they are smaller and paler, almost white.

My lens is smudged with rain, so the photos are unfocussed, greyed-out, as if the pale animals were barely there. Their heads are down, busy with their feed – no time to even look up for a strange noise, boat motor passing – if I was up right close they would be flesh and blood, I'd know the smell and breath of them, and those proud antlers, that strong reality, the sudden flare of nostrils and the fear.

A little later, a stocky brown muskox can be seen stepping slowly over the hill. Even from very far away, the muskox don't appear as ghosts; their brown stubbiness, the very manner in which they walk, picking their way over the stones, seems to embody stubbornness, and the statement: 'I am here, watcha gonna do about it? I can stand my ground in a -50°C blizzard. No need to fade into the background, not me.'

The muskox is a glimpse into our distant past – as close as we'll get to looking at a live mammoth – a last true remnant of the ice age, the one true Arctic land mammal.

A green spit of land juts out of the eastern side, near the head of the inlet, and we tuck behind here to anchor. After both engines are off, a profound quiet descends, other than the sound of water falling, tumbling down out of every rocky crevice. Occasionally a seal pops up his head, then dives, and never comes up again in the same place, so a photo is always impossible.

The usual ice charts and news snippets arrive from other boats. The cruise ship *National Geographic* has arrived at Beechey to the west of here, and can't get through the passage. Will we end up following them and their 40 decamping tourists? I don't much relish sharing an anchorage with them.

Clearly there is another week at least of waiting, as a lid of ice has blown from Lancaster Sound into Prince Regent. Peel Sound is still blocked, and although there is now a way of sorts down to Bellot Strait, beyond that the chart remains firmly coloured red, impenetrable. Beyond that, west, past Gjoa Haven, the way is clear – so close – and so frustratingly far! A heap of boats coming the other way, bound east are no doubt waiting there. Meanwhile our westbound gang has its shape – west of us are *Manevai*, *Lillian B*, *Drina* and *Moloda*, while in Arctic Bay are *Arctic Tern*, *Revenge*, *Gjoa* and *Katrin*.

NERA'S BLOG:
MUSKOX OF THE NORTH

The Australian yacht 'Drina' first informed us of these shaggy ungulates via a boat email telling us to keep our eyes peeled for Muskox and walrus on the rocks and tundra of Cuming inlet. We first spotted this lone animal as it grazed on the high Arctic meadow on the port side. All it was really interested in was grazing, and eventually lay down on the grassy ground.

After the first sighting, we were bidding for more: our wish was granted in the form of two beasts, this time on the opposite bank of the inlet, making their ambling way alongside and then past *Aventura*.

Muskox are, one could say, the remnants of ice ages which have passed; their ability to withstand -50°C blizzards due to coarse outer hairs and a thick, light fleece of wool which is called qiviut by the Inuit. They moult in summer and the qiviut hangs tattered around their ankles adding another skirt-like layer to the already hanging, long outer hairs.

As the ox walks, you can see the muscles rippling under the coat as his cloven hooves strike the rocks beneath him. He comes to a standstill and glances behind him, opening his muzzle slightly as if to usher on his companion. His headdress of curling horns sits above his brows and captures the attention as the pale contrasts with his dark mahogany pelt.

Another interesting phenomenon was when one chose to run into the water, splashing great washes of salty spray into the air. Leaping up and allowing gravity to pull him down, he sent water in every direction and finally, having satisfied his need he shook several times and came out of the cold water. As he joined the other, he charged and they galloped across the beach and towards the rocks.

You'd never guess that a calm-looking animal such as that would move so fast. Luckily, we were firmly planted on the boat rather than anywhere near their pounding hooves.

'We've decided to turn back.'

John from *Suilven* has come by in the dinghy to tell us their news; they're worried about getting into the Pacific too late when the autumn storms start to blow. So it looks as if *Aventura* will go on as the lonesome BPO boat, though *Drina* is considering becoming an honorary member.

Both boats move up to the head of the inlet so we can go ashore together. I quickly whizz up a carrot cake en route, left from one of the cake mixes bought all those months ago in London, and stored away until now below the floorboards. It gets cooked in the microwave which drains so much electricity it can only be used when the engine is running.

A broad U-shaped valley lies at the head of the inlet, where a long-gone glacier has flattened the land. The mud it created makes for good holding ground. The water is exceptionally clear. A huge red jellyfish drifts by, opening and closing like a giant jungle flower. *Cyanea arctica.*

The crews dinghy ashore for a farewell outing. Some had the intention to walk to the head of the valley but after a while realise it is too far. Distances are deceiving here and we aren't alone in observing this:

> *Parry was entranced by the tricks the Arctic could play... Distance was a baffling matter of guesswork: large outcrops of rocks which seemed at least half a mile away across the snow became, after a minute's walk, a small stone which they passed from hand to hand in wonder.* Barrow's Boys

Human footprints join muskox ones in the mud. A jellyfish has been stranded – beautiful, voluminous in the water, here collapsed to a red soft blob decomposing and oozing yellow matter.

We must keep an eye out for bears, although at least here we would see them coming for a long way off, but my eyes are mainly drawn to the ground, where there are so many rocks of different colours, red, yellow and purple, dragged here by the ice, embedded in the mustard-yellow mud. Many rocks are multi-coloured, compressed together into one, in intricate lines and patterns, smoothed, smashed or squashed by the power of the ice.

Emily and Nera stop and sketch the view.

We appear to have reached the most northern point of our summer, eleven miles deep inside Devon Island. 74°43'N... the numbers when I write them in my journal don't sound like much, don't give any impression of the long cold seasick way it took to get to this place, this place where very few humans have ever been.

Back by the dinghies, the crew of *Suilven* surprise us with sparkling wine and nibbles from their rucksacks for an impromptu farewell party on the shore. We toast our northernmost point and our parting from each other, our shared adventures, and sing a last rousing rendition of our beset in the ice song *Push with a Tuk!* to the tune of *A Drunken Sailor.*

Back on the boat Nera and I quickly decorate the microwave carrot cake for a last gathering of all of the crews, before *Suilven* weighs anchor and motors away. *Aventura* is left alone in the mirrored reflection of the mountains, a silver boat pinned like a Victorian butterfly specimen to the shimmering light of rock and water.

The songs and chat and the engine noise are gone, and the quiet descends on us again. It is the quiet you'd only find in a vast uninhabited wilderness like this – where even the animals don't draw attention to themselves – the white boulder of a Caribou, like a ghost passing, and even the doughty I-am-here Muskox mostly looks like a brown boulder if seen from a distance.

Of course, it is not a wilderness – what does that mean anyway? My Kindle dictionary is all I have recourse to – *an uncultivated, uninhabited and inhospitable region* – which I suppose is technically correct, although in the hearts of those who want to preserve these places they resist this word, as it implies an emptiness waiting to be filled (dug up, cultivated, exploited). Nothing there. In this sense, I shouldn't describe this place as a wilderness, as it is full of sustainable life, generation after generation, from the millimetre black speck of a jumping sand flea on the glacier valley mud, to the beautiful red flower of the jellyfish, to the one we all know, the white prince of the realm, the bear.

Other definitions – *a neglected or abandoned area* – no.

But its origin is from Old English – *land inhabited only by wild animals* from wild dëor, wild deer.

In its origin, then, I can call it a wilderness. Because animals certainly live here and humans certainly don't.

We watch the film *Moby Dick* as *Suilven* leaves us. It is a long sail for them, south back to Greenland.

We head west into the fog, motoring through the last remnants of sea ice, ghostly relics of the winter, white reminders of what has been, and will come again.

The sea is a cold grey steel, flat and shiny as a knife, and the ice floats on it like a jagged wall of white. Flat pieces, rounded and blue underneath, are pushed into shapes, fragments, slabs, slanted ledges and wedges. I wonder how it all stays together. The larger pieces bunch in the middle and where we are, travelling along the edge, all that is left are tiny fragments like shattered pieces of glass scattered in the water. They'll be gone soon. The ice floats in ghostly silence, enshrouded in its fog, shielded from the world. It has created its own weather as the warm air we were in earlier hits the cold air and the ice wraps fog around itself, resisting the melt.

Without a functioning magnetic compass, it would be quite possible to get completely lost in this fog, other than a smudge of sun to guide you when it breaks for brief moments through the cloud.

On the cold evening watch: -2°C air, while the water is 2.6°, nearly 5° warmer!

Nera comes out into the cockpit to say someone has helped themselves without asking to the Arctic Bay chocolate spoons. We are supposed to share them and ask who would like one. Spoongate! These small things create far larger tensions than they should amongst people stuck for weeks together in the tiny space of a boat. We've been a long time squished together, and fair to say, not all is well for us in the ice while there is still no end in sight, no way through.

BEECHEY

When the fog lifts, far away to the west a white flare reflects upwards into the clouds, a sign of the ice between here and Resolute. At last our destination can be seen a few miles ahead: we are about to enter the bay where John Franklin and his crew spent a winter in 1845 on the two ships *Erebus* and *Terror*, before heading south never to be seen again. This is one of the Arctic's most well-known mysteries and even today people keep searching for clues. No note or sign was left by them to indicate their route or intention, thereby sealing their doom, as those who came looking for them, found this place first, combed the bare slopes for any document or clue and found nothing more than an empty stone cairn, a pair of gloves left out to dry and three dead men buried in the stony ground. This lack of clues sent rescuers on fruitless searches north and west, but never south down Peel Sound which is where the Franklin expedition had sailed in a rare moment when the Sound became ice-free.

Many expeditions followed over the years to try to find the lost men and ships, and as a by-product a large part of the Arctic was mapped. Franklin became a household name back in Victorian England, but many others sailed this way, mapped and navigated, endured many winters, lost very few men, traversed thousands of miles by sledge, learnt Inuit ways – and then returned home, unlike the Franklin crews, alive to tell the tale. Their names are forgotten now except for a few traces in the places named after them on the charts.

For sailors who've steeped themselves in the history and tales of the Arctic, this place is the Taj Mahal, the Eiffel Tower, the place you must visit.

We anchor at the head of the large bay, to our southwest is Beechey 'island' which in fact is a peninsula linked by a slender causeway to Devon Island that is submerged at high water.

French *Manevai* and American *Lillian B* are here.

'I don't like this place much, it has bad vibes,' says Jimmy as we drop anchor near the other boats. 'We'll leave tomorrow and go to Graham Harbour where *Drina* are. Then we'll sail in company with them.'

I agree. It seems a godforsaken place.

NERA'S BLOG: EREBUS & TERROR BAY

Compared to the other harbours and bays our boat had nestled into over the past weeks, Beechey Island looked rather desolate. Of course, that's what we said when we set eyes on all the others as well, but there wasn't even any green spattering of meadows like in Dundas or Cuming inlet. Not that this meant there wasn't wildlife, a seal bobbed its head above the water and watched us curiously with beady eyes.

Everyone sleeps soundly after their night watches. I'm the only one awake, because Jimmy had let me sleep on for a couple more hours when I should have started my watch with him at 5. I make bread, and as I knead the dough, I look out of the cabin window. I wonder who else has looked out at this place, in the galley making bread for an always ravenous crew. Imagine being a sailor spending months on end here in the winter darkness. No scrap of colour, and even the birds have the sense to migrate, at least.

As the dough is left to rise in the warm oven, I step out into the cockpit for a moment. It is so quiet that the sound of a nearby fulmar washing itself is startling. A big black seal lies on a tiny ice floe not so far away. It slips into the water to be replaced by a smaller grey one. I think Nera might like to see this so I go wake her; she hasn't taken a night watch so I don't feel too bad about this. She is happy to see the seal, that rolls about in an amusing way as if performing morning aerobics, raising and lowering its flippers, before giving up and trying to lie and get comfortable on the ice which is barely big enough.

'How would you describe the colour of the land?' I ask her.

'Poo-brown.'

She has a point. The brown is dull, rather disgusting, almost green but not quite, like something that is decaying. The few scraps of ice caught in folds in the hill are grubby, not white. A pile of fuel drums are rusting on shore, man's noble relic – a monument to our wonderful Age of Oil.

We have managed to crawl even further north than before (74°43.55'N) – and that's really it, only southward from here on. *Aventura* has already sailed a quarter of the way round the world (granted the world is smaller at the top, but still).

The sun comes out and it turns into a bright, calm afternoon, giving the solemn hills some colour, trying to win us over, trying to seduce us into liking this grim place.

❄ ❄ ❄

I wasn't expecting much from this excursion as a tribute to the great failure of Franklin, it means far more to other sailors here and some of our crew. We've a book onboard which describes the autopsies that were done on the unfortunate sailors buried here, establishing evidence of lead poisoning from faulty canned food, although some now dispute that account. The fact is, Franklin and his crew did behave in odd ways that have never been explained, as reported by the explorer John Rae who came across Inuit people further south who told him they had seen some confused and aggressive men wandering about. As is depicted by the film *Passage* that we had watched back in Dundas Harbour, when Rae returned to England and reported what he'd been told, including suggestions there might have been some cannibalism, Victorian England, led by Franklin's wife and Charles Dickens, no less, went out of its way to discredit and vilify him.

Listening to indigenous voices, or learning their ways to survive in the deep north, was not the British Empire's way. This lost precious time, no one went south to check out the stories; all of Franklin's crew perished and his ships were never found. Even today people are still looking for the wrecks.

And yet, the Inuit stories of meeting the sailors on their 'death marches' as they abandoned their ships and trudged off into the Arctic, were passed down through the generations, as captured in the book *Encounters On The Passage: Inuit Meet The Explorers* by Dorothy Harley Eber.

In modern times, in the *Passage* film, an Inuit man confronts a bluff Navy guy who still, even all these years later, tries to claim the evidence points to an Inuit massacre. He stands, incredulous, in front of the Franklin memorial in London. 'Dead men can't find the Northwest Passage,' he says.

It is a long dinghy ride to the beach so we take turns for shore parties. I set off with Nera, Jimmy and Jean Luc and we aim for the graves spotted by the camera zoom earlier. A small black smudge I couldn't identify from afar turns into a notice board as we approach, which is so strange to see in the midst of this human-less nothingness.

There are also white grave posts facing west. Human-made but bleached so much, almost turned back into the landscape. No picket fence, no ceremony, a mere scraping on a long bare slope – there have been a handful of visitors in the past few years (more than ever since climate change) but before that, so very few people ever came here, and only then in the soft warm exhalation of summer, no more than a brief moment's breath in the year – and then plunged back into dark months of solitude, endless night, and no one here, no one for miles around.

My heart was beating slightly faster (could there be a bear? *Lillian B's* crew told us they had seen bear droppings ashore) as we came to shore. The water is clear and inviting, in the tropics you'd swim in this in a flash. We step off onto a grey beach of broken stones – and crunch up the hill. Really crunch – the stones are rough, somehow, like bits of broken cement, mostly flat and grey. Nera picks one up. It has a curious shape and texture, like a fossil.

On the way to the graves, looking down at the ground, I realise these are pieces of dead coral. This seems to be a supreme irony – some bitter joke of Nature – that in this iron, desperate place of cold death, men walked and died on a bed of forgotten pieces of long gone tropical warm seas.

Later, I find out that cold water coral does exist… I never knew, and in fact I don't think anyone much knows about the coral reefs deep in these cold seas.

Perhaps we could link the Blue Planet Odyssey, Beechey, to the South Pacific, dead to dying coral, a sad link, a chain of time and place, of natural and manmade effects upon the landscape, relentless, unstoppable.

On a large boulder beside the graves people have placed the most attractive coral pieces – in memorial.

We strike overland south to see the Franklin memorial. Nera and I lag behind, stopping to examine interesting stones and coral fragments. The crunching stones underfoot sound as if something is following us; we fall behind the two men, who are striding on, and we must hurry to catch up. I am tempted to take notes en route but we are walking at a fast clip and I don't want to fall further behind and feel a bear's breath, or worse, on my shoulder.

We cross over the high land of fallen shingle and soft ground. By the graves, nothing grew, but on the heights are yellow Arctic poppies – like pale partners of those red ones now blooming in Flanders – a memorial of life in death.

August 2014. It is a hundred years on, almost to the very day, from the start of World War One, and not quite 200 years from the Franklin expedition, and here are the poppies, scattered over the hill – the sun is just slipping over the peak, and she illuminates their petals, so many spots of yellow light that lift the spirits.

Poppies in the Arctic, who would have thought it? I've read the same few facts about Beechey Island, always the same, rechurned in each and every book we've got onboard. Even the best and most acclaimed of these writers, for all their skill, just regurgitate other people's words and experiences, and like me from the deck of the boat, watch the land from afar and draw conclusions. No one mentioned poppies and broken coral.

The decaying land seen from the boat was a figment of my imagination. In every single place we've visited, my first impressions have been proved wrong when I get ashore.

As we drop down to the other side, there are lovely views across the bay but Jimmy looks back and worries the dinghy might drift off with the tide. He doesn't want us to linger.

Suddenly there is a furious noise above us, a flash of feathers, as a large white bird and another, which is coal-black, have a dramatic scrap in the air.

'Get a photo!' calls Nera but my fingers fumble with the camera and I miss it. There is a blur and they are gone.

We spot our first rusty can nestled among the poppies, then many more. Rusty metal – cans and barrel hoops – and weathered wood, are scattered over the stony ground, and among the remnants of ruined Wellington House, like some sort of piece of conceptual art or gallery installation. Perhaps these tin cans are the very ones that had poisonous lead to seal in the sailors' preserved food.

The white wooden memorial to Franklin beside the house is grooved where bears have tested their claws. Nera runs her fingers along the long scratch marks in the wood.

'Daunting to think,' she says, 'that an animal has touched this too.'

On the cliffs above the shoreline, she spots that there are white gyrfalcons nesting – fierce guardians of this place, perhaps. One chases away a black bird,

a raven or skua and then perches on a rock not so far away. My cold hands struggle to rush with the camera but at least this time I get one blurred photo of the gyrfalcon.

Jimmy insists we head back. We try to keep up. Interesting things to poke and look at! At times we sink boot deep into the soft ground. No time for us to jump in the ice valley.

The dinghy's ok at least, and as we lug it down to the water, Nera notices a curious swimming creature about five centimetres long, for all the world like a transparent angel with gentle wings and a long draping tail. I guess this is a food for the birds. An angel seems appropriate in this living-dying place.

The creature, of course, wouldn't define itself as food. It'd regard itself as much in the here and now as the muskox. I hope it doesn't mind too much being scooped up into a plastic box for a trip back to the boat to be photographed. It is called a sea butterfly, or a swimming sea snail, although its shell is very light and transparent.

When I pour it over the side, it wafts away quietly, in a current or of its own volition, I can't tell.

As the others take their turn going ashore we get visitors from the other two boats, and hear their tales of being stuck in the ice and gales in bays as they came west. They've been here a week, hoping to go to Resolute for fuel, but the way is still blocked.

They describe a phenomenon which happened here a few days ago. Lots of fish crowded into the bay, hunted by packs of seals that herd them to the head of the bay. This is followed a day or so later, by pods of beluga whales that crowd around the boat in a noisy, musical frenzy. That must've been a tremendous sight… Nera and I are quite jealous.

At evening the sun almost, almost sets, colouring the sky west beyond the isthmus, and painting a red brushstroke, a band of red light, across the top of Cape Riley. Light can, it seems, change the grimmest of landscapes. We are reaching the mid-point of August: our summer is on the wane.

DECISION TIME

Thus vanished our golden dreams, our brilliant hopes, our high expectations!... To describe our mortification and disappointment would be impossible at thus having our increasing hopes annihilated in a moment.

William Hooper, Purser, under Parry's command, 31 August 1818

Even Beechey looks spectacular this morning, and molten gold runs over the sea from the bright new sun. There is a big high over us – light winds, blue skies. A red Canadian icebreaker *Pierre Radisson* has joined us in the bay. Jimmy calls them on the VHF radio to get some news. It seems that the large tourist exploration ship that they were supposed to help through the pinch-point in the middle of the Passage couldn't get through, and so they had to turn back.

The crew gathers and we talk about what we can do next.

Jimmy suggests going back to Graham Harbour, a little to the east along the coast, where *Drina* is waiting.

'What's the point?' says one of our crew sharply.

My father does not reply but I can tell he is not happy as once again his suggestions are dismissed. There have been many such small incidents, building up the tension.

In my account so far I have not dwelt much on any personal issues on board. Just say – there were crew tensions with those who were not family, which ran through our voyage like a thin steel wire – and in this we were hardly unique among Northwest Passage supplicants. It is relatively common on small boats to have such issues when strangers are cooped up together for weeks on end.

Jimmy, our captain, talks to the rest of the crew. There is disagreement about next steps. We have to accept that time is running out. How much longer can we wait for the ice to break? The worry is that it will be very late in the season when we get through, just when the autumn storms start to hit the north Pacific. Or we might end up having to over-winter in the Arctic: Jimmy doesn't want to leave *Aventura* alone here, and too many of us have jobs and families and school we must get back for.

I have no idea what the outcome of the talk will be. My blood runs cold up and down my body and I feel sick from all the tension. I wonder if we are about to join the noble or ignoble ranks of those – so many! – who turned back.

It is the quiet time of the afternoon. I think I'll hide in my cabin as long as possible. Jimmy comes in to find me and talk to me alone. The 'talk' has really not gone well. It looks as if we must part company with some of our crew, if they can find other boats to go on, or head home from Pond Inlet, the nearest airport.

At the point of failure – Beechey, the cairn with no words – the question mark, the sign that pointed nowhere – our own small fate is to be determined.

Ok – that's it. It has been decided. We are giving up and turning back.

❄ ❄ ❄

In this Game of Chess, the White Queen beat us. All those pawns and pieces moved so very slowly. The question mark hanging white to the west remained as illuminated and unreachable as an ice blink – and then snap! Checkmate. The white hand moved – remorseless, inscrutable – she got us, as she got so many before. In that sense at least we can partake of a noble tradition. We are true Brits at last, joining the polar fetishisation of failure. Franklin is a household name more than Rae, Scott more than Shackleton. And it was the Norwegian Amundsen who was the first to get through the Northwest Passage – he learned the ways of the ice, and of the people who'd called it home for thousands of years, before he headed south to the other end of the world to beat the Brits there as well.

Perhaps the metal of the wire was too close to the compass and made the voyage go off course just as the proximity of the magnetic pole affects real compasses.

Marianne wondered if the magnetism affected us personally, but I don't know.

She and I also often thought, when it was quiet and everyone slept, and we were alone on watch, that we heard faint voices on the boat, a murmur of words, but there was never anyone there.

NERA'S BLOG

I thought it was a little eerie that at the same time I was coming to an end of the book I'd been using as my diary, we decided to turn back due to the uncertainty of the Passage as the ice wasn't melting in the centre. Either way, it was now our turn to turn our bow around and head back east.

We head back a short way to Graham Harbour, round protected bay but dry and featureless. Although, just before we arrived, one of the other boats here had seen a muskox face off a polar bear.

Jimmy has arranged for Emily to go on *Drina*, with her plastic trawl, and she takes the Secchi disk too so the studies can continue. Nick and Nikki will go to *Moloda*. Jean Luc is staying with us as he needs to get back home. We donate some of our provisions – pasta, pâté, milk to *Drina*, tea and hot chocolate to *Moloda*, biscuits and chocolate spoons to all. I am glad when it is done and we raise the anchor to leave, waving our farewells. Will they get through? *Drina* might if no one else does because Michael doesn't mind overwintering in Cambridge Bay. *Drina* is now the sole representative left of the BPO Northern route. After all that effort, it has come to this alone.

Strong easterlies are predicted soon so we must move fast out of Lancaster Sound. As we emerge from the harbour, in the distant west the clouds have stretched themselves into freaky shapes. It is as if the horizon were stretched upwards, repeating itself over and over, white line after white line, and whether

the white is cloud or ice, I cannot tell. This illusion is known as the fata morgana, from the Italian for Morgana le Fay, as there was a belief that similar mirages in the narrow Messina Straits between Italy and Sicily were conjured up to lure sailors to their deaths.

Sirens, Morgana – females as ever get the blame for men's mishaps.

A band of ice appears ahead. It is scattered thinly across the sea surface, so quite navigable. The sun shines onto melted fingers of ice, poking up out of the sea like the tips of forgotten white trees. Our last sea ice.

A thousand miles lie before us to Nuuk. South to the warmth, and darkness. After a month of no nights – what does that do to the brain? Wide-eyed and wired, we are still deep in the Arctic.

The south-setting current, alive with bergs, awaits us.

Aventura feels empty and quiet with three less people onboard, and I feel very light, very light indeed. We are going home.

WE CANNOT GET OUT

All this sweetness and light ends abruptly in the early hours.

Marianne, Nera and I had been enjoying our night watch together as we motor east, keeping an eye out for ice, talking out the last few days and events when suddenly the engine starts to make a loud rattling noise.

In a flash Jimmy wakes and turns off the engine. He checks everything over but cannot determine what is wrong. Time passes, without answers. He sits with his head in his hands thinking, thinking, trying to work out what the problem is.

At some point, I cannot recall why, I look into the bilge below the propeller shaft and spot a small bolt in there. After closer examination it appears the propeller has sheared from the gear flange and there are broken nuts and bolts in the bilge. We do not know why. Jean Luc and Jimmy write an email between them to the French boatyard for advice. Not being able to use the engine could be a real disaster. There is no one here to help us.

During this delay, while we are engineless and hove-to, not moving forwards, the promised easterlies come upon us. The wind blows just from where we want to go, and it strengthens by the hour. As we cannot use the engine, we must tack back and forth across Lancaster Sound. The boat batters into cold grey seas, the sky grey and close above us. Water crashes over the bows and seeps into the cabin. The sea temperature drops to 0 and then -0.1 and there is fresh, clean white snow on the far mountains. Winter is coming.

And, despite all this effort, we make no progress east at all. The chart plots our course, tacking into the mouth of Admiralty Inlet and then back, north towards Dundas Harbour, and then we repeat it all over again. We find ourselves again in the place where we were once beset by ice, in one of these ironic little tricks this place likes to play on those deluded souls who chose out of their own free will to come here.

I remember how we arrived a few weeks ago fresh and full of expectation, the journey here seemed quick and easy, into the Sound with a soft breeze and sunlight – and all of summer lay open before us. Now we are fighting to get out, the season is closing – and behind us the other yachts start peeling away also. *Manevai* and *Lillian B* have turned around.

The Arctic doesn't want to let us go, holding on, beating us back. A trap is slowly closing around us.

The slow diagnosis finally ends with Jimmy having eliminated all options save one, that there must be something wrong with the propeller. Marianne has a Gopro camera which is lashed with cable ties to the pole of the long tuk, to stick over the side of the hull and get a view under the water. The camera is hauled back up and cold fingers plug it into a laptop. A perfectly clear little film appears on the screen of a black rope wrapped right around the prop shaft, one frayed and broken end flapping away like a sad ornament. No idea how it got there in this empty ocean, and a quick check shows no rope is missing from on deck.

'I'm going to put on my dry suit,' decides Jimmy, 'to try and get the rope off.'

Feeling seasick, I must help dig out the diving gear from the locker deep under our bunk, while Jean Luc and Marianne assist him getting ready in the cockpit. The image rises in my befuddled seasick mind of a king sat on his throne as two courtiers slowly dress him in stiff and awkward ceremonial robes.

Once ready, he can barely move, encumbered with the dry suit, heavy with weights and equipment. Neither Marianne or I are very enthusiastic for our 74-year-old father/uncle to plunge into these Arctic seas mid-ocean, with no functioning engine and no help to be had for hundreds of miles. We lash a line to his waist and fasten the other end to the hull. He hangs off the ladder at the back of the boat. I silently pray he doesn't let go. He tries to look below the waves but the boat is moving far too much to get underwater to see anything. He is in the icy seas for a minute or so only but it is already getting to him and he is starting to lose focus.

'Bring him back,' one of us says urgently.

He clings to the ladder but can't get onto the rungs with the large fins on his feet. With a great deal of effort, superhuman it seems, he lifts a leg and then another for us to grab the fins and pull them off. The mask is passed to one of us and our cold numb hands lose it overboard. It sinks quickly – claimed by the sea.

It is very hard to drag his weight back onboard. Finally he is back in the cockpit. The whole episode only lasted moments but he collapses onto the bench and for a while doesn't respond, blanked out with the bitter cold and the effort.

After this, two bad days follow. All our former watch routines, our organisation, mother watch, schedules, cooking for eight, slides into anarchy. No one eats. We sleep where we can, ragged, tired, quiet.

I've completely lost my sea legs. On night watch with Marianne, I wedge myself on the navigation chair, watching the radar for ice, braced against the heeling of the boat, but must run to throw up every twenty minutes.

When I finally come off watch, I lie down, pinned to my bunk, my eyes closed, unable to move.

'When will this end?' Nera moans as the bow crashes into the waves, up and down, our poor stomachs falling like malfunctioning elevators plunging down skyscrapers. The last few oranges bounce out of the overhead netting onto our heads and anything not wedged in falls onto bunks and floors.

At last the wind lessens a little and in a calmer patch we can test if the engine will function in gear, because the new bolts we've fitted, that the boatyard has emailed to advise us to cannibalise from other places, are holding, and the prop turns slowly while under sail. This is a relief, as the boat can be manoeuvred in an emergency and into port, and now, in the calmer weather which has come, we start to make progress once again.

We even manage to sit together for an evening meal and finish off the stew, our first proper meal in several days, that I'd had the foresight to make in the calm afternoon after leaving Graham Harbour.

'When the engine stopped working and the ice and fog was all around, I was so scared,' Nera tells me now, 'more than any other time so far on this journey.'

All summer my father has kept in close email contact with my mother, but not wishing to worry her, he hasn't so far mentioned our problems these last days.

He emails her at last with news of the propeller issues. 'I knew something was wrong,' she responds, 'I could tell from the tracker on the website you were not making progress.'

He doesn't mention the icy dive.

❄ ❄ ❄

Nearly four in the morning and the sky is a cheerful orange. Each and every time I feel wretched and fed up with this place, like in Beechey, or this morning, the light changes, and its beautiful again, seductive again. East, across the open sea, the horizon stays bright as the sun lingers. Behind, the land is geometric and dark by the shoreline, and all the hills are topped by pink-tinted snow and ice, while puffy pink clouds sail through blue skies. A new-minted lovely day, a day to be enjoyed, to begin again – here she comes, the White Lady, dressed in her brightest colours.

Jimmy takes over the watch.

'Get some rest,' he tells me. 'I can manage.'

I make a cup of tea and look back into the cockpit. Our captain is sitting there on his own, watching the sails and the sea, with his own company, content. In spite of our troubles, he has been rejuvenated by spending time alone with his boat these last few days, happy to put up and adjust sails on his own. For the first time, after all the fuss and clutter and clatter of the past months, quiet moments to be a sailor.

Watching my father, reminds me of something which happened much earlier this year, long before we left home.

OLD SAILORS, SEA SALTS

Back home, in the spring, long before we were due to set off, I'd switched on the radio and caught by chance a radio dramatisation of Dante's *Inferno*. The rich language washed over me, as we plunged deep into the miseries and torment of Hell. My listening was somewhat idly done (although I'd always been interested in the poem, and once learned by heart the first few lines in their original).

Nel mezzo del cammin di nostra vita
mi ritrovai per una selva oscura
ché la diritta via era smarrita.

In the middle of our life's journey
I found myself in a dark wood
Where the straight path was lost.

Idle, until one episode jumped out at me. Dante and Virgil have made it to the Eighth Circle of Hell, where they come across Ulysses, whom Virgil compels to tell the story of his last voyage. Ulysses is bound in fire with Diomedes, having together created the wooden horse that deceived the Trojans, from whom, it is said, the Romans were descended; there is no love lost by Dante for Ulysses, naming him a Counsellor of Fraud, and relegating the great Greek hero, pagan that he is, deep into Hell.

And yet, the poet puts into the mouth of Ulysses, these immortal words:

No tenderness for my son, nor piety
To my old father, nor the wedded love
That should have comforted Penelope

William Blake, Ulysses and Diomed swathed in the same Flame (1824–1827)

Could conquor in me the restless itch to rove
And rummage through the world, exploring it,
All human worth and wickedness to prove.

So on the deep and open sea I set
Forth, with a single ship and that small band
Of comrades that had never left me yet.

'Brothers,' said I, 'that have come valiantly
Through hundred thousand jeopardies undergone
To reach the West, you will not now deny

To this last little vigil left to run
Of feeling life, the new experience
Of the uninhabited world behind the sun.

I was transfixed. Nothing *could conquor in me the restless itch to rove.* These words spoke powerfully to me and the voyage we were about to set out on. My father was in his seventies and still consumed by a burning desire to set sail again, *to seek the new experience/Of the uninhabited world behind the sun.*

My mother had no desire to go sailing any more. She would remain at home throughout this planned voyage. Penelope, waiting at home for news.

Now, a long way from home, lost in the wild northern ocean, I observe my father sat in the cockpit, so profoundly content with the boat, the sea and the sky, these words return to me. Since his boyhood when he first glimpsed the sea on the Black Sea coast seven decades before, this was the life he has chosen. But how could Dante have possibly understood so well, seven hundred years ago, of the passion of the old sailor for the sea, never to be extinguished?

I'd subsequently found Tennyson's poem about Ulysses, inspired by this same scene.

I cannot rest from travel: I will drink
Life to the lees...
Tho'
We are not now that strength which in old days
Moved heaven and earth, that which we are, we are;
One equal temper of heroic hearts,
Made weak by time and fate, but strong in will
To strive, to seek, to find and not to yield.

Somewhat appropriately, Tennyson married Franklin's niece, and penned the words to be found on his Westminster Abbey memorial: *Not here: the White North has thy bones.*

There is a great deal of pleasure to be found in these fragments, linking our lives, our journey, the white Arctic, together across the span of hundreds of years of poetry and love for the sea.

WHAT LIES BEFORE US/ OUR WAKE BEHIND

A calm day. Ahead is always the unbroken water, the path not trod. We pass, marking the water, and we leave the wake behind the boat, as straight on the sea as a ruled line on a paper chart. The wake is made and then the waters close up, smooth over, once again, and our traces are wiped out, completely.

A trace of diesel oil. A piece of orange peel. A tin can sinking to the depths. If only that was all we humans left behind.

Practical matters drag me back to the unpoetic present – we have to sort out arrangements for travelling home and for getting a relief crew to help Jimmy sail back to Europe. But we are in the depths of the August holidays. It seems no one we know is available at such short notice. Nera, Marianne and Jean Luc all need to get home to their various commitments: school, children, work, and they need to leave in Nuuk. After some debate, it is decided.

I'm going to sail with my father back to Scotland, just us two.

I don't really want to do it – I'm so tired, I just want to go home. But I can't let him down; not one more disappointment after these last few days. We've two-handed before – years ago, from Gibraltar out west to Madeira and the Azores. We got on fine.

A lovely, relatively balmy day unfolds. It feels as if we have been through some sort of initiation – reborn again into this bright new day, after our trials. The mountainous spectacle of the coastline slides past, gatherings of glistening giant icebergs.

Nera comes out of her cabin after five days in her bunk. Smiling. I am glad she does, just as we spot a sleeping whale black on the water, spouting white breath forward in such a distinctive way that Nera identifies her as a sperm whale. A survivor of the brutal killing trade that coveted their oil.

We use the camera to check the propeller again – the rope is wound a little bit more tightly but the bolts hold. Beyond the rope, the water looks lovely, clear and green as far as the eye could see, illuminated, glowing on for ever.

Now we are nibbling toffees and marshmallows and it is up to 12°. Almost tropical.

Passed 5000 miles today since Cherbourg. Just over 500 miles til Nuuk.

News from the front line: *Le Mangier*, a 100-ton science and support vessel, is blocked by a plug of 9+ ice six miles wide just west of Bellot Strait. The icebreaker *Pierre Radisson* that we'd seen at Beechey, with the cruise liner following behind, crashed through there a few days ago. Money buys you icebreaking services and an 'authentic' Northwest Passage experience.

❄ ❄ ❄

With the winds so light, I help Jimmy to get the big foresail of the Parasailor ready, beginning with the spinnaker pole. The boat is covered with ropes, all convenient different colours, which would throw a novice into a cold sweat. He explains to me twice, 'this blue and green one is the topping lift' (I know that one – obviously I knew it as a child and I kept that knowledge), 'the grey is the something and the beige is the something.' The downhaul, the aft guy? I hear the words twice, I stare at the ropes, and then the words are gone. Why can I never remember? As I wait for instructions I stare at the ropes. I see them so very clearly, the detail of their complex weaving that makes the fibres so exceptionally strong; the green and blue and yellow are bright in the sun. Their very existence is powerful and I'm fully aware of it and yet there's a blank where the names should be. I wonder about this, because some words are strong in me: solid words for things like sea and sky, and colours like blue and green. But I'm also familiar with the high concepts, good and evil, all those abstract words as big as the universe. These two sorts of words – the physical – and the metaphysical – have been with us from the very beginning. The Greeks, and beyond them in the past no doubt some shaman scratching about and dreaming in an ice age cave, were as familiar with those as I am. These words arrived on earth with us humans.

It is the new words in the middle I have trouble with – what we keep inventing – the technical ones. No doubt there were once a hundred words for stone tools that a cavegirl like me would happily forget – but thousand of years have passed since then and the rate at which we fill up the middle is accelerating. Carburettor, downhaul, microchip – these words I can't hold onto are crowding in – so I guess I'm kind of old-fashioned in the words I can remember.

The Parasailor unfurls, all those little threads untangling like a great big man o'war jellyfish, soft and light to capture the faintest breath of a wind.

❄ ❄ ❄

Night is creeping back, as we slide southwards, and towards the end of August. We spot our first star in weeks, and red lights are needed in the cabin so we don't lose our night vision on night watch.

'Quick!' Jimmy shouts from the cockpit, and I rush out, thinking it's an emergency. He points upwards. The Northern Lights have unfurled themselves grandly across the western sky. I rouse Nera.

Sheets of light, like some strange cosmic mist, are falling through the sky. For a brief moment they curl in pink and yellow circles and then unfold again into falling ribbons of pale yellowy-green. A visible sign of what comes to us every day from the sun, a constant rain of particles, radiation, heat, light – now we can see it very clearly, and yet it seems so very insubstantial, so pale, frail, temporary. From the west the soft shapes spread to the east, strips beyond the masthead, though always most spectacular in the west. Just as they seem to be fading they uncurl again and for a while occupy half the sky from west to east in a glorious spectacle.

This is Nera's last night at sea, her send-off, her Arctic farewell. She stares intently, quietly. Later, she tells me off for talking too much, instead of being quiet and enjoying the show.

'Mum, can't you just be quiet?'

Damn, she is right. Why do I feel the need to fill silences with words?

The lights show as green in photos but in reality they are not green – a pale yellow, not bright, but faded and dusty, with rare hints of pink at times. A colour that is ethereal, and hard to actually get hold of with the eyes – feeling always as if it is fading and gone, slipping away, though in fact you can see it always – modest, hard to grasp, subtle, ephemeral. The show of the North. As fierce and blazing as the Sun is, these are gentle visitations, a soft sign from above. Unlike the physical brutality of the ice, which states its position with cold arrogance, these are apologetic and modest. As if coming towards you in all its beauty and yet trying to hide at the same time.

But in both cases, relentlessly temporary, water and air, soon quite gone.

The fleetingness of the *aurora borealis* is a reminder of what we are, faint lights that flare in this world for a moment and then are gone.

NERA'S BLOG: ROUNDUP AND FAREWELL

We've been stuck in ice, walking among ivory animal bones, talking with Canadian Inuit, and lots more over this 2014 summer.

We've seen Dundas Harbour and the great Polar bear (*Ursus maritimus*), Cuming inlet and the shaggy Musk Ox (*Ovibos moschatus*), Beechey island with its Franklin graves and Gyrfalcons. Among other, more marine wildlife, we've spotted Humpback whales in Greenland, seals practically anywhere you look, and a Sperm whale in the last week. This isn't really even mentioning all the birds such as Fulmars, Murres, Skuas, and Dovekies.

Other than what we have actually seen, this trip was meant to highlight something bigger, affecting the whole Earth: climate change. We've read about how there are indisputable facts and figures showing and proving the existence of this changing climate and how the ice in the Arctic is melting, but when you really go there it makes it all the more real. What with the Inuit finding the melting season is longer while the sea ice is lessening so hunting becomes harder. Even just looking around and seeing a Polar bear standing among grey scree with its stark yellowy-white pelt and seeing the contrast of the two it's not hard to imagine them becoming extinct. Just seeing the receding glaciers and how they are melting more and more makes an impact.

Even now, after so long, no boats have yet made it through the Northwest Passage; some of the ice still hasn't melted and boats are still waiting.

I guess one thing shows how amazingly awe-inspiring the Arctic really is, are the Northern lights. Last night, our last night at sea, we were presented with these shimmering, ethereal visions criss-crossing the night sky. What a wonderful, natural sight which seems totally untainted by human hand. The Northern lights, Aurora borealis are usually seen only in winter as the nights are dark and generally clear so it was a big surprise for us. They are sun flares which escape the gravity of the sun and are released into space and some are attracted by the gravitational pull of Earth. When they hit the atmosphere, the colour can be seen in high latitudes such as in the Arctic. Usually, they can be predicted as the sun is monitored.

So now, after my last night at sea, I can say I've seen an amazing array of all the Arctic has to offer and what everyone else should understand and see to realise how important all of this environment is to Earth. That's definitely been the point of these blogs for me: to allow not only myself, but others to want to work to keep the wonders of the Arctic alive.

SAILING SOUTH

Bustling Nuuk feels quite prosperous after modest Arctic Bay. Polar ships are loading supplies for the settlements to the north, and trawler men are packing up fish.

Jimmy asks at the fuel station if they would like to buy back our old Russian rifle. They politely decline.

We moor alongside a big old boat which looks as if it hasn't moved for ten years. There are quite a number like this in the harbour, like men's sheds, full of paint cans, varnish, jobs to do, guys in overalls fiddling around with tools. We're the only yacht in the port bar one but no one pays us any attention except for the guy on the man-shed boat next door to us (we eventually give him the gun).

A quiet night, and then time for our crew to leave us. Farewell to my daughter. Hugs are too quickly over, and then they are gone. After this our day is busy with a long list of chores. Jimmy wants to check the rope and I help him don his diving gear. It is so very cold he only stays in a short while, and cuts off the dangling part of the rope but leaves what is wrapped around the shaft.

'Two Arctic dives at the age of 74,' he says proudly.

He tidies the storage locker at the bow of the boat, which stinks of diesel, after the surplus fuel was stored there, and finds one long mooring line is missing…

'It is terrible,' he says, 'to get your own rope round your prop.'

We never solve the mystery of how the missing rope ended up in the sea.

Now Nera is gone I've so much space in the fore cabin. The books on the shelves reproach me with their titles. 'Arctic this and Arctic that', 'The Search for the Northwest Passage'. For sure, to have got through, would have been a story, it would have been an achievement. I check out the day's ice charts; the west of Bellot Strait is still plugged and Peel Sound won't open this year. I'm now thankful that we turned around.

My first night alone, without Nera, in 42 days. Tomorrow she'll be home. I meanwhile have 1700 miles to sail across the Atlantic.

Or do I?

In the morning before we leave, Jimmy phones the boat builders and they tell him that they would like to keep the boat in the States to exhibit her at the East Coast boat shows in the fall and winter. She is the prototype of a new design, the Exploration, and they are planning to build more of them.

So we have a last-minute change of plan – we are going to St John's, Newfoundland. At least it is 700 miles nearer – and it is one of the few places in the world neither of us have been to.

Slip the lines.

❄ ❄ ❄

The tide spits us out of the channel beyond Nuuk at a furious ten knots, and the water is white with the frenzy of fish panicking as seals hunt them in a pack.

Out in the open sea the islands no longer protect us from a gale force wind. For 24 hours we're pounded by it. The waves rise steeply behind the boat, and curl into white breakers. Water constantly breaks over the cockpit and sprays onto the electronic instrument display which shows the course and wind direction, essential indicators that we watch diligently to keep us on track. The sea spray interferes with the touch screen, and makes the boat image flip about. The autopilot struggles to cope, we watch it constantly as the alarm regularly goes off, until it gives up and we must steer by hand. It becomes increasingly hard to hold the course as the waves knock us about. Eventually it ends with a violent gybe as the main boom slams from one side to the other, making the whole boat shudder. The one thing we were trying to avoid at all costs.

Eventually Jimmy goes below to rest and I take over the steering. This requires all my mental and physical energy, to lightly touch the wheel to keep the boat within a degree or so of the course – if I go too much off course, the wind is so strong, the sails flap as violently as sheets of metal. After the gybe, I can't afford to let my concentration slip for a moment.

At some point I notice that the mainsail boom looks as if it is sitting in an awkward position against the mast, and although I'd rather not disturb him, I call Jimmy up. He attaches himself to the boat by his safety harness and against the movement of the waves goes struggling onto the deck to investigate. Turns out the metal goose neck fitting has broken in half and only a few slender ropes are keeping the heavy boom attached to the mast. Strapped on, bracing himself against the waves, he binds the boom to the mast as best he can.

'This is bad,' he says. 'I wonder if we must put into the nearest port.'

The nearest port in Greenland is over 200 miles away, the last 50 miles up a narrow fjord. We consider this option for a while, but then we decide to go on. In fact, once the mainsail is triple-reefed, and the boom lashed on with ropes, *Aventura* sails well. Surfing down the waves, she gets up to 14 knots speed, and we start to make good progress. We get the autopilot to settle down so don't need to hand steer all the time.

Aventura at least is not fazed by her troubles. When she goes fast, sometimes she hums with pleasure, vibration of speed through the hull, in harmony with the wind and waves.

Jimmy sleeps in temporary fashion in the main cabin, keeping his foul weather gear on, in case I have to call him. On my own in the cockpit, my seasick thoughts ping feverishly from one subject to the next. I watch the birds circling in the air and dipping to the water. Do they enjoy the storm? Is it easier to fly when the wind is strong? And what about the whales? What is it like to swim underneath a stormy sea? When they swim the world on their long migrations, from cold to warm waters, how does that feel on their skin? Birds and whales, what sense of time do they have as their days pass, and their years? I'm sure, never like us, waiting to get through the hours, wanting this night watch, this storm, this voyage, to end.

Great shearwaters

Just before dawn, on the horizon, faint smudges appear in the sky. A mist starts to spread … The Northern Lights have arrived again, and take over half the sky. Pale streamers spread out long and thin from the masthead as if it were some night-time celestial maypole – the metal mast a magnet, around which the Lights fall into patterns like iron filings.

In my tiredness, coldness and sickness I cry aloud with delight and lie on my back in the cockpit and watch, one eye on the autopilot, and hitched to the boat by my safety harness (the wind was still blowing 40 knots in the night). For a while it seems the whole sky is covered with pink and yellow swirls. Falling, falling so busily, our solar visitors. I trace the most dramatic with my arm to help me remember. Because it is hard to recall afterwards what these insubstantial faery lights really look like. One beautiful brief moment, and then gone once more.

Earlier in this voyage I had considered myself to have become a landlubber with no desire anymore to go to sea. But now I realise that I am a sailor, another thousand miles just made me so whether I choose or not. The sea makes it so. Days upon days, nights upon nights, and no ship nor living thing seen other than the wild birds – I don't even know what name this place has in the no man's land between the Davis Strait and the North Atlantic. This is the vast, unpopulated ocean. The waters we humans barely know – just glimpsed from beaches, from planes and the decks of ships – the place we all depend upon, and yet utterly ignore, and are ignorant of, and all too often fear.

The lungs of the world, the thermostat, the equilibrator, the nutrient generator, the mother.

Out of this place we came crawling once.

And like children growing into adolescents, we break free of mother sea, but sometimes visit her dutifully on holidays.

❄ ❄ ❄

South of Cape Farewell now, out of Greenland waters. We beat against a southwest wind – the air and sea are 10°C, it pours with rain – we are truly going south into the warmth and damp. The radar is on for icebergs, though we've seen none for a day or two, but instead we spot rain as the passing squalls show up clearly on the screen. Whoever invented radar was thinking of metal – ships and submarines. Not ice and rain clouds, not H2O.

Today *Drina* finally made it through an almost ice-free Bellot Strait and is now steaming on to Gjoa Haven.

I wish I could have seen Bellot. I'm desperate to get home and yet a piece of me is missing the Arctic, now we are so definitely not there anymore.

August ends. With the first September days, as we head south, it is getting warmer, half degree by half degree and now I'm only wearing one fleece not two in the cabin. We sat out in the sunny cockpit this afternoon with hot drinks, and I enjoy the fact I didn't need a hat or gloves.

'I wonder if the Canadians might confiscate some of our fresh food,' wonders Jimmy. We bought a lot of fruit in Nuuk, planning for the long transatlantic haul to Ireland. We'd better get eating it – the apples bruised from bouncing out of the netting – maybe we must take off their New Zealand stickers and say we bought them in Arctic Bay.

I've been here before... taking labels off Israeli tins. 1975, sailing for Egypt.

Nera emails to say she's made blackberry pie – from thousands of miles across the wide ocean comes a tantalising hint of autumn; of prickly tangled brambles, nuts ripening on trees, and school about to begin again.

There are no seasons, however, here.

Only seas.

ALONE

We finally spot our first ship on the AIS (the Automatic Identification System which lets you track vessels), 26 miles away and out of sight. Then they're gone and we're alone again. The boat is so cosy and connected electronically to the outside world, I forget sometimes we are two souls on the sea, quite alone, and the nearest land right now is 130 miles to the west. Out here we are further away from other humans than astronauts are, encircling the world.

If you crave solitude and retreat, nothing better than 1,000 miles of uninhabited ocean. Nothing but the canvas of sea and sky to fill up your idle meditations, your 3 am brain ache, your midnight revelations. You can retreat to the desert like the hermits did, but this is not a desert – what positive function holds the desert for the world? Retreat instead to this life-giving place, where you'll be washed clean. It may be that no single thought or insight comes to you: you only stare mindlessly at sea and sky and they fill you up, your mind salty fresh and blank. Sand and land would be far more distracting than this place, far too busy with growing green things, insects, other life. Out here, there are only the storm birds to give you a lift, a sailor's soul wheeling by, as the old superstition would have it.

Outside the fulmars are circling. They never stay long, but there are always new ones with a few seconds of bird curiosity to spare, coming to visit. They've been our companions throughout the voyage. Even in the fiercest storms they wing past, undaunted by any cold, any storm, any ice – our guardian spirits, a spark of life, freewheeling, sea-loving, tied to no land, no possession, no agenda. All that counts is the wind under their wings, the creatures in the sea to eat.

Simple, isn't it.

Unless the sea creatures vanish.

And I can't see into their stomachs.

A study published earlier this year just before we went north revealed how many seabirds have stomachs full of plastic. Fulmars are rare among birds in that they have an excellent sense of smell to detect fish in the waters below. Does this help them discern fish from colourful bits of plastic?

I toss my apple core over the side. The birds wheel in our wake looking at what has gone overboard and one settles in the waves – a strange odour to them, wonder if they'll nibble it? I hope they rely on their sense of smell more than their sight, because plastic at least has no scent, but I have an awful feeling this is not the case, as they pick red and green apple pieces from the sea, or red and green fragments of plastic. Colourful titbits they have no knowledge of and no way we can warn them against the dangers.

Outside on deck in the cold, on watch alone, I can exist in the moment, for a moment, with the birds and the sunrise, but when I try to write out all my clever thoughts, I can't help but look beyond to that place of terrible knowledge that caught me right at the start of this voyage and the awful state of our ocean and the life that depends on it, as we humans overburden them with our heat and our waste.

Even now after six weeks of trying, I haven't yet managed to work out this riddle, how to write this or understand it. The discrepancy between what I see and what I know.

❄ ❄ ❄

We've just over 300 miles to go. Other ships appear on the AIS though all are some 50 miles away – with grand names like *Atlantic Explorer*, laying cables, *Northern Navigator*, fishing, and the *Ottawa Express*, cargo bound for Liverpool. Newfoundland is a cypher to me but the names on the chart are tantalising – Red Head Cove, Knobby Hill, Quidi Vidi Harbour, Cow and Calf Ledge.

News comes from *Drina* – they have spent the day in Gjoa and are now rushing for Cambridge Bay where Emily will leave them. They must push on hard as the nights are dark now and the newly formed sea ice is already stretching out into the sea from the western coast.

Our wind dies and we motor all day through smooth and glossy seas. As the motor chugs on, every now and then I must check and top up the engine's header tank with diesel. I can see inside where the pale liquid, faintly green, is swirling around the filter and bubbling into the tank. There it is, the cause of all our troubles – fossil fuel, our glory and our destruction.

It strikes me that this diesel, as yet unburnt nor turned into motion and exhaust, is the same colour as the northern lights. That refined oil, however, cannot fool me with its faint, modest colour. It may appear to be as temporary as the aurora and the ice, but it is far more deadly, and in one form or another, it'll stick around.

And where did it come from? Out of which piece of deep ground was it sucked? Which trees and plants died for its life? We don't know the origins of anything anymore – on this boat, this fuel, this aluminium hull, the warm wood of the navigation desk beneath the palm of my hand – where did it all come from? under which skies, by which sun and which land was it nourished into existence?

The Inuit once knew – the origin of everything they used – men were hunters, women seamstresses, that was all that was needed.

However much we might want to be responsible, conscientious, ethical, this modern world, this system we ourselves created, defeats us with its complexity. We are trapped, trussed up helplessly by these long supply chains wrapped around the world.

Our conscience is global, but so is our servitude.

❄ ❄ ❄

The moon sets like a part-deflated orange balloon and my last sea-sunset is reddening the waters. After supper, I sleep until Jimmy wakes me at 1am to take over. I will not miss these broken nights.

The sky is dark and thick with stars, the Plough low behind us, pointing to the Northern star – we have turned our back on the North and are hastening south as fast as we can – hastening to St John's southern glow, now whitening the horizon. Flashing navigational aids, bright ribbons of coastal settlements: the coast is alive with lights, something new for our night watch eyes. People are over there, and all the accoutrements of life and civilisation.

A huge white bird flaps past to investigate us like a pale sea ghost.

The radar shows a boat dead ahead so I turn on the steaming lights so we are very visible and go outside to look. I can see its lights are close and wonder if I must change course to avoid it. Three huge birds suddenly appear off the starboard bow, with impossibly big wings, bathed in our green navigation light and flying, flying, close by, as if they expected something from us – perhaps attracted like moths to the light. The other boat draws nearer and the birds like guides stay close. At last I change course 10 degrees to port, away from a collision course. The birds still accompany us in the night, and once the fishing boat is passed safely, I turn off the steaming lights. At that point my flying companions leave me.

The radar screen is again black and empty, and ahead, Cape St Francis blinks a 3 o'clock welcome.

I daydream about still nights in port, a hotel room, and stepping through the front door of my house. 'The sailor home from the sea' is a quote that drifts into my head – a memory of the words inscribed on Robert Louis Stevenson's white Pacific tomb on the hill in Samoa where he spent his final days and where I visited with my family, as a child, during our Pacific travels. Past and present fold in together, and that scrap of verse now finally means something: I had these words in my head for forty years, and at last they make sense.

Too many night watches: selfie at dawn

However much we love the sea, landfall, for sailors, is always most sweet – and it is there now, the promise of the warm, still earth – the quiet purpose of a harbour – the lines and fenders and the boat, the crew at rest.

A faint feeling of anxiety comes over me, however much I've been looking forward to it. Perhaps it is the knowledge of what awaits me – work, emails, internet, TV, house – that will rise and break over my head, a salty wave of trouble and care. I want it and don't want it, and it'll be dirty, oily, difficult. The pure, disconnected world is falling behind, left behind in our wake, with the Northern Star, Polaris, receding.

Twenty-one days since we decided to turn around.

The netting is nearly empty.

For months before this voyage I had cabin fever in my house and my village. Now I let the cold breath of the Arctic in, and all the wide expanse of the sea, and I've fulfilled that yearning, I'll go home satisfied.

Until the next time.

NEW FOUND LAND

Jimmy wakes me at 7am and I rub my eyes, it is hard to wake. But when I get out on deck, wow! The coast has burst up out of the sea in all its detail, rocks are topped with green, and those are actually trees, the first we've seen in weeks. Through the binoculars their slender pale trunks can be seen, as thin and white as matchsticks. There are one or two buildings but otherwise there is no sign of the large town whose glare last night whitened all the horizon.

It is land. Land, beautiful, green and bountiful. Newfound. No wonder this became such a favoured place right at the start of this continent's white history.

A police siren drifts across the water.

Jimmy radios Port Control. A cheery Canadian voice instructs us to wait, as a tanker is entering the port just ahead of us. There is no obvious entrance to be seen amongst the rocks and green slopes. We watch as the tanker slips between two spurs of rock and then she's gone, swallowed by the land.

The image of my final landfall as that of being swallowed up by the land, into a harbour we as yet can't see, seems rather to the point, and very final.

Into the harbour – busy with ships, docks, buildings. Jimmy calls for me to jump to get fenders and warps ready quickly and we tie up as instructed by port control alongside a small pontoon. *Aventura* is dwarfed by huge metal ships moored nearby. They have masculine fierce names beginning with 'Atlantic' or 'Maersk' Destroyer or some such. Not like the dilapidated wooden little ships of Nuuk, the men's floating sheds – these beasts are for serious, metal work.

Beyond the harbour rise the terraces of a city square or park, people sit on benches, watching us with idle curiosity. There are green trees, and busy roads, cafes where young people sip frothy cappuccinos.

A world away from Arctic Bay.

Our new crew Lou and Ryan arrive with a box full of muffins and other pastries, their coffees in disposable cups, two healthy looking, cheery, practical American guys who will make very fine crew for Jimmy for the next journey south.

We sit in the cockpit and a wasp comes to inspect the sweet things. I haven't missed those. Jimmy attempts to check into Canada using Ryan's mobile phone but he is put on hold. Muzak faintly spreads through the cockpit.

'Welcome to civilisation,' I say.

More phone calls establish that the replacement part for the broken boom fitting is languishing in a DHL depot bizarrely somewhere in Texas with no prospect of arriving any time soon.

A guy ambles along the dock and looks with interest at *Aventura*. 'Hi,' he says and introduces himself as Frank. He met *Drina* on their way up north. The conversation drifts onto the broken gooseneck and it turns out that Frank knows a guy who has a machine shop and can get him to be here in an hour.

This is Terry – a quick look at our boom and then he is off to his workshop. By 4pm he's back with a piece made of aluminium, fitted on the boom, boom magic. Piece of Jimmy's luck.

A busy day. Cleaning, fixing – watermaker, boom, autopilot – the guys are like doctors busying with endless symptoms and trying to make diagnoses. They struggle to fit the replacement blades onto the wind generator – its blades had broken up north in the Dundas storm – the pieces get stuck together, they take a trip to the nearest hardware store for advice, where they get offered full use of the workshop.

Like with Terry, I guess it is the universal guy network, and I mean that in a very good way.

I'll put in a good word for visiting sailors here, who are more likely to contribute more than tourists flying in and out to all-inclusive resorts; they shop for provisions in local shops and markets, eat in local restaurants, and because things are always breaking on boats, use the services of all the local small businesses and specialist workers, putting money back into the local economy.

Music from a lunchtime concert in the park drifts across to us. And it is so warm. I go barefoot for the rest of the day, which is a joy.

That night I sleep in the forepeak for the first time since Nuuk. My ears are ringing with the final silence, and my heads spins with too much wine drunk at a celebratory meal in a nearby restaurant, that Jimmy had promised me back in the seasick, broken boom days far north.

I willed with all my power for time to pass, this day to come, and the block of time between me and now seemed far too big and long and heavy, but its gone, passed now, like a flick of cloud, and one should never, never, wish for hours and days to pass, it is a dangerous business, for these sorts of wishes always come true.

I relish the still, still, still boat, sleep one whole night through, the first in eight days.

GOODBYE TO AVENTURA

In the morning my head is sore and Terry arrives to give us a lift to check me with my luggage into the hotel, and then takes us off in his great big truck over the hill to the Costco wholesale supermarket. He tells us how oil is good for St John's economy, the Hibernia well is pumping on the Grand Banks, and more oil has now been discovered. Those big metal ships moored alongside us service the oil wells. Canadians work in oil all over the world. The city is expanding, and the house prices are going up. For him, this all seems to be a very good thing. Nursing my hangover, I say nothing.

Costco is one of those vast places that people flock to like temples on a Saturday morning. A vast warehouse piled high with stuff, TVs, and all the rest, and the food only comes in ginormous containers and multi-packs.

Back to the harbour with our groceries. Hugs from Jimmy – time for quick goodbyes – ropes cast off. Then they go, I watch until they turn the corner – right – South – and then the gap of sea between the two headlands looks very empty.

Very empty.

I go the hotel room, meaning to head out and explore the town, but sleep most of the afternoon, exhausted. I wake at three hourly intervals through the night. All those watches have wrecked my sleep.

❈ ❈ ❈

A free day before the flight home. A cruise ship has arrived and there are plenty of tourists.

'Are you from the cruise?' the woman asks in the bookshop when I buy the kids presents.

'No,' I say, and tell her a brief version of my story. She hasn't heard of Arctic Bay. I walk along to Harbourside Park, ignoring the empty space where *Aventura* was moored and am confronted by the following notice:

> *Close to this commanding and historic spot Sir Humphrey Gilbert landed on the 5th day of August 1538 and in taking possession of this New Found Land in the name of his Sovereign Queen Elizabeth thereby founded Britain's overseas empire.*

So the empire began here, in this mild-looking green square. After that first contact with the English, and other immigrant Europeans, all of the original inhabitants of the island, the Beothuk, soon died from infectious diseases. The fact they were already here, and the land couldn't therefore be taken 'possession' of, was of no consequence.

I sit a while and watch a vast ship reverse slowly into the dock. It is called the *Atlantic Raven*, a super tug that can tow anything – oil rigs – even icebergs. How can you argue with that brute reality? I feel as frail as the thin white matchstick tree trunks I saw on the shore as we arrived. The Industrial Revolution is still going on, has not finished, how can you possibly resist this metal progress?

Gandhi could do it, versus the seemingly unassailable British Empire, but who will mobilise a world against this new empire? The slow tow of the oil rig northwards, like a Satanic majesty, to the cold lands where it will sink its teeth into the earth, suck out the dark rich blood, and burn the blood into a vapour, a spell of the devil to poison the weather and turn the world topsy-turvy.

Rain starts bucketing down and I get utterly drenched running across the roads to The Rooms Museum. I want to see Pointed North, the exhibition of work by the artist Rockwell Kent. I'd first heard of him on this trip, mentioned in *The Magnetic North* by Sara Wheeler, that I read up north. Frankly, that mention underwhelmed me, as I found the lithograph she had chosen for the book, an illustration of Kent's mistress, a rather voyeuristic or at least a peculiar look at a woman. But I had a free afternoon, and I was also intrigued by this artist who became so fascinated by the north. He said (if I recall right) that his soul was *magnetised and pointed north*. Hence the title of the exhibition.

The experience of walking around a hushed gallery space is very familiar, but the fact I am thousands of miles from home disconcerts me.

Funny how you can never have heard of a person and then suddenly two coincidences blast him into life in your head and soul – the mention in Wheeler and the fact there is the exhibition here in a place we were never supposed to come to.

The show marks the centenary since Kent lived in Newfoundland. His visit here was cut short as he was deported, despite pleas due to his wife expecting her fourth child – suspected of being a German spy – he wrote a letter in German to a friend, courting trouble perhaps – and called his new daughter Hildegarde (which he later changed). Today they celebrate him; and in fact amends were made before he died in 1971.

I like this man who was an artist and a prominent socialist, supporter of trade unions, and fascinated by the wild places of the earth. He spent long stretches of time in the Arctic. As well as art he designed ads and illustrated books. His 1946 illustration in the Saturday Evening Post for an ad for the Bituminous Coal Institute, is accompanied by this text:

> *Truly, our whole civilisation depends on this magic mineral, and anything that affects coal mining also affects you – whether or not you actually burn coal! ...Thanks to the unlimited bounty of nature, America boasts a 3000-year treasure trove of Bit. Coal. What better assurance could any new-home builder have that his coal supply will always be available – will always be low in cost, no matter how high the prices of other fuels may climb?*

Promise made, not yet broken.

I buy the last remaining copy in the gift shop of Kent's beautifully illustrated edition of *Moby Dick*. They say this is one of the greatest novels of the sea (to my shame, I have never finished reading it; but I suspect I am not alone in that).

There are not so many artists that combine their art with the sea, or rather, work the sea right up inside themselves to let it out in words and images which have been properly chewed over by the subconscious. So I am pleased to have found one, so new to me, by chance, at the very end of my journey.

Literally, at the final moment.

On this same day, 7 September, as I wander St John's, far away north, in the central part of the Northwest Passage, a Canadian expedition finally finds the wreck of one of Franklin's ships, the *Erebus*, lost for some 169 years.

❄ ❄ ❄

Out of the plane window I can see the Plough and Polaris – I'm flying over the Atlantic, and far below my father struggles on. I thought going at six knots in a boat was fast. Now we are cruising a hundred times faster.

The east is bright red and yellow. Going east – the rope pulling me home.

To the west is always the unknown and the adventure, *an arch where through/ Gleams that untravell'd world.*

All of this story, in a sense, was a journey to find out what the end was.

And I found it. The end was Rockwell Kent, the empire, and the steel ships of oil.

Orange points of light below mark towns and villages, like homecoming fires burning.

I'm welcomed home by the warm green smell of the garden, the dog's happy greeting, and the children's cheery hello as they come home from school, ringing through the house pure as a bell when I was in the bath, trying not to fall asleep.

Teenage years were creeping up on Dan and he was cool – what can you expect from a twelve-year-old boy after all? Though much, much later, I got a hug.

And wishing them goodnight, after a bedside joke and a chat, was very sweet indeed.

Seated Figure, Rockwell Kent

NORTHWEST PASSAGE BIRD SIGHTINGS – FINAL TALLY

Once back home, I submitted the best of our seabird photos, along with records of where we had seen them, to Diana Doyle, one of the Founders of the 'SeaBC' Sea Bird Count who had been leading on the Odyssey seabird observations. Diana got to work confirming identifications. What was most gratifying, was that, the rare white morph Gyrfalcon cliff-nesting on Beechey Island had not been reported from that area since a historical report back in 1999. Diana wrote to us.

Hi Doina and Nera,

I can't tell you what an outstanding job you did photographing all those birds! I know how hard it is to photograph birds on a cruising boat — much less when you're bulky with extra clothing and cold hands!!

The system worked phenomenally well. I simply 'replayed' the photos, in order of time-date stamp, to then log them by location and date into Cornell's eBird database. I did a final summary using eBird of all the species and counts you saw (see below). To this list I'm pretty sure you can add Iceland Gull. Iceland Gulls and Glaucous Gulls are very similar, mostly differing by size, so I could never confirm a specific instance of Iceland Gull, but I'm pretty sure that of all those 'white-winged' gulls at least one of them was this species also. You might think, '17 species, that's ALL?? ' But for the Arctic, that's a good number. As you probably noticed, there aren't many species uniquely suited to breed in the High Arctic!

Some of the species you saw were captured in only a single sighting, so that was great that you nailed them with a photo: Pomarine Jaeger (your shot of the chunky, bulky jaeger species), Leach's Storm-Petrel (the blurred small seabird!), the Long-tailed Duck flock (the ones with the white spectacles), the Thick-billed Murre (aptly named), and so on.

So thanks again! Now that I've completed entering all your data (180-ish photos!) it's a little sad to have this vicarious trip end!

Best, Diana

You can find out more at www.birdingaboard.org. Anyone can get involved, and the more data that is collected and submitted by sailors, anywhere in the world, the better.

HIGHEST COUNT FOR A SPECIES (SAMPLE SIZE)												
Species name	Jun 2014	Jul 2014	Aug 2014	Sep 2014	Oct 2014	Nov 2014	Dec 2014	Jan 2015	Feb 2015	Mar 2015	Apr 2015	May 2015
Common Eider	- -	100 (3)	- -	- -	- -	- -	- -	- -	- -	- -	- -	- -
Long-tailed Duck	- -	- -	5 (1)	- -	- -	- -	- -	- -	- -	- -	- -	- -
Northern Fulmar	- -	1 (3)	9 (4)	4 (1)	- -	- -	- -	- -	- -	- -	- -	- -
Great Shearwater	- -	- -	- -	2 (1)	- -	- -	- -	- -	- -	- -	- -	- -
Leach's Storm-Petrel	- -	- -	- -	1 (1)	- -	- -	- -	- -	- -	- -	- -	- -
Pomarine Jaeger	- -	1 (1)	- -	- -	- -	- -	- -	- -	- -	- -	- -	- -
Long-tailed Jaeger	- -	3 (3)	- -	- -	- -	- -	- -	- -	- -	- -	- -	- -
Jaeger sp.	- -	1 (1)	- -	- -	- -	- -	- -	- -	- -	- -	- -	- -
Dovekie	- -	1 (1)	2 (1)	- -	- -	- -	- -	- -	- -	- -	- -	- -
Thick-billed Murre	- -	- -	1 (1)	- -	- -	- -	- -	- -	- -	- -	- -	- -
Black Guillemot	- -	1 (1)	17 (2)	- -	- -	- -	- -	- -	- -	- -	- -	- -
Black-legged Kittiwake	- -	281 (5)	5 (2)	- -	- -	- -	- -	- -	- -	- -	- -	- -
Glaucous Gull	- -	1 (2)	35 (3)	- -	- -	- -	- -	- -	- -	- -	- -	- -
Great black-backed Gull	- -	- -	2 (1)	- -	- -	- -	- -	- -	- -	- -	- -	- -
Gull sp.	- -	38 (1)	5 (1)	- -	- -	- -	- -	- -	- -	- -	- -	- -
Gryrfalcon	- -	- -	1 (1)	- -	- -	- -	- -	- -	- -	- -	- -	- -
Northern Wheatear	- -	- -	1 (1)	- -	- -	- -	- -	- -	- -	- -	- -	- -
Snow Bunting	- -	1 (1)	- -	- -	- -	- -	- -	- -	- -	- -	- -	- -

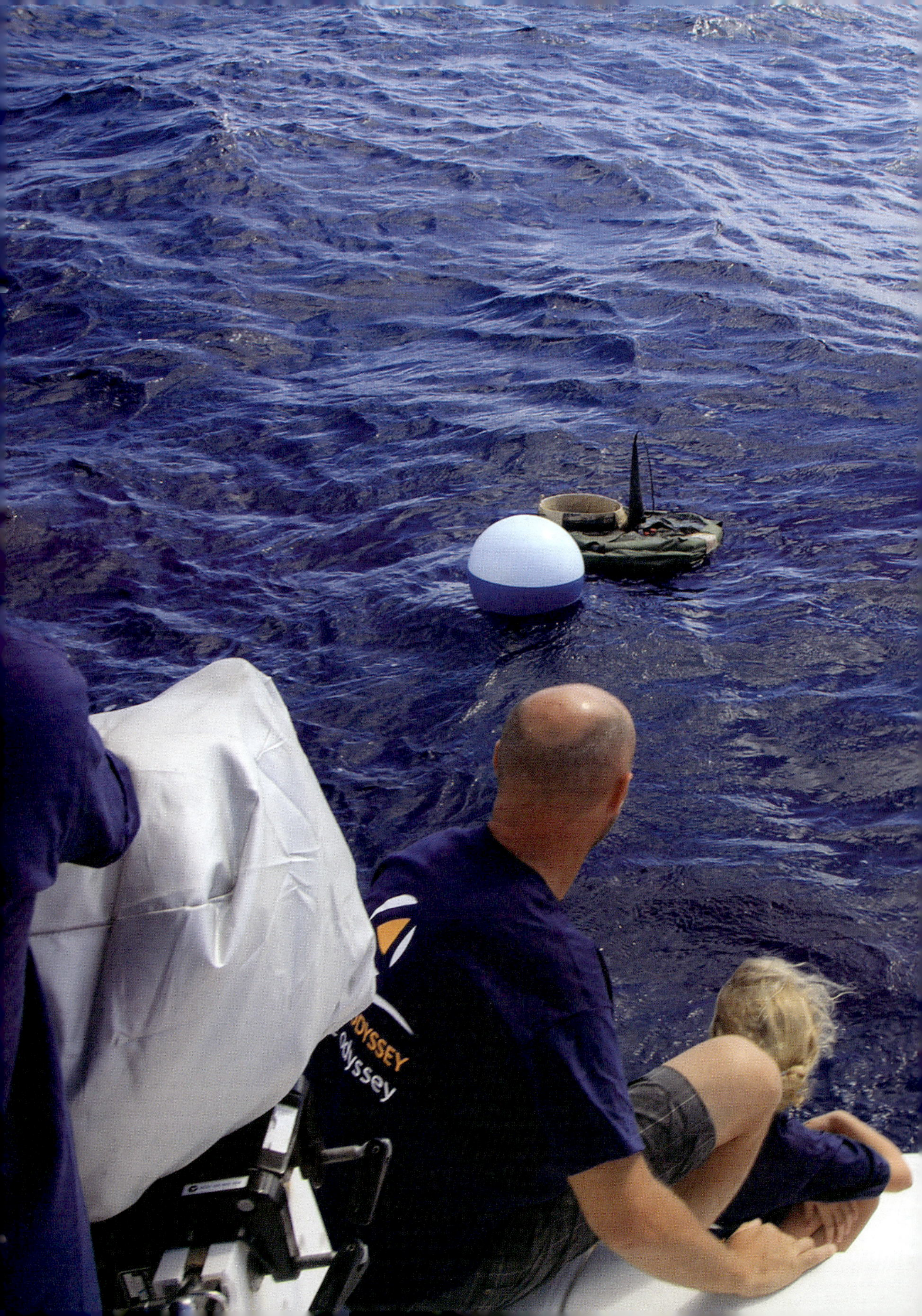
ODYSSEY
odyssey

WESTERN INTERLUDE

JANUARY 2015

A KINGDOM OF ISLANDS

BLESS ENGLAND! ... BLESS ALL SEAFARERS... BLESS the vast planetary abstraction of the OCEAN ... The English Character is based on the Sea.

Blast Manifesto, July 1914

I came across *Blast*, the Vorticists' radical art manifesto, in the winter of 2019 as we counted down the days to Brexit. We live in a kingdom of islands and nations bound together by the sea: I am struck that this is no longer a country of seafarers, and I wonder if this is perhaps a great loss – we've lost connection with the sea which made us, as the water we once worked and travelled on, place of our greatest achievements and our worst crimes. In the times before air travel, everyone who travelled came into contact with the sea, from a short hop across the Channel to the long journeys out to the colonies. These sea voyages tempered the pragmatic nature of the people of the British Isles with a glimpse of the beauty and infinitude of the sea and sky. We never saw absolutes and ideals in the same way as the continent. Our philosophies and our politics were always fundamentally different. From the glory of the precision of celestial navigation and the island creatures that sparked the idea of evolution, to the stink and shame of the shipholds of convicts and enslaved people, sea voyages forged our modern world.

The sea made us an idealistic and practical country, taught us humility married to a deep understanding of the world that never untethered itself from the craft of ropes and tar, internalised the wind and the endless waves, gave us poetry, the colours of Turner, and damned bloody Empire.

We have no contact with the sea anymore. Today, our leaders are now solely land dwellers, their egos untempered by the battle with the elements, lacking the humility the wind and waves beat into you. Sadly, we have not even realised this about ourselves. Our unique island character so beloved of many other countries, beloved even despite the cruelty and exploitation our appetite for colonies and extractive trade inflicted on the world, beloved because we gave the world so much pleasure, from the language of Shakespeare to the Beatles, is in danger of dwindling away, the sea salt which gave the flavour to the meat of the continent is now absent, and we are in danger of becoming little more than a laughing stock.

It is perhaps not too strong to say, that all of us losing contact with sea water see a withering of our souls. The ocean was our mother, out of her salty ancient soup our simple ancestors were born, and we do not know her anymore.

BLAST First (from politeness) ENGLAND …
A 1000 MILE LONG, 2 KILOMETER Deep BODY OF WATER even, is pushed against us from the Floridas, TO MAKE US MILD.

DATA DATA EVERYWHERE

Aventura spends the remainder of 2014 being exhibited at East Coast boat shows, before sailing south to Key West in Florida. At the start of 2015 I join her there, to help manage the American start of southern section of the Blue Planet Odyssey which is taking the warm water route around the world. I spend a busy week organising the event office and the idealistic, not so experienced, American crews who are getting themselves ready to sail around the world. At the last moment, two of the boats find themselves stranded due to crew and engine trouble, and one more is delayed by lack of cash. So now there are only four boats due to make this East Coast start, with others joining from the West Coast. Our Odyssey seems infernally unlucky.

There is time for a brief excursion out of the sterile marina confines (notable for the lack of insects or small birds, only Turkey vultures wheeling overhead, and the occasional osprey and pelican). We visit Hemingway's house where the writer lived in the 1930s. The house is set in tropical gardens of large-leaved exotic plants where nine-toed cats roam and lounge about, some of them descendants of the lucky felines Hemingway favoured. I have always been fascinated by writers' houses, and Hemingway has been a favourite of mine for a long time. When I had to choose a topic for an extended English essay at school, I wrote it on his concept of truth, as expressed through his sparse, pared back prose.

A short distance from the house stands the marker for what is claimed to be the southernmost point of the continental United States, at 24°33'N – and a long queue of tourists snakes along the road, waiting to get their photos taken by the brightly painted concrete marker. It strikes me that I've visited both the extreme north and the south of this continent in the last few months. Here, the south-eastern tip of north America crumbles away, coral crumbs scattering as cays and islands out into the Atlantic. Hemingway's house is built on the second highest point in Key West, but this is still only a mere five metres above sea level. The low coastline and cays of Florida are as vulnerable to rising seas as the faraway atolls of the Pacific and Indian oceans.

Back at the marina, we meet up with scientist Shaun Nolk, who manages the drifter buoy programme for the Atlantic Oceanographic and Meteorological Laboratory (AOML), which is based in Miami. AOML is part of NOAA, the US National Oceanic and Atmospheric Administration and the Odyssey has formed a partnership with NOAA and with JCOMMOPS (the joint technical commission of the World Meteorological Organization and the IOC, the Intergovernmental Oceanographic Commission of UNESCO). The IOC and WMO, in partnership with NOAA, and other national government agencies, navies and oceanographic research institutions around the world, manage the Global Ocean Observing System (GOOS). GOOS gathers data about the climate, weather, and oceans, from satellite observations in space, land-based weather stations, to buoys drifting with the ocean currents, and floats that descend into the depths.

The currents of the world's oceans are home to hundreds of drifting buoys that supply essential data for measuring the changes that our climate, our air and waters, are undergoing.

Shaun has brought us ten of these drifter buoys, to be loaded onto the Odyssey yachts, ready for deployment in the Pacific Ocean. As the Odyssey sailors gather, and help unload the buoys from the truck out on the dock, Shaun explains to us all the importance of the drifter programme, and how the buoys, once deployed, and floating with the ocean currents, will automatically gather data using their oceanographic sensing instruments and send it back via satellite.

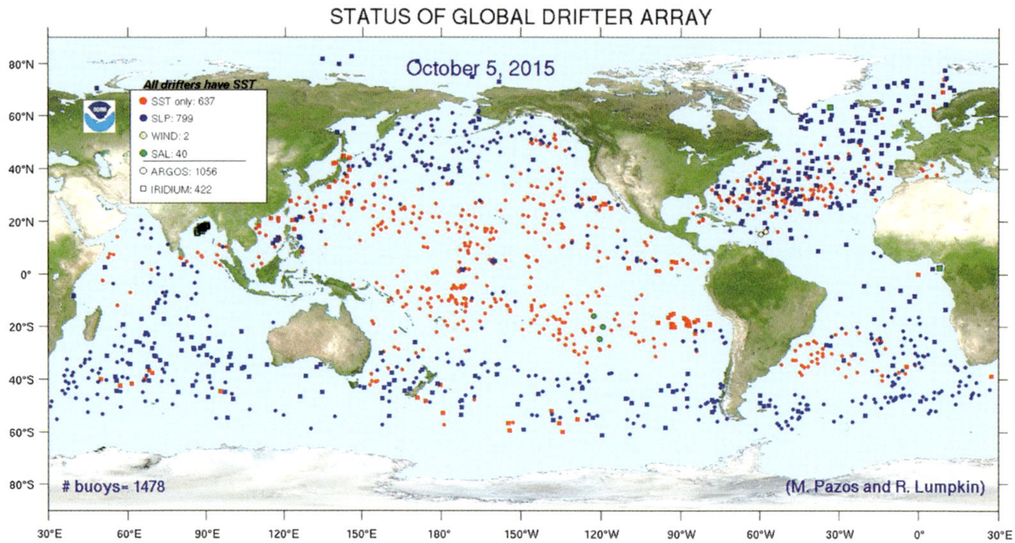

'There is a wide application for this data,' he tells us. 'It is important to scientists and meteorologists, but it is also used to help calibrate satellites, track marine debris and even assist with search and rescue operations. So we are really thrilled to partner with you.'

Drifters were first deployed in 1979 in the tropical Pacific, to study current changes associated with El Niño events, and then deployments extended over the years to include the Atlantic and Indian Oceans. Today a global array of over 1,000 satellite-tracked drifters, with further deployments each year, spans all the world's oceans. The data collected by drifters is crucial. They measure sea surface temperature, which is critical to predicting climate patterns. Warm sea surface temperature is an enormous source of energy, which fuels storms such as hurricanes and increases their intensity. Satellites also measure surface temperature but to ensure these measurements are accurate, drifters are used to confirm sea surface temperatures with the satellite data.

Drifters also measure salinity, which is important in determining the ocean's chemical make-up; coral, kelp and phytoplankton are all affected by changes in salinity, so identifying fluctuations is important. Salinity also affects water density which, in turn, affects the ocean circulation patterns that transport heat.

As the drifters literally drift, they measure the speed and direction of ocean currents. These currents carry much more than water. The Atlantic Gulf Stream, for example, carries vast amounts of heat and salt northward, and this affects the many marine species whose migration is shaped by seasonal temperature changes and ocean currents.

Until now, most deployments had been done from oceanographic research vessels and from the decks of cargo ships. But the idea of using smaller sailing yachts had become more attractive to JCOMMOPS as they realised that yachts sail outside of the main shipping channels, into areas where ships and research vessels rarely go. We have undertaken to use our Odyssey participants to deploy buoys in new regions of the ocean, some currently poorly sampled, and we are given precise locations, to fill in some of the gaps. Deployment from a yacht has the advantage of not exposing the drifters to the shock of being deployed high up from a cargo ship's deck travelling at high speeds. Our deployments are gentler, each buoy placed carefully into the sea at a slow sailing pace.

Sailors have already successfully deployed drifter buoys during the Atlantic Odyssey in 2013 and 2014, our sister event we have organised to cross the Atlantic from the Canaries to the Caribbean during the favourable trade wind months of November. We chose boats with families on board; the children illustrate the buoys with messages and pictures; some are adopted by schools back home.

And Jimmy deployed a buoy from *Aventura* in the summer of 2014, in the current off South Greenland en route to Nuuk.

In Key West, the ten buoys are divided up between the boats, and carefully stored above and below decks.

A gap in the global array has been identified in the Pacific Ocean between Panama and the Marquesas and our yachts have been instructed to deploy them there, at regular intervals on the 5-degree line of longitude.

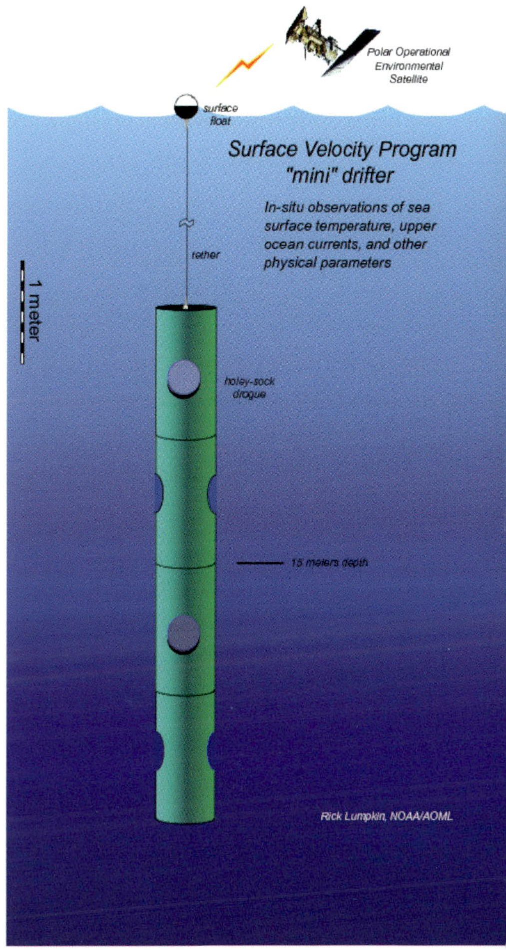

On 10 January we mark the 12 noon start of the Odyssey. Only four boats are leaving now – turning south, towards Panama and the Canal, but we leave them and go north towards Miami. Jimmy plans to join the fleet later with *Aventura*. I haven't sailed these waters since I was nine years old, 1977. I'm seasick and bound to my bunk, reading *The Old Man and the Sea*, bought from Hemingway's house, noting its fine and precise details of the sea, the very same waters where we are now. We are sailing fast, riding in the grip of the Gulf Stream. It's a rough and ready, watery warm highway – if it's in your favour you are ok, if not you will struggle. This mighty current drives warmth up into the northern Atlantic and across to the western shores of the European continent. Without it, our green and pleasant land, our temperate climate would not exist. The roots of British identity lie here, in the warm waters off Florida.

* * *

The Odyssey yachts which are leaving from the US West Coast, due to join the other boats in the Pacific, take on board Argo floats, a similar precious cargo to the drifter buoys. Named after Jason's ship the *Argo*, which set out to find the Golden Fleece, according to Greek myth, these battery-powered autonomous floats will typically descend to a target depth of 1000m below the sea surface to drift and then descend again to 2000m, measuring the temperature and salinity of the surrounding water. Floats can change their buoyancy by pumping oil into and out of an external bladder, which allows them to sink, drift with the ocean currents and measure data as they rise to the surface, from where they send their data and location back via satellite. Each float can drift in the oceans measuring data for as long as 4 to 7 years.

The Argo global array began in 2000 and is now a major component of GOOS, the Global Ocean Observing System. What is so significant is that recent data from the Argo floats has shown that much of the extra planetary warming has occurred in the deep ocean; while sea surface temperatures have risen more slowly in recent years, the data shows that heat has been absorbed through all layers of the ocean, even the depths.

Eight Argo floats are loaded onto our boats in San Diego from the Scripps Institution of Oceanography. Yachts *Libby* and *Om* will deploy the floats in a specified line along the 5°S parallel, between the Galapagos and the Marquesas, where there is a substantial gap in Argo coverage.

The trusty little drifters and the Argo floats, drifting on and through the ocean, give us a growing body of evidence that shows how the global climate is changing, with the ocean at the heart of it. In this at least our Odyssey has played a small part.

Studies are beginning to show the warming ocean is having an effect on the strength and direction of major ocean currents. Should so much excess heat be absorbed by the ocean (which after all is extremely efficient at doing so, a calibrating system that helps keep the air and land milder and more habitable than otherwise might be the case), we might see the Gulf Stream weaken considerably, even lose its direction. There'd be no more idle talk then of growing grapes in England – we'd be heading for a climate more like Canada, which sits on the same longitude as the British Isles.

Drifter buoys and Argo floats are expensive, sophisticated bits of scientific kit, but at the end point it is just a simple moment, a careful placing in the water by an ordinary sailor, not a scientist or an expert. An ordinary sailor who by this act has made himself or herself really quite extra-ordinary, as he or she contributes to the sum total of human knowledge.

And if the Blue Planet Odyssey achieves only this, we can be proud of this legacy left behind, these little buoys bobbing along or diving deep into the oceans for years to come, and sending back through the air little bits of data that add to other bits of data to provide the building blocks of what we need to know about our planet, of what is happening to the climate and to the ocean, on whose balance and health we depend for our very lives.

On *Aventura*, as we pass over the Gulf Stream, we watch the onboard instruments indicate the temperature changes which reveal the move into and out of the powerful current. At last we leave the Gulf Stream behind, approaching Miami as rain squalls gather and send the city into a grey mist. The high-rise buildings jut out of the sea like an improbable futuristic film – only the improbable future arrived a long time ago.

Just before we come into port, I peer once again into the engine compartment and see that the fuel in the header tank is a bright blood red. No more the pale green of the ethereal northern lights.

Three huge cruise ships are leaving as we enter Port Everglades. *Aventura* seems like a speck besides them. A security cordon encircles them and other vessels are not permitted to get too close; we are bossed around by a megaphone voice on a sheriff boat. For a few moments Jimmy misunderstands the barked instructions on where they want to us to go, and I briefly wonder if we are going to be shot at. A little boat passes, bristling with guns.

Welcome to America.

TO THE PACIFIC WITH LOVE

JULY – AUGUST 2015

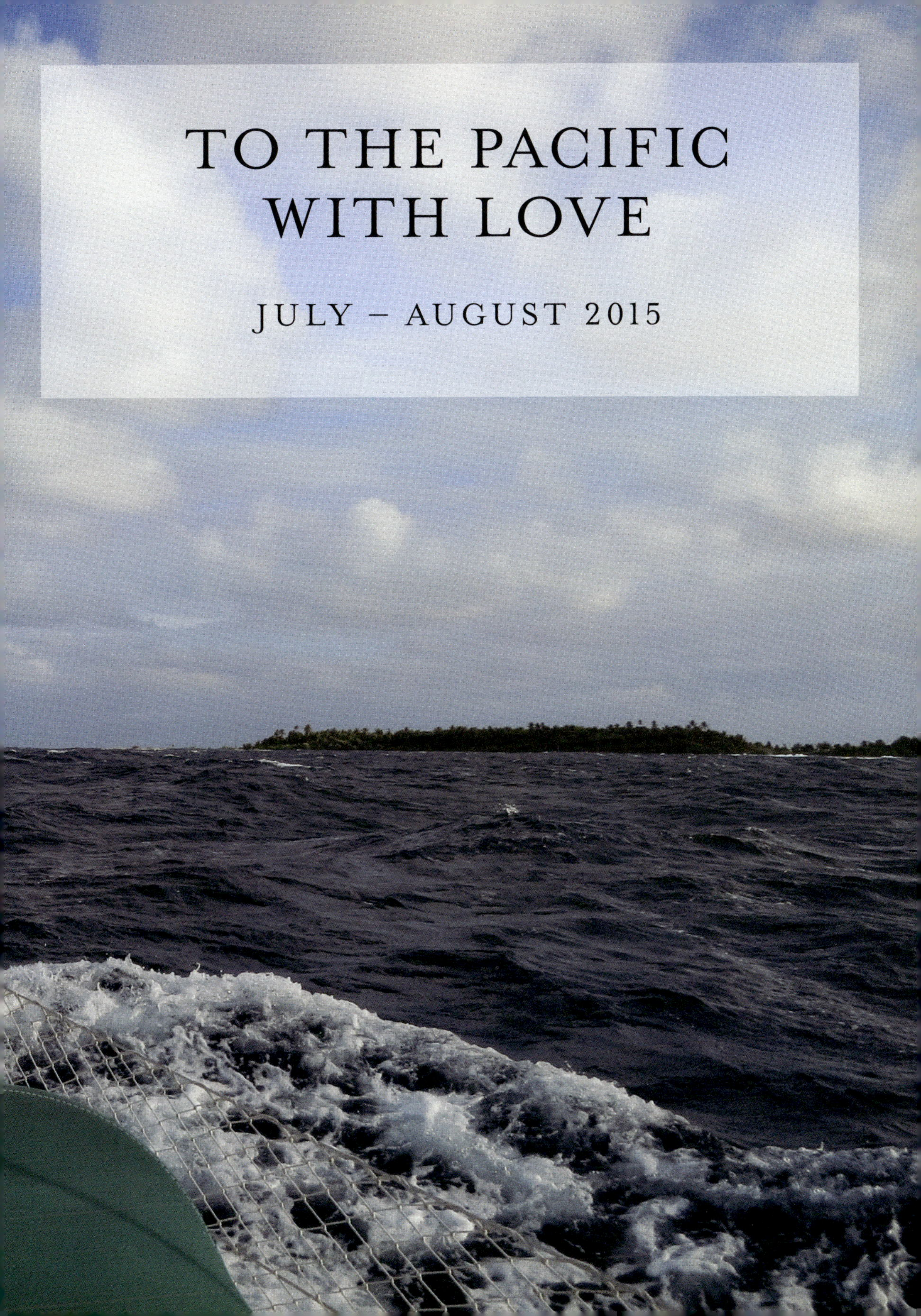

TROPICAL CYCLONE PAM

In March 2015 Tropical Cyclone Pam rips through the Pacific; the second most intense tropical cyclone the south Pacific has ever seen. Pam causes loss of life and extensive damage to some of the Vanuatuan islands and is considered possibly the worst natural disaster in Vanuatu's history. As a result this year's World Risk Index, which considers a country's vulnerability, and its exposure to natural hazards such as floods, storms, earthquakes, places Vanuatu top of the disaster risk ranking. For the low atolls of Tuvalu, so close to the equator and therefore located out of the cyclone zone, the storm surges caused by Pam are also catastrophic.

On the 8 June, leaders of the G7 countries, the richest in our world, meet in Germany and affirm their determination to adopt an ambitious agreement at the Paris COP21 summit which is going to take place at the end of this year.

On the very same day, leaders of six Pacific nations meet in the capital of Vanuatu, Port Vila, and announce the People's Declaration for Climate Justice:

We, the people of Vanuatu, Kiribati, Tuvalu, Fiji, Solomon Islands and the Philippines continue to experience the impacts of climate change – the single biggest human rights, environmental and humanitarian crisis of our time. It has claimed thousands of lives, displaced millions of people, damaged livelihoods, and caused a severe economic toll in relief, rehabilitation and reconstruction efforts.

The burning of fossil fuels by big polluters has been found to be primarily responsible for emitting large amounts of greenhouse gases. The concentration of said gases, especially carbon dioxide in the atmosphere causes climate change. An estimated 25-30% of the carbon dioxide emitted by these activities was absorbed by the oceans, causing ocean acidification.

As the people most acutely vulnerable to the impacts of climate change, we will not let the big polluters decide and assign our fate. Our rights and ability to survive must not be dictated by the continued addiction to the burning of fossil fuels. We refuse to accept the 'new normal' and demand for climate justice by holding the big polluters and their respective governments to account for their contribution to the climate crisis. Our people and our environment must be preserved for the generations to come.

We are from island states in shared oceans. We stand in solidarity.

We commit to holding those most responsible for climate change accountable. By doing so, we send a message of hope that the people and not the polluters are in charge of humanity's destiny.

EN ROUTE

I am sitting on a delayed train somewhere near Didcot Parkway, Oxfordshire. Outside is a summer field with ripe yellow wheat, dancing in the wind. The school holidays have just begun and I am on my way to the Pacific with Dan who is now thirteen.

Jimmy had intended to sail *Aventura* to meet the other Odyssey yachts in the Pacific, and Dan and I were to join him in the school summer holidays. But once he was through the Panama Canal, the Arctic called him, and he decided to head north for one more attempt at the northwest passage, only this time from Alaska and the west.

But I'd promised to take Dan on a warm sailing route; to visit those other parts of the world most threatened by climate change, the low-lying coral islands of Tokelau and Tuvalu. Tuvalu – where I had last visited more than 30 years before as a girl.

Thursday, July 2, 2015 gazetteseries.co.uk

Councillor sets sail on environmental mission

A DISTRICT councillor for Dursley is to embark on a six-week expedition in the Pacific Ocean with her teenage son – visiting a series of islands that are badly affected by climate change.

By Stuart Rust
01453 540217
stuart.rust@gazetteseries.co.uk
Twitter @stuartrust1

Doina Cornell, 47, of Everlands in Cam, is used to being at sea, having sailed around the world for more than half of her childhood.

Now, following a sailing trip last year across the Arctic Ocean with her daughter Nera, Doina will take Dan, 13, on a tour of several pacific islands under threat from changes in the earth's atmosphere.

Setting off on July 9, Doina and Dan will fly to New Zealand from London, followed by another flight to Samoa where they will meet their boat.

Over the course of several weeks they will visit Tokelau, Tuvalu and Vanuatu, three islands threatened by global warming and its effect of raising the world's sea levels.

"Climate change is not something that is an abstract thing to these people. It's something they can see every day," she said. "Whether it's flooding or the impact of sea water on their soil making it more difficult to grow the crops they depend on, these problems are a big issue."

Doina hopes they can offer support to people on the islands who may feel they go unnoticed by the world's major powers.

"We want to offer a message of support – to be able to say 'We know you're here and we are listening – and we'll do our bit'."

After taking her daughter on a voyage though the Arctic Doina promised she would take Dan somewhere hot.

The pair will be on a boat with just two other crew members and will, between some of the islands, be at sea for several days at a time.

As well as being a district councillor Doina also runs Cornell Sailing Ltd.

SR_2850_001 Doina Cornell with her son Dan

It just so happened that Michael of *Drina* was making his way slowly south through the Pacific after completing the Northwest Passage. His Arctic crew had headed home while he spent the winter in Alaska, and he was single-handing again as he headed back to his home port of Brisbane, Australia. And so Michael, who had been having sailing adventures in the Pacific and the high latitudes north and south since he was a young man – for some forty years – agreed to take us and make a detour. The other Odyssey yachts were slowly making their way west across the Pacific, and we hoped to meet some of them in Tuvalu and sail with them to Vanuatu.

On the day Dan and I were due to leave a rail strike has been announced so to avoid strike-breaking we leave a day earlier; no time to sit quietly with Nera before leaving her for the whole summer. We bundle ourselves hurriedly into the car. An accident on the way to the railway station has closed the road: a motorcyclist has been knocked down on the roundabout, so we must take a long detour through narrow country lanes. We arrive just as the train is pulling in and Dan and I grab our bags and run.

Unlike last summer, there is no question mark at the end of it as to whether we will get through or not. Our planned route, from Samoa to Tokelau, Tuvalu and Vanuatu, a portion of the Odyssey's Southern Pacific route, is more circular than linear, like a line with many hooks. Each hook might tether us to an island, and we'll get a silver glittering prize tugged out of the sea – how, like the old stories say, the islands were once pulled out of the waves by the Pacific gods of old. Or the hook might slip and just dig deep into the ballsy flesh of thumb or palm and the barb won't let it out. Each hook, each stopover, and all the blue sea-line in between, has risk and uncertainty veined right through it – all sorts of things could go wrong. Or maybe it will all go right – we'll leave behind the sight that still haunts me, now as I scribble these words on the train, of the man I'd seen earlier lying on the mini-roundabout (just as the Chancellor intones live on the car radio his summer budget speech how more money will be going into road building), leave behind the garbage truck and the fallen motorbike, the horror coming to the quiet centre of our village – and take the train going east to the city, then further east, to the glorious blue Pacific – via the golden wheat fields of summer England, via the jet trails of international travel, and of course, in my supremely hypocritical way, I will suppress any thoughts about the gas-guzzling airmiles and all the fuel and all my own personal contribution to pollution and carbon emissions so I can enjoy my pilgrimage and my holier-than-thou concerns about climate change. I hope I'll get away with it, no one will spot me for a fraud.

The next day I hear that sadly the motorcyclist died of his injuries.

Then an email arrives with the news that our contact in the tiny Pacific nation of Tokelau, government minister Aliki Faipule Foua Toloa, died recently after a long illness. His death is a great loss, as one of those eloquent leaders from a SIDS, or Small Island Developing State, which are most at risk from climate change. Death follows us.

These things do not seem to be good omens for beginning this long journey to the other side of the world.

As Dan and I arrive in London, another SIDS leader, the Tuvaluan Prime Minister, Enele Sopoaga is on a whirlwind European tour, speaking in Brussels and the Vatican in the lead up to the Paris COP:

> *We need to collaborate as one human face to save humankind. To make an agreement in Paris in December a meaningful one. We are told that even 2 degrees global warming is too dangerous as it would mean that Tuvalu would disappear under the water. Yes we can move the Tuvalu inhabitants to other peoples' lands but it will not stop climate change. We need to save Tuvalu to save the world.*

Dan and I travel on to Paris, with the business travellers, the global elite, those who can afford this travel, a world that exists and functions smoothly, quite separate from that of my councillor work at home – helping with people's issues, tax credits, food banks and benefit sanctions, checking if a bid for a council house has been successful. Quite separate from the island nations where we are headed. Worlds that never seem to meet, even if we share one land, one climate, and one ocean.

MESSAGE FROM TOKELAU

Tokelauan minister Foua Toloa had been an early friend of the Blue Planet Odyssey, writing the following for our Blue Planet Log magazine in April 2013.

In the middle of the Pacific Ocean, between latitudes 8 and 10 south and between longitudes 171 and 173 degrees west, lies a cluster of four tiny atolls named Tokelau. Its total land mass is about 12km2 with the highest point only 3 metres above sea level. It is home to about 1500 inhabitants. Its nearest neighbour is Samoa, which lies about 500km south of the most southern of the atolls, Fakaofo, the island I call home.

"Despite the impacts that climate change has had on Tokelau, our nation has not sat back and accepted its plight without action"

Aliki Faipule Foua Toloa

MESSAGE FROM TOKELAU

IN THE MIDDLE OF THE PACIFIC OCEAN
LIES A CLUSTER OF SOME
TINY ATOLLS NAMED TOKELAU

Tokelau like other small low-lying atolls is very susceptible to any changes to sea level and to the effects on sea temperature as a consequence of climate change from increasing emissions of greenhouse gases globally. Surrounded by sea, Tokelau relies heavily on the provisions from this resource for food. Its EEZ[1] is the only source of economic return available to it.

The impacts of climate change continue to be widely debated, and the annual Conference of Parties (COP) to the UN Framework Convention on Climate Change (UNFCCC) draws global attention to the fact that large developed nations will not commit to measures that will seriously mitigate their greenhouse gas (GHG) emissions. For tiny atoll nations such as Tokelau, the impacts of climate change are a way of life.

Tokelau contends with more cyclones and storm surges than it has ever had before. The cyclones and storm surges are more intense and occur more often. The impact of this is evident as our beaches and shores erode and some species of plants no longer flourish due to the high saline levels of our soil. The storm surges leave salt on the land; without rain, this crystallises, hardening the soil. A large quantity of rainwater is necessary to flush it out. This threatens the production of crops that we can grow such as coconuts and pandanus. The extreme weather conditions we are experiencing, with an increasing number of hot days during the year and unusually high temperatures during times of the year when we normally expect cooler temperatures, have caused droughts and affected the health of our more vulnerable groups of our population, such as the young and the aged.

As a consequence of the elevated sea temperature, our reefs are stressed, causing coral bleaching within our lagoons. The corals are noticeably in poor health, which has affected the quantity and quality of food supply for our in-shore fish population. The life cycles of our in-shore fish are also affected by the extreme weather conditions, which have seen a decrease in the number and gradual disappearance of some species of fish from the lagoon. Our food supply, with fish as our main source of sustenance, is threatened. Additionally, the rising sea levels have caused some smaller islets to disappear completely.

The changes to Tokelau and her surrounding environs, as a consequence of global warming, make it more and more difficult for her inhabitants to live sustainably. And though we do not want to consider it, with the rate of global warming not subsiding, our small island homes may no longer exist in the near future. With the loss of our lands, we will lose our culture, our traditions and our language.

Despite the impacts that climate change has had on Tokelau, our nation has not sat back and accepted its plight without action. In October 2012, the Tokelau Renewable Energy Project (TREP) Stage One was completed, whereby electricity needs for the three atolls are met with an off-grid solar energy system. Stage One of this project allows for 93% of total electricity production through solar energy,

1 A country's EEZ or Exclusive Economic Zone is an area of sea that extends up to 200 nautical miles out from land; Tokelau has an EEZ of 318,990 square kilometres and fisheries licence fees for this area contribute significantly to Tokelau's budget.

making Tokelau number 1 in per-person reduction in greenhouse gas emission in the world and fulfilling its global obligation. Stage Two will involve the production and use of renewable fuel to provide for the other 7% of electricity needs.

This project, while costly, has put Tokelau on the map. TREP is Tokelau's way of telling the world that while it may be one of the smallest nations, it can still make its contribution towards decreasing emissions of greenhouse gases globally. It is the principle of the matter. If a nation with an annual GDP equivalent to a fraction of the fees earned by directors of small businesses in developed countries can do this, shame on those nations and their leaders for not doing what needs to be done so that our future generations have the benefits of our environment that we currently enjoy.

And if they are not willing to turn off their carbon dioxide taps, at least they should be keen to keep the ocean healthy in every other way – robust fish stocks, clean water and protections for marine life are all things that science tells us can soften the impacts of climate change.

A plethora of literature and research identifies the serious losses from climate change and the expected damage in terms of health and agriculture on vast land masses. The impact that climate change has on the ocean, and the consequential effect on life-forms that provide food and sustenance and livelihood to small island developing states in particular, is not widely known. Oceans make up 71% of the Earth's surface, and the high seas provide resources such as food and minerals. They are key to global trade, and maintain essential ecosystem services including the production of oxygen. It is scientifically estimated that up to 50% of the earth's oxygen is produced by the oceans. The ocean also acts to absorb carbon dioxide; but that is making the water more acidic.

These facts, while mind boggling, still do not stir up enough concern for world leaders to act in ways necessary to address the underlying issues. I want my grandchildren and future generations of my family to enjoy the same benefits that my generation has enjoyed from the oceans. The urgency necessary to reverse the damage being caused with the effects of climate change on the high seas, which seems out of sight and is therefore out of mind, is the challenge being taken on by the Global Ocean Commission. This resonates with one of our Tokelauan ancestry laments:

Tui e!
Te ata kua kakau
E laga kita ko te fanau
Aue te alofa e faigata

Tui please wake up!
Wake up as dawn has broken
We must wake up because of our children
Oh, our endless love for them causes so much pain

FIRST NATION, FIRST BLOOD

For me, a visit to the Pacific is more than just a trip to a place some like to call 'exotic'. The year I first sailed to Tuvalu with my family was 1978 – I came of age that year – first blood, womanhood – as the new nation, shed the name of 'Ellice Islands', and gained its independence from the British empire. Although in fact, not a 'new' nation but rather an ancient one freed from the brief imperial interlude.

What was your freedom worth though, when the world's dirt binds you now in invisible chains?

The Pacific is no paradise but people love to call it that, and truly Paradise is under threat now from the dead things burning.

We can, if we wish, seize our energy from the invisible air, from the warm sun, from the relentless tide's ebb and flow – air, light and water that move over and through our earth and our sea regardless. We can catch that dance and use it to light up our little blue screens for pleasure.

Or we can dig and blast and dump and burn. That is no dance that is the march of demons.

There is a shard of ice embedded in the eye. No, not ice. A speck of black dirt. Fossil dirt. Dead dirt, dead eyes, dead men, and the fires, for now, still burn.

When I was barely twelve years old, my first blood came, and that was the hand extended to me to join life, and the dance down through the ages.

Out of the pain of it, I danced. I loved the dance.

I am going back now as a mother, not a girl. I will go back with knowledge, and there is no innocence left for me.

I expect you islanders may care little, for I will come and go and I'll be one of many.

You often speak out to the world.

So it is important that you know – some of us are listening.

TELLER OF TALES

The heat envelops us as we land in Samoa, and the sweet soft sounds of music as a band plays a welcome in the baggage hall, and beyond immigration and customs, a sea of Samoans in colourful shirts wait to greet friends and family. The taxi ride to Apia takes us past tidy villages, open-sided houses, breadfruit trees, coconuts, huge taro leaves – familiar things I've not seen for so long. Things Dan has seen in books or films but never in real life.

The familiar green-hulled *Drina* and Michael are waiting for us in the marina. Last time we met was so far away, up north, in Graham Harbour as we turned round last summer and abandoned our quest. We drink tea and Michael shows us his photos: an ice-free Bellot Strait, and Emily washing her hair in a blue ice pool of sea ice. A pang of regret seizes me that I never made it through.

Jimmy and Michael together in the Arctic

Stripy fish jump in the water by the boat, little black birds with red under their tails sing and perch on the rigging, and the tropical heat squashes us with a large sweaty hand. By 7pm, I'm falling asleep on my feet with jetlag. I take up a bunk in the front of the boat; Dan sleeps in the main cabin. It is so ferociously hot, sweat pours off me, I cannot think straight. At least there is a fan at the end of the bunk.

In the morning we make a long trek into town to find some Wi-Fi and check emails before heading on to the office of Tokelau affairs, as Tokelau is to be the first of our destinations. I had hoped to meet Paula who works for the Tokelau administration; we've been in email contact for some time now, about the purpose of the Odyssey, and obtaining permission to visit one of the three main islands of the tiny nation.

At the office we meet the Director who sits at an empty desk with dark shades on, and he tells me that Paula isn't there, he doesn't appear to have had my email with our arrival details, and he says we must phone tomorrow after the elders of Tokelau have met. They will decide if we are to be given permission or not to visit. Tokelau is a small place, made up of a few islands only, with few resources, and understandably, they protect themselves from too many visitors.

We leave and explore the market – Dan tries a fresh coconut for the first time, deftly cracked open by the man selling it, with a machete, and we buy a big knobbly fruit which is a custard apple (*siaki* in Samoan) which we eat dripping and dribbling with juice from the white flesh. Dan revels in all these new, simple pleasures. For myself, I enjoy the familiar sights and sounds remembered from my childhood and the three years spent roaming the Pacific.

Later Dan and I snorkel at the Marine Reserve. The water is like a warm bath. With his bare hands, Dan tries to dehusk a coconut washed up on the beach, a beach of broken dead corals. We are a very long way from Beechey.

A short distance inland is Vailima, the house which was the final home of Robert Louis Stevenson, settling here after wandering the South Seas – locally he was given the title of Tusitala, the Teller of Tales. I want to climb up to his tomb, to revisit that walk I made as a grumpy prepubescent eleven-year-old when I'd hated every step of the hot walk up the steep hill.

We plunge into the damp and heat of a tropical forest – strange bird song, black lizards, giant snails, bright red and orange flowers, so many unfamiliar plants and trees. Clusters of pale grey fungi on dead wood around which swarm clouds of tiny flies, rising as you pass. Small brown birds on the path ahead vanishing as you approach. Lianas entangling trees, hanging down like green waterfalls. It starts to rain gently, which is refreshing, until it turns into a ferocious downpour and we are soon drenched through and through. Dan leaps on ahead as I trudge up the hill. He has taken the rucksack and the water bottle, which starts to irritate me, as I would have liked a drink. Grumpy and wet and puffing my way to the top, I chance upon a bottle of water Dan has left for me on the path. I laugh, forgetting my bad temper: this is quite Dan's style, inserting something amusing, or unexpected, into the mundane or the serious. He is always able to surprise me. And it seems, I am not so far removed from my tetchy eleven-year-old self as I had thought.

At the top, the simple white tomb is there, just as I remember it. We are alone except for a couple of red flowers left as an offering and a wooden platform built 'by the people of Japan' under which we shelter ineffectually from the rain. Its presence seems quite inappropriate, having nothing to do with anything about the spot.

The views to the sea and Apia below are mostly obscured by cloud, but there are many houses large and small in the valley beneath us and I guess they were not there a hundred years ago when Stevenson lived here. I read the epitaph aloud. When, feeling sick for home and land, I recalled and wrote about these words last summer in the north, I had no idea that I would see them again so soon.

Under the wide and starry sky
Dig the grave and let me lie.
Glad did I live and gladly die,
And I laid me down with a will.

This be the verse you grave for me:
Here he lies where he longed to be;
Home is the sailor, home from the sea,
And the hunter home from the hill.

Down the steep muddy path as the rain clears, to visit the house. This is my second writer's house this year, after Key West, and I wonder how these creative souls manage it, landing in a place that suits them so well, becoming part of the landscape? I envy that.

The Samoan guide who takes us on the tour of the house, at the end hugs us and sings the epitaph beautifully. Although the hug and the singing are done, I guess, for every visitor, it is a little touch of something, a spirit that lingers on, though very hard now to find, it is fleeting.

Back in town, I check our emails. The elders have denied us entry to Tokelau.

So it seems, as with the Northwest Passage, the passage will not be smooth, we cannot draw a line or route as we wish upon the globe, our desires prevailing over others. I reflect that, the world of sailors and their boats is changing, and the people and the places they visit, are different, and my childhood world is vanishing fast. Michael is part of the old generation and there are ever less of his sort. Boats are more complicated, sailors more pampered, islands more bound up in paperwork and fees, and islanders have had enough of welcoming uninvited strangers.

Back at *Drina* we consider our options, and consult the chart. Michael proposes that we head straight for Tuvalu tomorrow. Dan is eager to get sailing. He is cheery and positive and I appreciate that at his age it is still so simple to enjoy and not overcomplicate everything like me.

One thing is sure – you cannot get your childhood back, you cannot get those places visited back, not in the same way. Perhaps this trip will be a closure, and a final end to my Pacific childhood dreams.

That evening I read in the book I'd bought at the house, *Prayers Written at Vailima*, some rather appropriate words:

with our broken purposes of good,
with our idle endeavours against evil,
suffer us awhile longer to endure and
(if it may be)
help us to do better.

This is from the very last prayer R L Stevenson wrote.

❄ ❄ ❄

In the quiet of a jetlagged morning, waking up far too early, I feel unsure what to think anymore, the way ahead is unclear, I don't know the meaning of any of this. No grand thoughts come to me, I'm like a tourist water-skater skimming on the surface – a white person, a *palangi*, who walks the streets with a white face and the history of whiteness a cloud around me or a bunch of baggage dragging behind me with a great clatter, disturbing the peace. We must own this, the white person coming here or to any similar place, and what the islanders might think of us after all those centuries of us coming uninvited. I know, in my case, this has been personally tempered by often being mistaken by white people for a local girl in different parts of the world – is your identity defined by yourself or by how others treat you? White tourist? Or person of colour, that cute island girl with brown skin and bare feet?

I wanted this trip to be positive, life-affirming and to have some sort of purpose. But at present I doubt anything much will come of it at all.

But the heat doesn't really let me think this through properly, and perhaps it is far simpler than that in the end, we white people, me, Dan, Michael, walk down the road, and the Samoans give a cheery greeting and a smile.

We accompany Michael to the immigration office to get our outward clearance. At the internet café I email my contact Paula to say it is a shame we didn't get the permission for Tokelau. She replies almost instantly: 'I waited in for you all day on Monday in the office.'

How puzzling. Just then Michael returns from the customs office. 'They said they think there is another Tokelau office!'

Paula emails back to invite us for coffee. It turns out where we had gone was in fact just an office overseeing transportation to the islands, while the remainder of the administration moved into new offices years ago. We never get to the bottom of why the guy in shades failed to explain about the other office. With hindsight it seems obvious but at the time how could we have anticipated this chain of misunderstandings?

Paula is lovely, and so very sorry about what happened. We could probably have got permission from the elders of her own island, but Michael says that the timing is out now as we'd have had to wait at least another day, so as not to arrive at the weekend, and then that would have had a knock-on effect all the days beyond that and our schedule. He is the captain and we must accept giving up on Tokelau.

Paula explains she and her colleagues are preparing for COP21 and have just returned from a meeting in New Zealand where it appears that as Tokelau is a NZ protectorate and not an independent nation (independence having been rejected by the islanders in two referenda) they are not going to get their own seat at COP. There are such a plethora of official bodies, organisations, coalitions and alliances involved in all of this, that it is impossible to keep track. It seems that there is a never-ending business/busy-ness of international meetings to attend here and there and speeches and declarations to be made. One next week in Tahiti, and another somewhere else, in this case, meeting to discuss the new climate fund, which matters a lot to the SIDS.

Paula's frustration is obvious in that her tiny nation, where only 1400 souls live (five times as many Tokelauans live in New Zealand and Australia) has no real voice when, as she says, 'we are drowning'... although New Zealand isn't directly threatened in the same way, she feels it is more interested in its own delegation and reducing the number of delegates that Tokelau gets to send to Paris.

She kindly presents us with a Tokelau flag, which shows a blue background of the sea and sky, the stars of the Southern Cross, and the traditional sailing canoe on which her peoples crossed the ocean all those centuries ago.

We have the flag at least.

Early the following morning we leave. Four young men are taking a net into the sea. Some fifty men are practising with a long canoe for a race, paddling fast across the harbour as a drum played keeps the rhythm. The drumbeats echo across the bay as one fisherman pulls the net into an ever-tighter circle and the others splash and dive to drive the fishes closer to the centre.

SEA PASSAGE

Flying fish leap away from us, golden-green smaller ones, and larger white and dark ones, cresting the waves.

'Look at the waves,' Dan says, his usual cocky self, as we leave the harbour. He has been eager to leave ever since we arrived in Apia. Not long after, as the sea begins to move the boat a little, he feeds his breakfast to the fishes. He remains in the cockpit, half lying down, pinned to the deck, unable or unwilling, to move, until I finally get him to his bunk in the main cabin, where he remains in misery, but refuses stubbornly to take an anti-seasickness pill.

We coast past Samoa's two main islands, Upolu and then Savai'i, their mountains clouded in grey, clearing the last of the land before nightfall and making good time under sail with the wind behind us. The birds are far and few between – white far-off specks, wheeling above the waves.

We are heading some 700 nautical miles northwest across the Pacific towards the few specks of land that are the island nation of Tuvalu, and there is nothing but hundreds of miles of sea before us now, the vast Pacific ocean. For my part, I am happy to be heading into the ocean once again, towards the bright and far horizon. The sea all around is comforting and familiar. We do not know, we never know, what awaits us there beyond the horizon, but the blue waves will carry us on, and the wind will have our back.

Michael adjusts the sails as the wind changes and politely refuses my offers to help. I don't know how anything works on this boat, and feel very conscious I am just a passenger rather than a member of the crew. He is very self-sufficient and used to doing it on his own.

He is so very much as you would imagine a seventy-year-old man who has spent his life at sea – skin the shade and texture of soft leather. He is a sailor through and through as is my father, and although in character rather different, in the sailing part, I observe, quite similar, in his preparedness, caution, and above all, a love of sailing.

Jimmy meanwhile is 280 miles from the Bering Straits. Some 4000 miles away from us, but it is the same ocean.

Unlike Jimmy, Michael doesn't bother with regular night watches and I sleep through the night in two halves with a spell in the cockpit around midnight. The southern stars are bright and their patterns alien to me although at least I recognise the Southern Cross. A few bright sparks of phosphorescence jump away where the seas break on the boat, like stone striking stone.

Days pass. The sea temperature has risen to 25.7°C. That is warmer than usual. Michael worries about the danger of cyclones forming as they are caused in part by higher sea temperatures. Above 27.5°C, the risk is high.

Drina, green-hulled and well-travelled old girl, is a treasure chest. There are paintings of Pacific scenes hanging in all the cabins, and each has a story to be told, and the bulkheads are covered with thirty years' worth of plaques and souvenirs of races and places. She is named after Michael's father's estate in Papua New Guinea. Jack Thurston searched for and found gold and later led a six-month expedition through the jungle to escape from the Japanese in 1942.

Michael reminds me of a character out of a Joseph Conrad novel, sailing these southern seas for the past forty years, and regaling us with tales of gold and lost fortunes, coastal trading adventures, and island loves. He is eventually going to head back to his base in Brisbane after six years away, in which time he's had a great many adventures, twice across the Atlantic and right round the Americas from Cape Horn to the Arctic. But the wealth from the gold and all the rest is gone now and pretty much all he has is his beloved boat.

Drina is a comfortable well-lived-in boat of character and experience but I don't feel the same affection for her as for any boat named *Aventura*, although she's sailed to every part of the Pacific, and almost every island, not to mention the Arctic and Cape Horn, so as good as any vessel to bear us to Tuvalu on what increasingly feels like a mission of fools. That is how it feels at present. The other Odyssey yachts have chosen to sail from Tonga and Fiji straight on to Vanuatu and not make the detour north to Tuvalu to join us, save for the American catamaran *No Regrets* which plans to meet us there. Our grand plans for a flotilla to arrive together, sailors declaring their ocean solidarity with the islanders, has come to nothing.

A few scraps of hope sustain me. I wonder if I will find anyone who remembers us from all those years ago? My family sailed these waters in 1978 when we made a detour here from Fiji to experience the independence celebrations of British colony the Ellice Islands, soon to be the tiny independent nation of Tuvalu. We made friends with Tuvaluans, above all the Tinilau family from the tiny island of Nukulaelae that we briefly visited. Two books described these magical childhood days: my own *Child of the Sea*, and my mother's *Pacific Odyssey*. Pacific islanders were not renowned for letter writing and we lost contact with our friends over the long years far away. I'd discussed with Michael whether we could stop in Nukulaelae, but the island has no safe anchorage, just the same as when we visited before, and Michael doesn't want to take old *Drina* there. We are heading instead for the main island of Funafuti.

No Tokelau; no Nukulaelae: what is left of this voyage? Right now there seems to be no more meaning than a hot boat where we toss and turn, sweating in our bunks. The heat below is overwhelming, we swelter like sweating beasts with no respite. We can't use too much water as Michael doesn't have a watermaker.

The waves slap us to and fro and the wind dies. No wind, no birds, nothing. We've seen not a single bird or any other sign of life the whole passage.

The ocean is blank.

This is turning into a watery ocean desert, with the fish all gone, fished up out of the sea after the islanders sold all their fishing rights to the Chinese or Japanese or whoever – thirty years ago when they got their freedom back, they had nothing else to sell but the fishing rights to thousands of miles of ocean.

Perhaps this blank ocean is the sign of what's to come. It reminds me of the planet visited in the film *Interstellar*, nothing but sea, no life, and a terrifying wave engulfing

the spaceship. If there is to be nothing left in the end but the waters, which have risen to swallow the land, and not even any creatures left who could live out a life on the salt sea, if this is to be, perhaps I catch a glimpse of it on this five-day passage.

❄ ❄ ❄

During these long days, I read the history of this part of the ocean in *Pacific Worlds.*

We remember and commemorate the European explorers, there are many statues raised of them, and their names are printed on every one of the charts sailing boats use to find their way, but what of those who came before? The Europeans were amazed to find people in the Arctic, and on almost every tiny Pacific island they came to, surrounded by thousands of landless ocean miles. Long before sextant, compass and GPS, humans found their way through icy northern lands and vast oceans, to make new places their home. These specks of land, surrounded by vast swathes of ocean, were populated by people on long distance sailing canoes, found by the skills of those ancient navigators, not just once, but many times over. For thousands of years the islands were self-contained and self-sufficient, happily ignored by the outside world. Polynesians, Micronesians, Melanesians – today we know them by the words crafted by Europeans out of Ancient Greek.

For Tuvalu, the first European contact was probably in 1567 by the Spanish expedition led by Mendana y Neira, sailing west from Peru searching for Terra Australis, the 'Great Southern Continent', a mythical place of untold treasure and 'souls to save'.

Just like the Northwest Passage, a quest was laid by those Europeans upon the ocean, an idea based on no evidence whatsoever, nevertheless laid upon the map, trying to bend reality out of myth, to bend the lands and ocean to the white man's will and desire. Never simply taking it for what it is. All must be named, converted, exploited.

Once it was silver, gold and spices, it was people in bondage and slavery; today it is oil.

Across these waters where we are sailing now, commercial routes came into being, sailed by huge Spanish treasure galleons, taking Indonesian spices, Chinese treasures one way, and then Spanish silver back – five hundred years ago, the beginning of the trade that links us all today (China is mighty now; and Spain has frittered away all its stolen gold and silver).

And then, for generations after those early visits, most of Oceania remained on its own. China – and Oceanian cultures – folded in upon themselves, focussing on ever more complex local structures of politics, hierarchy and custom, and there were no more visits from treasure fleets or long-distance seafaring empires. Spain's power declined. But next rose up the Dutch, and their driving force was not God, but Mammon, and the business of trade and merchants.

❄ ❄ ❄

Our progress seems impossibly slow, creeping for days through this heavy heat, the empty ocean. Rains on and off, engine on and off. Grey clouds bunch on the horizon as threats which don't always come to pass, and white fluffy ones sit far away like mocking icebergs in the heat.

Sea temperature is up to 26°C.

Jimmy emails to say he is heading straight through Bering Strait and Barrow. Michael had asked his advice about the risks of a storm and he replies to say that the water could get up to 28°C and not necessarily produce a cyclone. As the world expert in weather systems and routing – it is good to have his advice from afar.

Michael prepares a full Sunday roast beef dinner with all the trimmings. Dan feels a little better and eats but I still can't dislodge him from his bunk for a breath of fresh air even though the waves are negligible and the boat is barely moving at all. He lies there like an invalid aunt, fretting about how far it is, in-between scribbling cryptic notes and drawings to himself about World of Warcraft, which whenever he tries to explain to me what they are about goes in one ear and out the other without touching any understanding faculty of mine. We do find random ways to amuse ourselves however; today we invented a 'wimpy' high five with a clammy warm hand and a shriek.

Michael is more tolerant. 'Leave him,' he says. 'At least it's peaceful in the cockpit while he's in his bunk!'

We play I-Spy.

'I spy something beginning with p,' says Dan.

We can't get it so eventually ask for a clue.

'You can see it everywhere and all through space,' he says.

Impossible! After some time, we give up.

'It is p for the past.'

'What!' I say.

'Well,' Dan responds. 'We are looking always at the past, because all we see is light that has come from or bounced off things. It takes time for light to reach our eyes!'

Michael raises his eyebrows quizzically.

These are the sorts of thoughts that preoccupy Dan as he lies on his bunk.

❈ ❈ ❈

'The boom has broken in two.' Michael wakes me at 4am with this news. At first I don't believe him. It can't be – the winds are so light. But he is right — a welding job done in Ushuaia to fix the mainmast boom after a violent gybe in the Patagonian channels has finally weakened and given up. When day breaks Michael dismantles the ropes and lays the two halves of the boom on deck. Poor *Drina*, without a boom she seems missing something like a limb, and there is an unnatural space on deck behind the mainmast.

Boom trouble seems to follow me like on the passage from Nuuk last year. Now we must sail slowly on, under foresail, and we're estimated to make landfall in the middle of the night, so we will have to slow down to arrive at the reef pass only in the morning.

We are now heading for the setting sun almost exactly and pale yellows turning into a vibrant red spread across the sea and sky. The first bird in days circles us – a dark-winged gannet takes a good look and then flies away.

Dead ahead, high in the sky above the evening star, hangs a crisp white slice of white new moon. The clouds are rimmed with gold ahead, where Tuvalu waits beneath the horizon.

LANDFALL

Sometime during the night Michael drops the foresail and we drift with the current. Waves roll the boat to and fro so I slide from side to side in my bunk, unable to lie still and sleep, sweat pouring off me until I stink of it, while the wind whistles overhead and lightning flashes sharp and bright through the hatch onto my closed eyes.

At first light he raises up the sail and we start moving again. I come on deck to see a crowd of birds, black and white, behind us on the waters, the first seabirds seen in days, sharp silhouettes against the low morning sun, whose light is brazen yellow on the water.

Turning forwards, there, at last, is land, quite close by – not that much land can be seen, a dark huddled mass of coconut palms rising above bare slivers of yellow sand, as if giant segments of lawn turf had been unrolled upon the ocean. After six sea-slow days, seasickness and sweat, heat rashes, broken nights, questioning and self-doubt, all was washed away in this moment.

I know that nothing that had been or was to come on this voyage could ever match this brief morning moment seeing these green places spring out of thousands of miles of empty ocean.

It is very clear that there's no other way to arrive here than by sea, to appreciate the isolation, the vulnerability, but above all, the sheer magical miracle of the fact these dots of land had ever been discovered and populated in the first place. What superior knowledge drew those first navigators unerringly to the coral lodestone of refuge, not only once, but over and over – to here, and all the other islands scattered across the Pacific. What signs could they read in star and cloud, in wave and bird, that are invisible to us today, with our blank godless universe of scientific laws, blind to the thin veil beyond which lies meaning and all that is sacred.

And now, of course, that godless progress and science threatens these places first and foremost, our own modern miracle that spun heat and motion out of dead plants, out of our wonderful technology that was to bring us health, education, prosperity and equality, freedom from toil and labour, and even freedom from the very laws of nature, at least that was what we were led to believe – liberty from the random tyranny of drought and flood and unexplainable natural phenomena. But the freedom never quite came as promised, and there was a heavy price. There is always a price.

After the islanders' first European contact, chiefs and kings and rulers across the Pacific overcame the islanders' natural reluctance to accept Western ways, hoping for the goods, the guns and the words, that came with the acceptance of the white God and the white men's rules. And now, after all the Pacific centuries of contact between islanders and outlanders, the colonisers, missionaries and blackbirders[1], the complexities of give and take, harm and benefit, continuing today with aid packages and resource exploitation, alliances and trade missions, one thing stands new and tall that never did before, a storm cloud rising high above the horizon, as invisible and deadly as the common viruses that once ravaged island communities – the industrial pollution of the earth.

The meaning of my voyage lay there before me, a six-day passage by sailing yacht, to this remote Pacific landfall, whose name is on everyone's lips. Tuvalu and climate change: today inseparable.

The wind is blowing well, and the seas are high following behind us. There are one, two, three small islands to starboard, and the fourth beyond is Fongafale, the main island. The coral atoll of Funafuti, a band of islands enclosing a vast lagoon, is the largest of Tuvalu's atolls. 'Tuvalu' means 'cluster of eight', although in fact there are nine atolls, all inhabited: a total area of only eleven square miles of land, set in about half a million square miles of ocean.

These narrow atolls form a broken ribbon of islands that encircle a vast lagoon within – and we must find a safe pass through the barrier reef. We slowly approach the southeast pass into the lagoon, where some red and green markers are just about visible above the waves which are rolling in from the ocean. On each side of us the ocean swell breaks in fury onto the outer reefs, turning the water white and the air misty with the rising spray. Spindly green palms bend to the wind; they and the grey shores are all that hold the seas back from the lagoon beyond. The swells push and squeeze themselves towards the narrow opening of the pass, through which we must go.

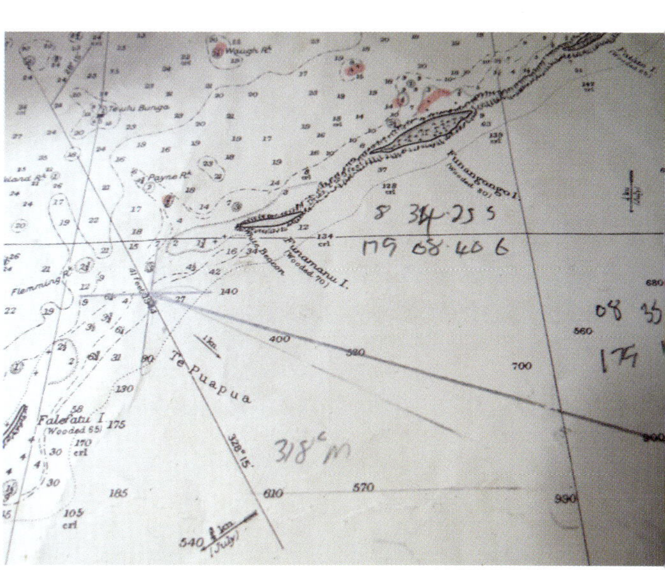

1 Blackbirders were those who forced many Pacific Islanders during the 19th and 20th centuries into slavery or forced labour through kidnapping, coercion or deception.

Drina's depth-sounder is not working which makes it a little nerve-racking that we cannot measure the water's depths by instrument, only by the old method of looking at and judging the colours of the water. Darkest are the ocean depths, and light blue and green are friendly to small vessels like ours, indicating enough water safely beneath the keel. The browns of coral heads, lurking just beneath the surface, are where the threat lies. There is no fear out in the open ocean for me, but here, as we draw into the pass, a cloud over the sun suddenly obscures the reef colours of the water, turning to grey the useful blue and green shades, and as I glance behind to see the ocean swell sharpening and rising to – not quite a white breaker – but starting to become one due to the shallows – an old and familiar childhood fear rises in me, and an old and familiar prayer, *please, please, just let us get through.*

FIRST STEPS ASHORE

Despite my worries, *Drina* and Michael bring us safely through the Te Pua Pua pass and it is an easy motor sail across the lagoon which stretches on for miles, its waters protected from the ocean on the other side of the narrow encircling band of reef and islands. The sun is hidden now, so there is no good visibility in the choppy waters. The main town appears ahead, out of the trees, and the grand government building, solar panels silvering its roof.

The only yacht there, we anchor north of the new wharf, besides the old crumbling one with concrete cancer; we are unable to raise officialdom on the VHF radio, so take the dinghy ashore to complete our clearance formalities. The port is busy with men loading sacks of flour and sugar onto the small ship, the *Nivaga II*, which takes supplies and passengers to all the other islands, the only means of travel as outside the capital there are no airstrips. We wind our way through shipping containers and large puddles in the white coral sand to the customs office. The officials are polite and not terribly curious about us but we engage in general chat about where we are from and why we are here.

One useful piece of information we glean however is that Fuolo Tinilau, son of my father's old friend, is living here in Funafuti. His wife works at the Women's Handicraft Centre by the airstrip. This is very good news.

After customs clearance is complete, we walk up to the Quarantine Office but it is locked up: it appears the officials are at the airport as the plane is arriving from Fiji on one of its twice weekly visits. Just beyond the office, the main road threads its way up the centre of the island; immediately beyond the road, and a single line of houses, is the sea again, the reef close up against the beach – there is literally nothing to this place at all, no more than a narrow coral strip. The slightness, the narrowness of the island, surprises me. I don't recall this from before, but like all children, I perceived distances differently, and perhaps I was also more in tune with the islands at that time.

The young customs officer offers to give us a lift to town to find the quarantine officials. The road up the spine of the island is very busy with mopeds and motorbikes, each carrying two people, riding up and down in a constant stream of traffic. A quick glimpse of life en route to town: houses close together, and open-sided areas on stilts with beds or mats where people lie or sit and talk; banana groves, papaya and pandanus trees, and frangipani flowers spots of yellow and white spreading fragrance into the air; big green rainfall storage tanks, churches and small Chinese stores, places to fix motorbikes and the infamous 'borrow pits' which were excavated during the war by the Americans for soil to build the airstrip and

One of the many 'borrow pits' on the island

have been the island's bane ever since, filling up with rubbish and water. The Americans who dug these holes all over the island never came back to rectify the damage they'd done. Now there is foreign aid funding a plan to fill them with sand dredged from the lagoon. The dredger is working near the anchorage, north, sucking up the sandy seabed. The land gained would be invaluable.

The grassy airstrip, the war's legacy, occupied the broadest part of the island, and when the planes are gone it reverts to its other role as football pitch. Today the airport is bustling, as it was when we came here all those years ago, although there is a terminal building now, and more buildings built on the further side of the airstrip where once was not much other than the radio comms centre from where my father made Tuvalu's very first international telephone call, calling in the story that Princess Margaret had been taken ill during her visit for the Independence ceremonies. The UK press were more interested in a royal illness than the fate of a faraway island nation.

At the Immigration Office in the airy government office building we fill out forms and while we wait for the officials to be done with the plane I look at an exhibition of children's paintings pinned up in the lobby on makeshift hardboard panels. Colourful pictures of islands, blue seas and skies, coconut palms, sea creatures, ships with funnels pouring out green smoke, and simple but poignant messages. *Plant more trees. Don't catch small fish. Life is more than a single breath.*

By now Michael is getting weary; the sea voyage has taken its toll, so once we are done we head back to the boat. For me, even that brief land trip was nourishing. We shift *Drina* to the anchorage nearer town and then Michael ferries Dan and me ashore again.

'Internet, find a decent place for dinner, and see if you can find your friend's wife,' he tells us are our three tasks.

It is a long hot trek to the internet café, winding through the puddles left by tropical squalls and avoiding the endless moped traffic. Spindly trees improbably bear large papaya fruit besides Christian exhortations pinned to the trunks: *Wanted! Lost souls – Marvel not... You must be born again.*

Everyone is friendly and smiles and greets us. I think this is great but Dan feels overwhelmed; he has to get used to this friendliness. We pass two grumpy-looking Russian men obviously looking for the internet cafe also. Do we look as pale and uncomfortable in the heat and as out of place as them? The Techspot Cafe appears very inauspicious from outside, but inside we're greeted by a host of monitors with young boys gathered round playing games which they could pay for in 20- or 30-minute slots. The connection is pretty slow but at least it is cool and quiet. The Russians sit opposite us, the one in black looks thoroughly miserable, unless it was his habitual expression.

I pick up news from the other Odyssey sailors, who are experiencing a motley collection of weather, unseasonal cold, lack of trade winds, tropical cyclones out of season. Bit by bit, the world's climate is unravelling. These days, knowledge of weather patterns and predictability is used for our leisure as sailors going to sea for recreation. But once it determined the world. This knowledge allowed the remotest of Pacific islands to be populated by sailing peoples skilled in navigation. And thousands of years later, this same knowledge meant that the north European nations became explorers, pirates, traders and slavers, roaming the seas at will, transforming from maritime nations into maritime empires and bringing those free sailing people of the islands into a new bondage. That was in the days before coal or steam, the days when the wind alone, or the brute strength of men to row, was the only thing available to power ships across the ocean. The British Empire was founded on its dominance of the seas, and what powered it at its peak was simply the wind – clean and renewable energy.

Our seasons in our old country are, for the moment, still recognisable. In other parts of the world, the binary of wet and dry, of cyclones and not cyclones, is falling apart – a predictable star of centuries collapsing upon itself into one long drawn-out season of storms, flood, drought – no respite anymore, no winds to trade upon, no patterns to sow and reap. The sailor, the islander, and the farmer watch the sky and the waves and look into the unknown.

The rain sweeps over us as we head back to the centre and we shelter in the deserted airport building. It is the torrential rainfall you only experience in the tropics – warm, fierce, and sweeping quickly through. We make our way to the women's centre but there is no one to ask if anyone knows Fuolo's wife.

We radio Michael to come ashore and meet us, so we can go eat at the Chinese restaurant we found earlier. Two out of three tasks complete; save for the one which was the most important.

While we wait for him, I return to the women's centre a couple of times. There are a few handicrafts hung up and sewing machines surrounded by bales of material and half-sewn clothes, but no one there. I feel very low.

I have pretty much given up, but at last I spot a woman sitting on her own at a sewing machine and go and speak to her.

A FAMILY REUNION

She is Fuolo's wife, Vienna.

'Oh Doina,' she says, overwhelmed and beaming from ear to ear.

My name, my father's name, are fresh and alive to her, and it turns out our family is no more forgotten to them than that briefest of brief stays on their island, Nukulaelae, is forgotten to us.

My heart leaps. After all the months of preparation, the little failures en route, the long sea passage with no clear end in sight, after all of this, I am so very happy to have made this one small connection.

Vienna's colleagues return and I show them the old photographs that I have carried with me all this way, and they exclaim over the pictures at people they know, some grown so much older, some who have passed on. They comment that the houses don't have thatched roofs these days.

'You must come to our house,' Vienna insists. 'At the end of the island. Fuolo is there.'

Soon after a young man arrives on a moped.

'This is my son, his name is Ivan.'

On Nukulaelae, my brother Ivan and Fuolo, both ten-year-old boys, had become firm friends in the few days they spent together, and as a sign of the bond between our families, they had swapped names, in the traditional way. I'm sorry that my brother hadn't stuck with it, but Fuolo had passed 'his' name on to his son, a slender quiet-spoken 22-year-old.

Ivan whisks Dan away. My son is gone into the night. Michael arrives, they have ordered a taxi for us to follow.

It is dark by now, the tropical dark which falls very fast, the day ending quickly, without any twilight – and we drive for what feels like a very long way, over countless speed bumps, unable to see where we are going, right along the length of the island. We arrive at a small house surrounded by vegetation and find Dan in the company of the young people and children, watching a film on a tiny netbook.

I meet Tinilau's elder son, Saosaoa, a venerable grey-haired man in his sixties, who holds my hand a very long time, I wish I could remember what he said but the emotions I experienced overwhelm my remembering. However, I still

Me getting a lift by canoe in Nukulaelae

can recall now the warm hand clasp, and warm words, and welcome, pleasure.

As a young man, he paddled in his canoe out through the tricky reef pass at Nukulaelae, to where *Aventura* was anchored in the ocean swell, as there was no inner anchorage, and he helped Jimmy fix the anchor more firmly into the coral so we would not drag and lose *Aventura*, our home. These worries have not changed, as tonight Michael worries about this unexpected trip, and leaving *Drina* for too long, a long way from the anchorage.

Fuolo is here too, of course no longer a skinny boy as I remember him, but a vigorous stocky man of 49. There are others too, the husband of Lieli who was my friend and taught me to dance in the Tuvaluan traditional way. Lieli has gone back to Nukulaelae to work and I am sorry not to be able to see her again.

We have quite taken the family by surprise and they apologise for not having anything ready to offer us. We drink very sweet tea and talk. Saosaoa tells us news of his home island.

'I was working on a government scheme there. We wanted to increase food security by making home kitchen gardens, and to protect our coasts from the rising seas by planting more diversity of trees along the shore.'

I am encouraged to hear this. But then he tells me about Tropical Cyclone Pam which had torn across the Pacific just a few months earlier.

'When TC Pam came,' he says, referring like everyone else we meet in Tuvalu, to the tropical cyclone as 'TC', 'the seas were so high they washed right over our island and washed away all the gardens and the kitchens. All our work was for nothing.'

These few simple words from Saosaoa, told in his halting English, are enough to break my heart.

The effects of Pam meant nearly half the population of Tuvalu had been displaced; some of the worst hit islands saw most of their crops and vegetation destroyed, and the saltwater left behind poisoned the land. The surge from the cyclone was made more destructive because of rising sea levels; because of the industrialisation of the planet in which my country and many others are complicit. The islanders had lived in self-sufficiency on their islands for a thousand years: and yet, today, despite their best efforts at mitigation, they cannot anymore. What crops can you grow in salty earth? The sea is rising and the Tuvaluans are the first to feel its effect.

Tropical Cyclone Pam storm surge on Nukulaelae

Tuvalu keeps trying; there are plans for the country to be powered 100% by renewables by 2020. Fuolo works in the government power plant the other side of the airstrip. Their ambition puts other countries to shame.

Solar panels on the government building

Meanwhile, Michael rests on a hard bed the family have spread with finely woven mats and pets a ginger cat who has wandered into the house to greet us.

'I need to get back to *Drina*,' he says. 'I can't leave her on her own for too long. And I'm feeling pretty tired.'

Although I would love to stay, we need to get Michael back and the taxi collects us. I feel bad about leaving: the family so wanted us to stay and eat with them, but we promise to see them again the next day.

I'd thought that the landfall sighting moment of Tuvalu would be the highlight, but that was just the beginning, and this moment of meeting the Tinilau family is so special, I can't explain why – why should it be so important to me as it is to them, but it just is.

I wish the rest of my family was here to share it with me.

FAMILY LIFE

Drina's VHF radio crackles into life, 'Doina Jimmy, Doina Jimmy, this is the Police Station.' I stare at it and wonder if I heard correctly. 'Person on the green yacht called Doina, this is the Police Station.' The police officer tells me that Vienna and Ivan are ashore and want us to come for a 'feast'.

Dan and I are collected on mopeds by two colleagues of Vienna's from the women's centre. Male from the island of Nanumea takes me on the back of hers. I cling on to her, perched right on the back and feeling I am going to fall off at any moment. The speed bumps are the worst. We talk as we go, that men and women should stay together (she finds it strange that I travel without my husband, and I can't really tell her that I am in the middle of sorting out my divorce), and that Satan is at work in the world. Faith is strong in these islands.

At least it is light so we can see the way. We pass over the huge pipe which is sucking up the lagoon sand to fill the borrow pits. Ancestors' graves are kept close by the houses, in the front gardens I see people spend time with them, lying or sleeping there in companionship.

Ivan gives us a tour of their bit of land beside the house which leads down to the lagoon, a fibreglass boat for fishing hauled up on the shore, pig pens, a plantation of the *pulaka* root crop, with their overlarge dark green leaves. There are bottles tapped into the trunks of the palm trees, gathering the sap; Ivan gives Dan a sip to try of the sweet toddy. Bananas, papaya and breadfruit hang green and ripening on the trees. These few crops remind me of the reasons why the islanders were able to maintain their self-sufficiency through the centuries: pork and fresh fish, and fruit and vegetables that grow freely, not to mention the miraculous coconut which provides sweet flesh and refreshing milk as well as much more.

A few paces away from the Tinilaus' house, just across the narrow band of asphalt, is the ocean. The ocean: you could never call this the sea. For beyond the thin green line of trees and scrubby vegetation, and beyond the grey coastal line of broken coral slabs, lies the vast expanse of the Pacific. The island curves along the outside of the atoll and so there is no off-lying barrier reef here to break and temper the waves, rolling in from thousands of miles away. Should the ocean ally with the winds and beat upon this unprotected shore, there is no protection. If she rises, she rises in all her power and might and she is unstoppable.

At the end of the island near the house they are filling a huge borrow pit. Despite the sign saying 'no entry' we walk into the site past a heap of rubbish, rusting metal and paperwork, discarded government papers, to see the deep pits filled with water. Men are lining the pits with material then adding layers of giant sandbags, which will eventually be covered with more loose sand. There are tiny shells scattered in amongst the excavated lagoon sand, which is a beautiful pristine colour, a pale yellow tinged with pink. The man in the digger waves at us to go back which is fine as we've seen enough by now.

Back at the house, fine mats woven from the dry strips of the pandanus tree have been unrolled for us to sit upon the ground. I have brought gifts of *Child of the Sea* and *Pacific Odyssey*; we look together at the chapters recounting our visit to Nukulaelae where the Tinilaus are mentioned. Saosaoa's son Soseala has arrived with his wife Vaipuna. He was only very small when we visited Nukulaelae.

'I work for the government,' Soseala tells us. 'I was part of the COP team that was in Peru and I'll be going to the Paris COP later this year.' Tomorrow he is off to Fiji for the Green Climate Fund meeting, as part of the work that Paula from Tokelau already told us about. He and Vaipuna both work on government schemes like that on Nukulaelae, implementing positive steps to mitigate climate change, by which the rest of the world could be inspired.

Filling the borrow pits

Over the last few years I've travelled from a distant place, on the edge of the issue, learning from books and the internet, and now at this point, we come right to the personal heart of it, to the island gardens being washed away by the sea, and the young island man, with his degree in atmospheric science, travelling with his countrymen and women to the world's summit – where these small island nations will do their very best to use words that the industrial polluting nations will hear, words which will have some heft.

Who would have believed it, from the Tinilau family I'd find such a golden piece of serendipity and all the threads tying together.

A great meal is laid out, a feast for us, after much work by the women, while the men hang up lights and nail protective sheeting to the windward side of the house. They recently took over the house from an older brother and have been doing it up, having ripped off the rotten second storey. Ivan's dog Simba wanders in and out, they block off the doors, so he then tries unsuccessfully to jump through a window. We eat, except for the women, who made the food, they eat last; Vienna, and Saosaoa's young second wife, Palanitina. I believe his first wife, Soseala's mother, has passed away. There are vast quantities for all the family, fried crisp pork, white rice, chicken pieces, breadfruit in coconut milk, and after, fruit and large round sweet donuts almost the size of footballs. As well as plenty of sweet tea.

After eating, Soseala and Vaipuna leave us as they have small children at home. The family already invited us to stay the night, which we'd agreed as it would be a long way back to the boat in the dark and it seems important to accept their hospitality. The youngest children have long before gone to sleep on mats, oblivious to the light and the talking. Vienna stays busy sewing until late as everyone else falls asleep. She works at the Women's Council which makes uniforms for work and church. Matching outfits for these roles are common here. There are bolts of bright island cloth in all the shops and most outfits we see are hand sewn. Now she is finishing an orange dress for work. She asks me if I can sew or cut and I must shake my head, no. Certainly not as skilfully as that: she measures, cuts and finishes all without a pattern, just by eye.

The two best beds have been moved into the corner for us, with the mosquito net over. I lie and listen to the sound of the ocean, and the wind in the palm trees. Beside the house the coconut palms grow very tall, creating a green space like the tallest of airy cathedral vaults reaching up to the sky, full of rustling noise – palm fronds in the wind. The rustle of the palms and the roar of the nearby ocean breaking on the outer reef, is constant in my ears throughout this stay. As a child I described this in a poem as a wonderful orchestra of sound as it was my constant companion for six Pacific years.

As I drift off to sleep, I reflect on how here the extended family is in full flow, with brothers, sisters and their spouses and children all living together. Living in one house, three rooms – everyone seems to rub along in a mild, supportive, companionable way. There may be friction and quarrels unseen, when we pale observers are absent, and naturally there will be other bindings that I cannot see, as this is still very much a traditional society. The roles of men and women are clearly defined and separate, for example, the women who made the food ate after the men and the visitors, but this is now being tempered by the modern world: women like Vaipuna can get educated abroad; Vienna goes out to work; and there are women in government ministerial roles.

I cannot help reflect, that for all the huge gains in our material and physical well-being in the so-called modern era, we have paid a terrible price in the losses to our mental and spiritual health: at the heart of our lives, is a terrible darkness, and you'll find there loneliness and isolation. You might see the bright lights shining, of our medicine and our comfort and technology, but what is lurking in the shadows of our houses, our streets, our old people's homes, our hospital wards? In the teenager's bedroom lit blue by the small screen?

These thoughts temper the profound peace I feel as I listen to the wind and waves: a constant rushing sound of noise, air and water meeting the land, the ocean roar and the rustle of the high high palm leaves; wind and waves that never cease their movement. In all the world I don't believe I'd find two sounds that would be so comforting. I feel as if I have come home; and want for nothing.

MAKING CONNECTIONS

Our fellow Odyssey participants, American catamaran *No Regrets* arrive. They made the effort to get here, despite strong winds and an unpleasant passage. It is good to see them again, as they have come a long way since Key West – when I thought they would never get to leave as engine trouble delayed their start. The three owners, Zeke, Tim and Bill formed a partnership to buy the boat and take part in the Odyssey; for this portion of the voyage, Zeke and Bill have taken on Canadian Bob as crew, as Tim had to return to the US. In their own words:

> *A magical bit of synchrony brought us together and culminated in our registering for the Blue Planet Odyssey. Remarkable were the facts that we had never met, that we lived in different parts of the US, had a fascination for the same catamaran model (the Chris White-designed Atlantic 42), had circumnavigation on our bucket lists and... were looking for partners to share these nautical interests.*
>
> *I guess we could say the Blue Planet Odyssey was the glue, the icing on the cake that made our partnership finally happen. Our additional lifelong commitment to progressive social and environmental causes has found the perfect compliment to our sailing passion. We are almost beside ourselves knowing that we will have the opportunity of contributing to such a worthwhile mission, which may just shake a few folks loose from their complacent non-activist moorings.*

The event of the day is the plane arriving from Fiji. We hope to see Soseala before he leaves for his meeting, but we are just a little too late. We watch from afar as he boards with the other passengers and there are tearful goodbyes and much waving as the plane taxis away and takes off. Moments later the all-clear siren sounds and people race onto the grassy strip, reclaiming the runway again for their football match: in that sense, little has changed since my last visit.

We make our way over to the government buildings to meet Selapa Kofe, an old friend of Michael's, who he's reconnected with, and who works for the Ministry of Finance, traipsing into the office to explain about the Blue Planet Odyssey's mission. He says we might be able to meet with the Prime Minister next week. This is encouraging.

I buy a Wi-Fi card so back at the boat I get connected and send my first email to my parents who I know will appreciate it, Jimmy having made the first international phone call here all those years ago. To get a signal I have to squash myself into *Drina's* small wheelhouse in the dark, trying to protect the laptop against the rain dripping from the dodger, as down below, there is no chance of a signal through the aluminium hull. In real time, I exchange some emails with Nera which makes me happy.

The following morning I hitch a lift ashore with Bob and Zeke. Dan passes on another shore excursion. A young man who works in Selapa Kofe's office meets us at the dinghy dock.

'You are invited to a workshop,' he says. 'By the Prime Minister.'

That's an invitation you cannot refuse. With no idea what to expect, and some excited speculation on our part, we make our way over to the Vaiaku Falekaupule which is the open-sided hall, used as a meeting place next to the airport terminal. There are lots of rows of plastic chairs where people are sat waiting and various dignified looking elderly men, though none quite looks like the PM. Someone hands us a programme. It turns out the occasion is to mark Tuvalu's signing of the UN Convention Against Corruption. At last the PM, Enele Sopoaga, takes the central seat, a pastor gives a blessing and prayer, then various long speeches take place. As these are all in Tuvaluan we are a bit lost but we sit there patiently, enjoying the atmosphere.

The concluding speech comes from the Prime Minister. He throws some English words into the Tuvaluan mix and as the speech proceeds there are some longer sections in English, which we wonder are for our benefit as there is only one other white *palangi*/foreigner present, a young guy I've seen in the government offices.

'The Green Climate Fund is far from democratic,' says the PM. We heard about this Fund from Paula when we were in Samoa. It has been recently set up to provide funds to nations such as Tuvalu, with some £9bn pledged by the developed world and is supposed to help with mitigation against the worst effects of climate change. This is the subject of the meeting in Fiji, to which Soseala has gone. Our Tokelau friends will be there too.

'The fund is controlled by donor countries,' Sopoaga continues, 'but it is not a charity as they seem to think, rather it is a survival fund for small nations like Tuvalu. Vulnerability is enemy number one for Tuvalu. We will be going to COP21 in Paris, and to New York before that, to find means and measures to save Tuvalu, our people, our home.'

The speech is done. He signs the anti-corruption convention and a 'tea break' is announced, after another prayer from the pastor. Laid out on several tables along one side of the hall are bowls of sliced fruit, cucumber and lettuce, sweet pancakes and small round doughnuts, pasta and crispy chicken, toasted sandwiches, sweet flan, chocolate and sponge cakes, omelettes and boiled eggs. Along with weak beakers of Milo (though they call it tea). This is the grandest 'tea-break' I've ever experienced. They don't do things by half – at our district council meetings back home, we might get a cup of tea if we are lucky. Cuts in our local government funding saw the end to biscuits long ago.

'I'll introduce you to the PM,' offers Selapa who has been sitting near us through the proceedings.

Soon enough we are having a chat and a cuppa with the PM and explaining about the Odyssey. He asks after my father: I am sorry that Jimmy is not able to be here now with us.

'I am happy that you will try to help raise awareness,' Sopoaga says. 'Look at the speeches I gave on my recent trips to the UK and Europe.'

The Green Climate Fund, he explains, as we sip our tea, is too bureaucratic; the paperwork to get any funding, for example for sea walls, is 'as high as the sea level rise threatening Tuvalu'. He has tasked Soseala with pressing Tuvalu's case forcefully in Fiji.

'Save Tuvalu, save the world' is the motto he gives us to take away. It is up to people now, not politicians, he says.

We are of course extremely pleased with our unexpected contact, brief but meaningful. Zeke (who has really committed to the Odyssey's purpose, and built links with his local schools back in the US state of Maine) is over the moon. He suggests we have t-shirts done with 'Save Tuvalu, Save the World' on them.

'It'll be too cold in Paris in December for t-shirts,' jokes the PM. 'Maybe they chose that date on purpose to put off the people from hot countries.'

'Tea' done, we are introduced to the ministers for Education, Foreign Affairs, Home Affairs and the Deputy PM, so I think we've met most of the government now. Some drama 'skits' follow, and then we must all get up and take part in some dance and movement. Obesity is a problem for these islands (no wonder, when you see the spreads they lay on; the creamy cakes and sugary doughnuts in the bakery; the sacks of white rice and sugar sold in the shops). We are amused to see the government front bench, sat in the front row, all taking part. At least they are trying to set an example.

When we get back to *Drina* Dan is still in his pyjamas. I am glad I didn't suggest he came ashore as he would have found it as boring as it was interesting for me. I'd promised him we'd go to the beach that afternoon where we make friends with two curious five-year-olds, a boy and a girl, and make sandcastles with them, while their old dog Beauty lies calmly by, keeping a watchful eye out.

It isn't perfection. There's more rubbish on the beach than there should be – a pile of discarded metal drinks cans – a shame no one thinks to recycle them.

A couple of boys Dan's age come along and they climb trees together, swim, and play rugby on the sand with a squashed plastic bottle. The boys want Dan to play football with them on the runway, but he says he is tired. We wander over to say hello to Vienna where she's working but decide not to go by the house today. Instead we accompany the *No Regrets* crew to the island's only hotel for dinner and listen to the Friday night band, The Underkavas, who sing a mixture of Tuvaluan songs and golden oldies. Slowly the place fills with young people, notably more men than women. Dan, who has revived somewhat, is invited by one of Lieli's sons, Antony, to join their group of friends sitting on the beach. They offer him a surreptitious can of beer. It amuses me that Dan thinks I don't notice. By the time we leave the place is getting crowded and our vacated chairs are gratefully taken; the drinking is starting to take effect on some of the men. The bright and cheerful music follows us as we row over the dark lagoon back to our boats at anchor.

The day starts sunny and promising for our plans to explore. The usual lagoon business begins the day – men wading out until the water reaches their armpits to fish, with a floating container beside them for bait or the catch – a man paddling an outrigger to anchor out in the shallows and cast the lines where he'll spend the day, staying through rain or shine, patient, with many lines out, tugging one now and then, gently. A shoal of fish jumps out in a flash of silver, trying to avoid some threat, real or imagined, and a white tern with a sharp black face swoops and dives for a fish with a quick splash. Otherwise it is quiet – the island's activity is much more focussed along the spine of the road.

Just as we mean to go ashore, the rain sweeps in fast and hard. We finally make it ashore in a lull between squalls but the wind gets up and a trip we'd planned to one of the smaller islands on the Tinilaus' fishing boat isn't going to be possible. Lieli's husband and one of Saosaoa's younger sons take us on their motorbikes on a tour, driving past the borrow pits and the airport runway, at the end of which kids are playing an improvised sort of cricket with a ball and wooden bats, past the Governor's and PM's house, past rusting hulk remnants left over from WW2 and people reclining in hammocks, resting by the sea, to the tip of the island, where the road comes to an end.

Back at the house, the family have done more work and have put up lattice blinds for the windows. I hope our visit isn't too much of an imposition, but Saosaoa is welcoming.

'I stayed up late reading your book,' he says. He enjoyed the mention he got in *Pacific Odyssey*. He plans to return to Nukulaelae soon to stand for election as President of the Kaupule – village council – as his father was before him.

Fuolo is also home: suffering from gout, he couldn't sleep and so he isn't working today. He would like to return to Nukulaelae also, but they are short of operators at the power plant so he's needed here. Yesterday, he says, they tried connecting the power from the solar panels, on the roof of the government building, into the island system, which he said was dangerous, though I didn't completely understand the technical details why. Something to do with keeping the power constant even when the sun goes behind a cloud, and solar input drops; they are hoping soon to get a new system with batteries for storing the power.

Meanwhile, the neighbours' pigs have escaped their pen, which gives the family's dogs some amusement, or work, chasing them round the houses. The brown bitch goes beneath the house and has her pups. The wind and rain come and go, beating hard on the house. At least they have the window coverings now. The young men haven't been seen at all today; their parents said they drank too much last night.

Saosaoa, his little daughter on his lap, tells me the story of how Christianity came to Nukulaelae; in 1861 a boat from Rarotonga was wrecked on the island with what he calls the 'laymen' on board. At first the islanders came with weapons but then were persuaded to help the strangers, who stayed and evangelised. I believe this is the same layman, Elekana, mentioned in the book I am reading, *Pacific Worlds*, who brought literacy to the islands, something that was most sought after.

At the end of the island, the sea waves rise higher than the land

Saosaoa's daughter falls asleep in his arms, and he goes to lie her down beside the other children. We talk about where the men have travelled when they worked as merchant seamen, a common livelihood for Tuvaluans. Fuolo sailed to Africa and took cargoes of logs back to northern Germany, and went up to Russia in the ice and snow. Lieli's husband transited the Panama Canal and travelled up to Taiwan. They have seen something of the world; but they prefer to return home. Fuolo plans to go fishing in his boat, but only when the work on the house is done. They will plant flowers and grass out front.

Before eating, we gather for the evening devotion. The family sit in a circle together on the mats, Saosaoa says a prayer and then they sing a hymn. The two women lead it, high, and the men with the bass – the harmonies are astoundingly beautiful. Afterwards, I ask Saosaoa why we didn't have evening devotion the other night.

He laughs. 'It was because Ivan and Dan started to eat too soon!' I suppose they were too polite then to say anything. I am reminded of RL Stevenson's evening prayers at Vailima as captured in the book I'd bought there – the homely tradition continues, a thread connecting us across time and across the ocean.

Protect the innocent,
restrain the greedy and the treacherous,
lead us out of our tribulation
into a quiet land.

When it is time to return to the boat, we get a ride on the 'bingo bus', a red minibus that you can tell is coming from far off by the loud music blaring out of the dark night. Some of the household join us heading back into town, picking up a few more passengers on the way, and dropping them at the meeting house where they play bingo all evening. We radio Michael to collect us. Nights come, like the rain, quick and fast and dark here.

THE MOTHERS

At the entrance to the church two young men place necklaces made of paper-wrapped sweets strung on cotton threads around the necks of the women going in. It is Sunday; Mothers' Day. They look at me and hesitate a moment then I am given one too. I'm gratified to be recognised as a mother. I've dug out the green dress I packed specifically for these sorts of occasions to look a bit more respectable. I knew Sunday worship is important here and I wanted to attend out of respect.

Dan wanted to sleep in, but I persuade him to come. 'For the singing at least,' I say. Michael comes too, with not much more enthusiasm than Dan.

Woven mats are laid down on the floor for sitting; there are no chairs. I find a place near the back, while Dan follows Michael nearer the front.

The church is filled with women, and they are all wearing long white dresses, with flowers in their hair and colourful garlands of sweetie necklaces. They are mothers and grandmothers, mostly middle-aged or elderly, and only a few men and children are present. A group of women lead the service, taking it in turns to come to the front and talk or read, prayers or scripture, I do not know which, and it all goes on a long time. I get stiff and fidgety: I've lost the habit of sitting for so long cross-legged and I admire how it is easy for the Tuvaluans, their backs straight and knees low, sitting easy for hours on the floor.

The church is very plain inside and out, with its doors wide open to the elements. The only decorations are four wall hangings in neon colours that appear to be from Ecuador and a sign saying 'Happy Mothers Day', picked out on the wall in pale blue letters behind the altar, which is adorned with bright artificial flowers. Although I say 'altar' it is very simple, two tables covered in blue and white cloth, on each a blue satin cushion holding a Bible. The women sat reading at the higher table sometimes seem to disappear behind it. There are no images, no written words on display – it seems the power and potency and life of their faith is in the spoken word, in their hearts, and in the music.

Because we really came to hear them sing – to experience again the Pacific harmony that I recall from my childhood. And we are in no way disappointed. Someone stands up to conduct; there are two different groups that sing at different moments, with the congregation at times joining in. The voices rise up with the hymn, women's high and men's underneath, and it weaves a compelling powerful harmony, beautiful, but not in a soft and mellifluous way, it has an edge of harshness to it, or perhaps I should say, saltiness – not sweet – it is as bracing, as all-encompassing, as deep and strong as the ocean – a blend of many things made into one.

I listen, easing my stiff knees. My eyes fall to the open doorway beyond which I can see the lagoon and *No Regrets* swinging peaceably at anchor. It is so very beautiful, this singing. Who would want this beauty lost to the world? So much has already been destroyed, never to be recovered. This music, this faith, these communities and lands, should be preserved. Because they are alive, because they are good. Because if the Tuvaluans are forced to leave, dissipated as climate refugees to one antipodean city or another, families broken, kids departed to study and jobs, and the islands left to erode and be washed over by the waves – the Tuvaluan people's spirit will be broken and all the good will be washed out of them. Can you imagine in a generation's time to walk down an Auckland street and meet a Pacific Islander when their ancestral island homes are no more, and it will be in part our fault, and we will all be the lesser for it.

Tuvalu is not a blank at the end of my journey, not a problem to be solved, but a living place to keep alive and treasure.

There are many hymns, and much talking, one woman is overcome with tears. Sometimes a woman stands up from the congregation, siezed by the moment, raising her voice in song which all join as she goes and speaks to us from the high table altar. And sometimes in the singing someone falters and an open wave of laughter ripples across the solemnity of the hymn. We hear a lot of laughter today, strong, easy and heartfelt.

At the end of the service, the pastor rises, the first man to speak. He welcomes us visitors – we are invited to join them next door. Everyone stands up, lines up to shake hands and to thank the mothers, hugging the ladies in their white dresses, their smiling faces wet with tears.

Next door where we've been invited is a smaller meeting hall where we sit awkwardly beside the pastor while two large cakes are cut, a slice for each of us thick with coloured icing. We're served first and must wait for everyone to get a piece. I hold the sticky cake for what seems a long time, as speeches are made, and then everyone joins in a blessing which involves moving your cake-holding hand around in a complicated pattern weaving through the air in response to the words; we try to copy without much success. Only then is it permitted to eat the cake. More speeches follow, some of which make people laugh, and the young people sing. We're invited by the pastor to return for the evening devotion and further celebration.

Neither Dan or Michael are keen to join me for the evening, but *No Regrets* crew Bob says he will come along. Evening devotion begins at six and people are called there by a man beating a rusty old cylinder outside the church. It is deafening. Two men preside over this service: it seems the morning dominance of the women was exceptional. The preaching is animated and vehement. The hymns are as lovely and compelling as before.

Afterwards we are invited again into the neighbouring hall where mostly women dressed in white are gathered. Bob, being a reticent and polite Canadian, tries to lurk near the back, but the Reverend insists we come and sit at the front with the elders of the gathering; I realise they are the only men present other than the younger ones who are part of the group of young people sat behind us. Tables are laden with food. One boy is celebrating his 18th birthday so cakes are produced as before, and we wave our slices about for a blessing before eating as guests, singing happy birthday, and 'happy long life to you'. Grace is said again, we are asked to serve ourselves first.

While we eat, Reverend Tofiga Falani tells us this is the Vaiaku Vaialofa Church, part of the Church of Tuvalu, formerly the London Missionary Society, LMS, and he has been pastor here since 1981. The older generation did their training in the Samoan language as that's where most of the original missionaries came from, and until recently the bible and hymns were only in Samoan. There is a Tuvaluan Bible now, and hymns. Samoan, the Reverend tells us, is very similar to Tuvaluan, with only a few letters different like thank you *fakafetai* (or *fa'fetai* they say), as there is no 'k' in Samoan. If a Samoan and Tuvaluan talked to each other in their own languages they would understand each other, although the younger people are starting to lose that ability now.

When the Reverend stands up and speaks to those assembled, in his smart jacket, and smart lavulavu wrap around, the long skirt that men wear formally in many parts of the Pacific, I observe he is not so tall, but broad, solid, and with strong feet that are used above all to being barefoot, like all of his compatriots. I wonder if the Tuvaluans are a not little like the nation of Hobbits (the analogy only goes so far, and I hope it is not disrespectful to make the comparison, so profound is my love and respect for this island people) in that they are a sturdy, strong, peaceable people, for whom family and celebrations are very important, who have lived in their lands for hundreds, even thousands of years unaware of the outside world (and the outside world quite ignorant of them; as still even now is the case – Zeke would tell you, his experience is that most people in the US haven't heard of the place), and now, through no action or fault of their own, they are at the centre of the world's story, threatened by the dark forces of Sharku and the Satanic Mills. Having been considered of little importance, they now found themselves to be at the heart of the troubles concerning the 'Wise and the Great'.

It would give me great pleasure to be able to say to one of those climate-change denying American rightwing politicians who profess to be God-fearing and knowledgeable about God, come and sit in this church, listen to the hymns and preaching, and when you are face to face with these people of deep faith, tell them climate change is all a lie and nonsense puffed up by some lefty environmentalists and scientists pimping for research money. Those internet sources backing up their denialism would be flimsy blue hyper-links blown away in the brisk wind whipping over the islands from the ocean.

Once everyone has finished eating, the real business of the evening begins. A square is formed with four groups of people sat facing each other around an open space: on each side of us are groups of white-dressed ladies, in front the young men and women. A woman who is the MC of the proceedings, who has led on the speeches, the thank yous and the birthday greetings, says (so the Reverend translates) Bob and I will have to judge the singing. Cue much laughter from the assembly at this. Each group sings a hymn in turn. Bob, who likes to sing himself, is impressed by the harmonies, and the amount of bass the women manage to belt out. At first it seems there are only one or two 'choirmasters' but as the evening progresses, many different individuals step out to 'conduct' and the singers watch that person attentively.

Hymn after hymn after hymn, the music pours over us. Hard to imagine it is a block of voices and nothing more, no instruments; the volume and power is strong enough to make your ears ring. Each song – here and earlier in the church – begins with one woman like a human pitchfork singing high. She gives the notes to follow, a line of words to get everyone in tune. The harmony of the women's voices in the first group to sing, to our left, is astounding, as salty as I said before, like a wave that

breaks over you, knocks you down, leaves you clean and breathless and wanting more. You could never have enough of it. My only regret is that I wish I knew what the words meant.

Second up, on our right, what we find are two groups of ladies. These are the jokers of the pack. As the evening notches up a gear, they start to goof about, which sends everyone, especially all the young people, into peals of laughter. Merriment comes with various speeches which we don't understand, then different ladies get up to conduct hymns. During the singing, some of them make silly dances, others steal each other's hair combs, sunglasses and flowers, one gets quite carried away and animatedly conducts the empty corner of the room before hugging a pillar. Huge gales of laughter erupt from the gathering. A younger guy comes and kisses her (much laughter) and all the while the hymns go on and on, pouring over and through us. Appreciation is shown by spraying singers and audience with perfume.

It just so happens that I'd re-read in the last few days my mother's *Pacific Odyssey* chapter on our visit to the Tuvalu island of Nanumea and how the older women entertained us in the exact same way with their dancing and joking.

Even the PM's wife is here as part of the congregation and is singing in one of the less serious groups. The Rev'd tell us that this church, of the Vaiaku community, includes the government and official residences on its patch so has the PM and Governor General as part of its congregation.

I am struck by the lovely way humour is shared between generations, I can't imagine at home a bunch of teenagers and twenty somethings so unreservedly enjoying their mothers and grandmothers larking about without being embarrassed, let alone at a meeting after church. (A few days later, we find out from the PM's wife that this humour is usually reserved for women's gatherings only, and although for the last couple of years the youth have been included, there are no men present – the three male elders on this occasion are considered *palangi* like us, foreigners, she says, so we don't count.)

There are many rounds of singing and larking about and laughter. It is well after 10 pm by the time it ends, with speeches and thanks. I'm not sure what happens to the judging aspect (what was the best? I couldn't call it). I stand up to thank them as that's expected and present them with a couple of parish magazines from my village and a history of my parish church that I'd brought with me all this way in case of such an occasion.

The Rev'd says the ladies are involved in fundraising to rebuild the church which is old and needs renovation. It is the least I can do to promise I'll take this message back home.

Speeches done, and we go.

Throughout the evening the squalls came over, the rain beating fiercely against the hall's lattice windows. At least there is a brief lull for us to get back to the boats; Dan and Michael are already fast asleep. I go to bed with the laughter of the mothers, and the music, still ringing through my head, body and soul.

THE HIGH LEVEL DIALOGUE

The Acting Secretary to Government requests the pleasure of the company of ... Ms Doina Cornell... to a reception to welcome our Development and Donor Partners to the High Level Dialogue on the TC Pam Recovery & Vulnerability Reduction Plan to be held at the Vaiaku Lagi Hotel on the evening of 28 July. Attire: Island Formal.

Monday morning begins with a radio interview for me. I'd visited the Media Centre, as my cousin Marianne has asked me to try and track down a journalist contact of hers. She has her own personal contacts with Tuvalu, having made a documentary here, *The End of Tuvalu*, in 2003. Her first meeting with the islands and islanders of the Pacific was back in 1999 when I was too pregnant with Nera to do any sailing, and she crewed with my father part of the way as he sailed on his third boat, *Aventura Trois*, from the Antarctic to the Arctic.

Marianne's contact isn't there, but I speak to another journalist, Diana, and when I start to explain my story she asks me for a quick interview for Radio Tuvalu. It'll go out tonight after the news.

When I get back to the boat after a morning of trudging round offices, I can see Dan isn't very happy with me although he tries to hide it; I'd left him all morning when all he wanted to do was go for a snorkel.

'Let's try swimming to the beach,' I say, to snap him out of it. Tiny bright fish have attached themselves hopefully to the boat, imagining her to be a large creature, hoping for scraps, and there are some small jellyfish here and there, which when Dan spots them, makes him shriek and leap out of the water. So much for our swim... We sit on deck hoping for rain to shower us with fresh water, but the line of the rain squall bypasses us and drenches *No Regrets* instead, just as I have soaped my hair. I just about manage to rinse it off; when the wind blows the rain is as sharp as needles.

That evening both the crews of *Drina* and *No Regrets* get dressed up for the reception, to which we have all been invited, hoping this will do for 'island formal' as per the invitation. A gathering of eminent-looking people have gathered at the hotel, and despite our best efforts, we sailors feel rather shabby in our scraped-together 'finery'. It is hard to look very formal when you've dinghied ashore, dodging tropical rain squalls, and my one dress is ever more crumpled.

Our new acquaintance Rev'd Tofiga greets us – it turns out he is the Acting Governor General – and introduces us to the PM again and his wife Salilo Enele. We recognise her from the Sunday singing. She takes the time to talk to us at length, and we learn that breadfruit trees, long a staple food in the Pacific, can no longer be grown in the traditional way, planted in a deep hole, as in her garden and across the island, the salt from the rising seas kills them off. A makeshift solution has been found to plant the trees in raised beds. Her great passion though is to raise women's rights up the political agenda, and to ensure women pass their skills on – the old crafts are in danger of dying out as women have traditionally only passed their knowledge onto their own kin, so if there is no kin left, their skills die with them.

Breadfruit tree planted in raised bed

❄ ❄ ❄

Another invite, a card delivered with our names written out by hand.

> *The Prime Minister requests the pleasure of the company of ... Ms Doina Cornell... to the official opening of the High Level Dialogue on the TC Pam Recovery & Vulnerability Reduction Plan to be held at the Tausoa Lima Falekaupule on 29 July.*

Dan, Zeke, Bob and myself get ourselves early to the *falekaupule* or *maneapa*, the traditional island meeting hall. The open-sided hall has been decorated with shell necklaces pinned to the edge of the upper walls, and finely woven mats with names of all the places in Funafuti. The floor is also laid with mats, and a long table has been placed in the centre. Fans turn in the ceiling. A great deal of work has been done to organise this day by unseen hands. When I see Vaipuna later on, she tells me she was working here until 4am and so overslept this morning.

The VIPs arrive with flower garlands round their necks, which they keep on for a while, and sit around the table. We find ourselves some seats at the back.

Protect and Save Tuvalu: Our Home, Our Island Home, is the title of a short film, only five minutes long, that begins the High Level Dialogue. The titles roll, island by island.

VAITUPU ISLAND

Photographs on the screen: broken concrete, rubble and strewn vegetation, boiling white seas towering over the shore, crashing over the land, collapsed buildings.

A song begins, a woman's voice, over the images:

Six years I've been in the city
And every night I dream of the sea

NUKULAELAE ISLAND

Photos of the sea, white and furious, covering the ground, beating against the trees.

The song continues.

My island home
Is waiting for me

NANUMEA ISLAND

When the waters recede, they leave behind debris, concrete ripped apart and strewn across the ground in broken white chunks, uprooted trees, foundations split in two, walls collapsed.

NUI ISLAND

The sea beats against the shoreline, spray fills the air, the thin trunks of the trees no longer form a protective barrier but are forlorn, broken, washed over. A dim figure of a man appears out of the mist, leaning towards the sea, watching.

The white sea fills all the space, the land has disappeared: grey-white water has flooded the groves of trees, nothing to be seen but water, drowning the roots of the trees.

A woman and a young girl, knee deep in the grey water, carrying a piglet to safety.

The bright green leaves of the *pulaka* root, planted in traditional pits in the ground, inundated by sea water. The sun shines on the tranquil scene, brightening the green plants and reflecting off the silvery water, whose salt will slowly poison the soil so nothing more can grow.

Another flooded *pulaka* pit, the leaves remind me of angel wings, large enough to strap onto a child's back. The brown shapes of coconuts float half-submerged like drowned heads, bobbing amidst the debris.

A woman sits on the threshold of her house, the water rises to just below the lintel of the open door. With her hand she pushes away at the seawater, a gesture at once curious, and futile.

Flooded shops, full of water inside and out.

A smashed monument, half of the white-washed steps to its plinth still in place, the rest broken into pieces that tumble down to the destructive sea.

A shoreline swept clean of vegetation, and two small lone figures of women looking on.

We always lived by the sea.

A boy stands beside the fallen roof of an island meeting hall: the green metal roof has folded and fallen down like paper, and white coral blocks have been left, stranded, by the wall.

NAUMAGA ISLAND

Another collapsed building. And another: walls, floors, fallen down where the ground has been swept away.

Corrugated roof metal bent and broken, ripped off buildings and scattered across the sand.

NUKUFEATAU ISLAND

A metal fence that has no purpose, as the sea water rushes in. The land has ceased to exist, it is only water here.

Children wade through the water. There is no respite, no dry place, no refuge – it has covered every part of the land. Homes piled up with the debris that the waves have brought with them.

For four minutes we look at the photos, one after the other, from different islands, and the music plays. The photos are vivid, and tell the picture quite adequately. We'd seen many of them on display in the government building the day before, in the place where the children's pictures were when we first arrived.

But then the music abruptly stops, and a film starts. We see an open-sided shelter, and water draining away across the floor. A man's voice calls out urgently. Beyond the shelter is the sea, the waves are rising, and then 'boom!' calls a voice, and suddenly sea water crashes against the side of the shelter, right up to the roof. Then the sea rushes in and over everything, there is nowhere to go that is not covered with the sea. People are running away. You cannot see where the island begins, and the sea ends – the waves and water cover it all. As quickly as it came, so it recedes, pouring away back into the ocean, as if now it is obeying gravity, and the proper demarcation between land and sea, when only a few moments before it made up its own rules. Inside the rooms, as the water starts to recede, is a jumble of furniture where the sea has tossed them around, tearing off cupboard doors, breaking tables.

I felt a chill all through me at the shock of what I was seeing. I hadn't expected that. A bare minute and a half of film brought the abstract knowledge, of rising sea levels being a threat to these islands, to vivid life. As the song said, we are saltwater people, we lived by the sea. The sea was their companion, for them and all their ancestors, a familiar place to them and me, and yet now it had become a threat... not because of anything they had done. It was elsewhere, the greed and growth of the world, without a care, that tipped the fine balance of this nation. The Tuvaluans had become the canaries in the coal mine and we had better heed what they have to tell us.

❄ ❄ ❄

This film sets the sober tone of the long day of the conference, with presentations from the Tuvaluan ministries about their plans to deal with the impact of TC Pam.

The World Bank has estimated that the damage and losses caused by Pam amounted to more than 25% of Tuvalu's GDP: islands were cut off from the outside world, food crops and water supplies affected, people displaced, islets lost, as well as damage to boat ramps, roads, health clinics and sanitation. The government's plan has three objectives: support households to recover; support the construction and repair of damaged infrastructure such as coastal protection and sea walls; address chronic food insecurity and build resilience. The government and the international community have already pledged significant funds to assist, but there is a shortfall, which is what today's conference is about – asks of funding from those who are present today, and there is a good gathering here in the hall of partners and donors – representatives from the World Bank, Red Cross, WHO, UNICEF, UNDP, EU, Japan, New Zealand, and many more.

One of the ministers says to them, this is not 'begging', but a dialogue. 'We are here to be able to tell you the stories, so you understand why we are asking, as our partners, for your assistance.'

The eye of the storm might have been a thousand miles away, but its effect was so brutal, it was a 'wakeup call' for the government, 'a blessing in disguise', as they realised quite how vulnerable their islands were – and at its heart, they tell us today, this is not just about the survival of Tuvalu, but all of you, the world at large.

At a recent meeting in New York, a politician from Africa asked, 'why don't you just move away from Tuvalu?'

The answer they got was, 'We were born here in Tuvalu, we will live here, and we will die here in Tuvalu.'

Photographs from Tropical Cyclone Pam and messages on display in the government building

Fast Facts

Tuvalu Tropical Cyclone Pam Report and Vulnerability Reduction Plan 2015

Partner with us to give Tuvalu a better future, making the country resilient to climate change and contributing to society and for our communities to be stronger and healthier.

Support for Tuvalu Tropical Cyclone Pam Report and Vulnerability Reduction Plan

Between 10 and 11 March 2015, strong winds and high sea waves caused by Tropical Cyclone Pam (TC Pam) but also a Category 5 Cyclone whose eye passed through Vanuatu Islands swept across the low-lying islands of Tuvalu. The sea waves, estimated to be from three to five metres in height, caused significant damage to food crops due to salt water intrusion making island communities food insecure. Water supplies were contaminated by seawater and hundreds of people were temporarily displaced. Island communities are also experiencing challenges on managing debris: boulders, coral, damaged coconut, banana, breadfruit trees and other debris are littering the island environments. Significant land losses due to coastal erosion were also experienced with some islands reporting as much as 20-50 metre sea encroachments. Three islets were totally lost while another three from the islands of Nukufetau, Funafuti and Nukulaelae partially destroyed. We strongly believe these effects are caused by Climate change, there is general consensus that Tuvalu is losing land due to coastal erosion not only to cyclone effects but the rising sea levels and high tides. Building coastal protection is critical to mitigate coastal erosion and to reduce land losses.

During one of the tea breaks the PM greets everyone going to get a cup of tea and we ask him boldly about making our own presentation. Just before the session starts after lunch I'm invited to the front with Dan and Bob and make a speech about the Odyssey in front of all the dignitaries, giving one of our small BPO commemorative plaques to the PM. (If only the other BPO boats had come here. Even six of us, we might have had a discernible impact. If we had come with 20 or 30 boats that would have been a great show of solidarity. But we didn't, it was really only me in the end, and *No Regrets*.)

What moves me most today is when the head of the women's council stands up and speaks about how the impact of TC Pam and climate change is most keenly felt by the most vulnerable, women, children, disabled – by households headed by women, by single mothers – from where will assistance come for them? Other women speak up too – and it is notable that public speaking happens a lot, on every public occasion we've attended there is an 'MC' and many speeches of thanks, and women do it with as much confidence as men. The top table of the Tuvaluan government however is almost exclusively male and the fact that the Acting Minister For Education is a woman is positively remarked on by an Australian (woman) diplomat. The PM points out that the Attorney General and Acting Secretary are also now women.

We meant to leave after our own presentation but then I find out the man filming the proceedings is Iakopo, the journalist Marianne wanted me to speak with, so I hang on until the next tea break to get his contact details for her. After hours of speeches we are fidgety and impatient and not concentrating, wanting to be away, and Dan counts up the many hours we have been sitting here. He has been patient until this point, reading his science book, and I am grateful to him for sticking it out; my tolerance level for meetings is far higher than his, as I know all too well from my three years as a local government councillor. Finally when the next break comes we get away. We were supposed to meet Vienna and we are now late.

Later I read back my scribbled notes from this day, jottings of ministerial speeches, and a few lines I think are from a song, but I can't now recall. I'll end with them:

Alas my country
when that time comes
where shall I turn?

A FAREWELL FEAST

The long day of speeches and hard facts is to end with an evening of celebration – *fatele*, traditional music and dance. For this to happen, during our own short visit, is a truly glorious piece of luck. But best of all, the Nukulaelae dancers are one of the island groups chosen to perform tonight. I know how much I harp back to those days when we were here for the independence celebrations, but I recall how they were the best dancers then and I am sure will be again.

We are now on borrowed time. We must sail west to Vanuatu to meet the others from the Odyssey, and after that, home to work and school. A big low has formed over Vanuatu. Michael and the *No Regrets* crew consult each other on the weather and when it will be safe to leave – it will be soon.

We've just enough time tonight to meet the Tinilau family for what they call our 'farewell feast', a meal in the Chinese restaurant. We are given parting gifts of a small pandanus mat, and pillowcases embroidered with 'Tuvalu'. In return, I give Saosaoa my only copy of *Pacific Odyssey*. We do not have long as they must get ready for the evening's performance.

'We must go,' says Saosaoa, as he wraps a green lavulavu round himself. 'We are needed for the music.' Dan walks off with the men towards the *falekaupule*, and Vienna gives me a lift on the back of her motorbike.

The *falekaupule* has been cleared of all the furniture from the conference earlier, save for a line of plastic chairs for the VIPs. They are having a grand buffet dinner, with more speeches, at the hotel, so it is a while before they arrive. I sit on the floor at one end of the hall with some of the Nukulaelae women, each wearing something a bright shade of green, fresh garlands of frangipani and other fragrant flowers on their heads which send warm perfume into the air.

The bright colours of the flowers, but even more so, their sweet smell, remind me of the women making garlands on Nukulaelae with me and Lieli all those years before. So many years! It took all this time to bring it all back to me, like out of a dusty forgotten trunk in the attic, and the colours and the fragrance are as alive as ever – it is not the same flower garland we tossed into the sea when we departed Nukulaelae with a wish we might return – but flower begets flower, down through the generations, now, and yesterday, and thirty odd years ago, and hundreds of years ago, the same flowers, that are the custom of the Pacific islanders, to greet travellers from near and far away. Welcomes and farewells to travellers have always been a significant part of sailors' and islanders' lives, this we share: all journeys of arrival or departure come over a thousand miles of open ocean, and when you leave, can anyone be sure you will ever come back again?

Meanwhile, men haul in the long, flat wooden box which is the only instrument, other than voices. Now I see familiar faces, Saosaoa, head crowned with a wreath of fresh flowers, Fuolo, and the young men, Ivan and Antony, quick garlands of green stuff hastily arranged in their hair.

The people representing the other island who will perform – Nukufetau – sit down at the far end of the hall, dressed in orange and red.

Everyone gathers into a square, facing each other, sitting tight and close, with the wooden box drum and the men at the centre of it. The youngest ones, like Fuolo and Vienna's youngest daughter, stay on the edges. They are learning.

Having met and got to know them in their daily lives, I feel quite overwhelmed seeing them all come in ready to perform. I'm only a *palangi* after all, and I can't speak their language, nor sing or dance as they do, but I feel a part of me belongs, and the feeling, if I can ever describe it, is of pride, the pride when your family does something well.

Perhaps the Tinilaus made it so, because of their great hospitality now and then; perhaps it is because I was so young and impressionable then, and the songs and words and poetry you hear in your childhood are more potent than any that comes later in life, as I remember Gandhi writing once about the epic poems heard in his youth; or perhaps it is just some sort of magic or silver thread that has struck us and bound us. For they are my beloved brothers and sisters, and that is how it is.

The VIPs are all in place now on their chairs, and everyone else sits around the edges or stands watching from outside.

The dancers enter and stand in front of the seated group, women dressed in all their traditional finery, bulky skirts of brown pandanus layered over brightly dyed strips, that sway dramatically as their hips move. Vaipuna is there too – from a self-assured educated young woman and mother that I'd first met, to a Nukulaelae dancer, she was herself and yet quite transformed.

The dancing begins. It is the same as it was: the fine detail of hands weaving slowly through the air, the beautiful smiles, the slight swaying of hips, set against the slam into the box, the clapping beat, and the volume of the voices. A few steps from the singers, the sound is intense, overwhelming. The men are at the hard centre of it, drumming on the box, down to the earth, and the women sat surrounding them, sing with high salty harmony. Now and then an older woman leaps up and dances too, when the moment takes her, and all the while the rhythm of the music builds faster, faster, and faster – then when it seems almost too much, too intense, there is the breath of a pause, the dancers stop, whoop like birds and whirl about, and it all begins over again, slower, and building to another crescendo.

The dignitaries, as is the custom, are invited to join; the Tuvaluan government ministers join in for a few gestures, easily done for them, and then the other awkward VIPs are dragged up out of their chairs, and there are spare skirts to hand to wrap around their hips. Perfume is liberally sprayed onto the dancers, as is the custom, a sign of approval.

PROTECT AND SAVE TUVALU.
MY HOM

HIGH LEVEL DIALOGUE
TC PAM
THEME:PROTECT AND SAVE TUVALU.
MY HOME

Some four, or five rounds take place, alternating between each end of the hall, as each island takes it in turn, like a dignified dance off, without any posturing. Nukufetau are good, with sweet smiling girls, and men dancing too, but of course Nukulaelae are the best. For their very final dance the Nukulaelae dancers spell out 'T C P' which reminds me of when they did the same for 'Tuvalu' once. It is their signature move.

Across all the islands of the Pacific, they dance. After the hurt of the crashing waves, the swept away gardens, the betrayal of the richer nations of the world, the need to be supplicants to the powerful for aid money to mend the damage – the dance is there for healing, for the simple joy of celebration. This is who they are, dancing, equal among nations.

❄ ❄ ❄

The dancing has ended. Formalities follow which take some of the magic out of the evening: speeches and a prayer, and then the ritual giving of gifts. The VIPs leave promptly, and the singers too, leaving only the wooden box alone in the middle of the floor, surrounded by scattered empty soda cans, which fuelled the singing.

Michael and *No Regrets* have been watching the dancing and now discuss when to leave. Looks like it might be tomorrow. Our time here was only ever fleeting. A quick few last photos and goodbyes, just in case we do leave first thing. I wish there was more time for this.

Fuolo must head off for his overnight shift at the power station.

'You are our sister now,' he says, and Vienna's eyes are wet with tears.

'Come back before I die,' says Saosaoa softly.

I feel like I'm leaving a piece of my heart behind. I never wanted to leave last time and I don't want to leave this time, so why the hell do we leave?

❄ ❄ ❄

By morning, it looks like the Vanuatu low is dissipating. The decision is made to go straight away; we cannot miss this window of more favourable weather – no time for more goodbyes.

Please let me not wait another 37 years before I come back.

PASSAGE WEST

A line squall passes to our south, a grey shape moving along the horizon, darkening the islets strung along the outer reef with a white veil of rain, and writing a dark forbidding line across the sky between itself and the bright blue sea and the sun-stroked islands beyond. We are heading across the lagoon towards the western pass. The buildings of Funafuti recede slowly behind us, and I wish we could have said just one more goodbye to the family in the morning light, by the sea, a moment before departure, not in the dark by the meeting place, but this was not to be.

There are a handful of scattered, small islets on the western side of the lagoon, top-heavy with thick growths of green vegetation above low sandy shores, except for one which is just sand, stripped bare – a victim of TC Pam.

The passage through the reef between the coral heads is narrow and crooked but the sun is behind us so visibility is perfect. This was the big ship's pass once, says Michael, but all the buoys are gone – only the other pass is marked now. *No Regrets*

follows not far behind. On each side of us the beautiful bright turquoise, symbol of tropical dream holidays for city dwellers, but a lethal colour for a boat, a siren call you would not want to heed. The tide is low, brown nubs of the reef visible above the water. Birds rest and preen on thin strands of sand where the sea breaks white onto the shallows. I am relieved when we are through, out into the calm and deep ocean.

For an hour or two the islands stay with us, sand and then green trees slowly slipping beneath the horizon, until only the sea is left. Our destination is Vanuatu, some 800 nautical miles to the west. Michael estimates this will take us less than a week.

'I'm worried,' he says, that first evening at sea. 'It isn't clear which direction this low is headed, it could develop into a cyclone and so I think we will stay north where it is safer, above the 10°N line where the storms don't generally track.'

He decides to drift, all night and the following day, no sails up, borne on the current at about one knot in the right direction, *like a painted ship upon a painted ocean.*

My father, far away north, sends us weather reports by email, he thinks it unlikely a cyclone will develop, as we are out of the season, but Michael is very cautious and as the captain I can't argue with that. I trust his experience. So we are sticking to the north.

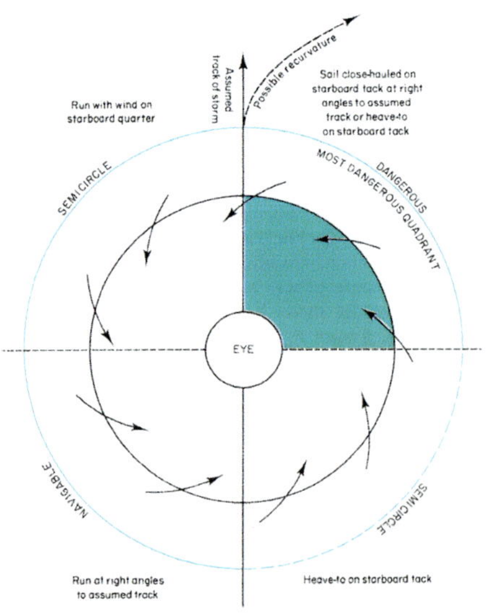

Tropical storm tactics – northern hemisphere

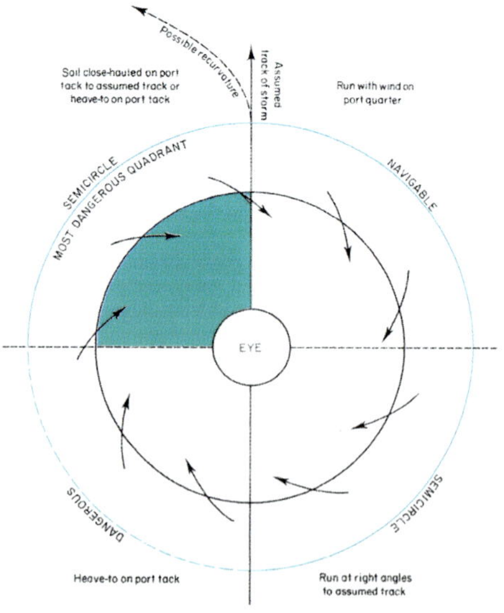

Tropical storm tactics – southern hemisphere

I study one of Michael's meteorology books, and old newspaper clippings fall out of the inside cover with diagrams and explanations of tropical depressions, how they form and which quadrant of the spinning circle is the most dangerous. In the southern hemisphere the cyclones rotate clockwise (anti-clockwise north of the equator), the wind moving in a spiral, being sucked into the storm's core. You wouldn't want to be anywhere near one of these beasts in any part of the circle, but for sure, the lefthand side is the most dangerous. My father has a great explanation of this, and the tactics to avoid storms, in his book *World Cruising Routes*.

There is nothing for it but to go on, making progress as best we can, sweaty, stinky, eating the Captain's cooking (much corned beef, and few veg – even Dan is beginning to dream of fruit, our apples and pears are nearly gone).

No Regrets is some 10 nautical miles away, also heading north. Only two ships are seen, in the first 24 hours – a Taiwanese fishing boat and a cargo ship bound for Port Moresby the Papua New Guinean capital. An occasional brown gannet or tropic bird.

I talk to Jimmy on the satellite phone, he is 400 miles from Cambridge Bay. The central part of the Passage is still blocked with ice but the prospects look good. News from home is not so good, as my 98-year-old grandmother Irene is not well, she has an infection, my mother is spending all the time she can visiting her in her care home.

We drift on an indifferent grey sea. Confused swells from the northwest and southeast meet and merge, and the boat rolls in between, the sails flap in the light winds.

Damn this ocean, no more trying to wrestle poetry out of its damn blue, three days in and I've had enough and want to get to land. I feel sorry for Dan, once again sick and pinned to his bunk in the main cabin, desperately wanting to get to the end of this. Lying there, pale-faced and lacking the will to move, he reminds me of young Colin in *The Secret Garden*.

He and I play games to pass the time, making up riddles for the other to guess.

I have many names but one body
I can hold you but you can't hold me
I'm the mother of all but few know me
I am light and dark, light and heavy
I have no colours but painters love me.
What am I?

Two little creatures like Gollum and Bilbo, exchanging riddles deep underground.

I am black but if you work on me you can see through me
I am dead but I bring things to life
Animals shun me but man loves me
Riches are built on me but I will make the earth poor
What am I?

We spend a day slopping about and although we are drifting very slowly in the right direction, there is still more than 400 miles to go. I really hope that the latest weather information we get through via email tonight will show a final weakening of the low and that it moves south away from us.

A small black bird with white on its belly swings low over the waves with one leg hanging down, just skimming the surface, barely, barely.

'Storm petrel,' says Michael. We can't work out what type of petrel it is, but it comes from the family *Oceanitidae*, the southern storm petrels, and it is a pelagic creature, spending most of its life far from land, flying over the deep waters of the ocean.

The low still remains. The night is black, now and then illuminated by lightning. I manage to prise Dan out of his bunk to see the evening stars and the phosphorescence which goes tumbling in our wake, the bright tiny stars of glowing creatures disturbed by our passing. These are the good and glorious moments to be at sea.

We wallow and roll around all night, so it is hard to rest. I mumble a sleepy invocation, *Go away front, stop blustering and blocking our way west like some big old cross lady demon. Pick up your skirts and fly away, mother storm.*

At last, after three miserable days, the wind shifts to the southeast and the air turns cooler – 'because the wind is from the south' Michael explains. As a Northerner I am not used to that. For us 'north' means cold and 'south' hot. The cold south wind feels all wrong to me, but reminds me that I am in the other hemisphere, far from my northern home.

The southeasterlies mean *Drina* is now slamming into the waves. The wind grips us tight, like iron. My forepeak bunk is the worst as the bow rises on each steep wave and falls slam down again, and then again, and although my body stays on the bunk, all my insides rise and fall. How to rest in all this movement? The boat's wood panels creak loudly, in every drawer and locker items clank back and forth, the waves crash over the bow, water rushes over the window of the forward hatch above my head.

This voyage west, each individual mile of it, must be wrested by force from the ocean, as if the ocean does not want to give it up. The captain brings all his will and wit to bear, reading the weather maps, the clouds and the air, adjusting the sails, and the compass course this way and that, pitted against the wind and waves. Bit by painful bit, we progress, pencilled marks on the chart showing our snail-movement onwards. Dan feels like he has fallen into his own personal circle of Hell. He started to feel marginally better until the southeasterlies come and sent him back to square one. Tonight he was sick again several times. Terrible mother, inflicting this suffering on her son during the summer holidays.

Nine days – a slow, frustrating passage.

We should see the first island, though, at daybreak.

❄ ❄ ❄

Michael gets up often to check the boat and how near the land is. Around 4.30am I join him in the cockpit. The skies are overcast but the stars and moon behind the clouds means there's light enough to see the circle of the horizon, and off our port bow, the dim shape of the island of Maewo.

This dark, indistinct shape seems to sum up what I feel about Vanuatu – my memories of this place are dim and few, and despite reading the guidebook, I don't know what to expect or what our visit will bring us. I have less affinity with Vanuatu. I don't feel that same link to the people and the place as I had to Tuvalu. Of all the islands in the west of the Pacific, labelled 'Melanesia', 'Black islands', by the Europeans, because of their darker-skinned inhabitants, I felt more of a link to the Solomon Islands, and Papua New Guinea, both north of here, where I wrote my first poems, became a teenager and had my first boyfriends, local boys a few years older than me – my parents were not very approving.

By morning Maewo is fading behind us and the next island to our port, Ambae, is clearer, its heights veiled under pale clouds. I inhale on the breeze an unmistakeable scent of honey. Am I imagining this faint sweet smell, or is it truly drifting over the water from the land?

Some 40 miles yet to go. Dan dreams of hot showers, swimming, fruit, ice cream and drinking lots of Vimto.

Espiritu Santo comes into view. The Vanuatuan archipelago consists of some eighty islands of volcanic origin – quite different from the low atolls we have left behind, and Espiritu Santo is the largest island in the archipelago. No sign of human habitation except for one or two strands of grey-white smoke drifting up lazily from the trees. The shores are lush with thick forests, rising up to high volcanic peaks. The peaks remind me of Lanzarote, but this is a very different place from the Canaries, and although the islands look like islands, and the sea is blue and familiar, for a moment, I feel very far from home.

A PAUSE. GLOUCESTERSHIRE, SEPTEMBER 2022

I have typed up my handwritten Arctic and Pacific diaries, revised, researched, shortened, revised again. It has taken me ten years to get here, leaving Tuvalu behind at last. Now the notes from Vanuatu sit reproachfully on my desk.

What next? Should I continue to recount the end of our 2015 Pacific visit – to Vanuatu and New Zealand, where Dan and I spent time before going home? This question turns in my head for days.

I read my notes over and over, and all I've come to know in the intervening years, all I've become aware of, make me realise how my observations, my eye, are barely different from the white explorer who gazed upon those Vanuatu shores a few centuries ago. My words and descriptions feel 'othering', with the curiosity of a tourist, the sympathy of a traveller, but no belonging. Can I continue this story with any legitimacy?

The layers which wrap around this story, from the time when I began it, in 2012, and the years and years that have come since as life got in the way of my finishing the book, these layers grow each time, another added, a gleam of understanding, a pearl that drops unbidden into my hands and astounds me – and this makes me want to continue the story to this black, ancient archipelago whose people's culture is so rich and diverse, place of a hundred languages and the black volcanic stone that inspired the Vanuatu poet Grace Mera Molisa. Because, in my pause, by chance I discover Grace. Amazing Grace, they named her, the first woman of Vanuatu to get a university degree, writer of the new constitution when the country threw off the yoke of its unique and absurd joint Anglo-French colonial administration. Black stone represented most what she wanted to express in all the fire of her poetry and words, her righteous anger for her people, the volcanic stone of the islands, but above all the women of Vanuatu, as she called them, the 'Colonised People': *Vanuatu is now free of foreign colonial domination but Ni-Vanuatu Women are still colonised.*

And so I resolve to go on.

A few words to wrap up this Pacific journey, fragments I have found again to shore against our ruins.

I must continue just a moment longer, until I find the end point.

A MILLION DOLLARS IN THE SEA

A cheery voice comes over the VHF radio, 'Greetings *Drina*, from Blue Planet Odyssey Rally Control!' This is Luc, who has been running the mobile Odyssey office, looking after the yachts as they make their way through the Pacific – *No Regrets* is already anchored here, while the rest of the fleet is in Port Vila, the Vanuatu capital. We plan to meet them in a few days on the island of Malekula.

We sail into the Segoe Channel past Million Dollar Point which is so named because at the end of the war, the Americans wanted to sell their excess military vehicles to the French and British, who said it was too expensive. So the Americans just dumped it all in the sea instead. The underwater jeeps and diggers are a divers' attraction now. A million dollars – rusting on the seabed.

We step ashore as dusk is falling. After nine days at sea, it is hard to walk in a straight line, rolling from side to side like sailors of old.

Luc is there to greet us. I finally get to meet him in person after 15 years of us working together on different projects, starting with the Noonsite website for sailors I founded back in 2000 with my father and brother. He is from Belgium originally, and with his American partner Jackie, and a collection of Schipperke boat dogs, have lived on their trimaran *Sloepmouche* in the Pacific for many years. He is just as cheery and positive as I had expected, after all these years. Based now in the Philippines, he spent many years in Vanuatu, sailing and working, and he has arranged two island visits for us and the Odyssey fleet, where local festivals are taking place.

We first spend a few days in Luganville, the main town of Santo. At dinner at the resort off which we have anchored, we talk with a New Zealander who is here with others from tourism offices to promote Vanuatu again – visitors stopped coming after the news told the stories of the destruction brought by TC Pam. Tourism is very important for the islands' economy. The resort seems a pleasant dreamy place perhaps to pass a holiday with the beach and sea all before you. But on the land side you can only enter through a high gate and all the complex is fenced in – except towards the sea. Beyond the fence and the perfect green lawn, the bush grows thicker, a jumble of weeds and trees, and there are little houses hidden amongst the growth.

Dan and I play our part as tourists now and go on the Millennium Cave tour, taking a bone-shaking ride in a minibus through the forest. At the top of the hill the bus turns onto a stretch of concrete, a long pale strip surrounded by vegetation.

'The Americans built an airstrip here,' the bus driver Philip tells us, 'during the war, in 80 days and 80 nights, working 24 seven. My father helped build it.'

A dirt road takes us deeper into the interior. The famous Santo cattle are pastured under the coconut palms. Other than tourism, the cultivation of cattle for their much-prized beef is one of the economy's mainstays. Exotic flowers grow wild in the bush, and decorate the neat front gardens of the houses, yellow and brown spikes standing to attention, and long spiky tongues of red. The ubiquitous binding weed has white trumpets at least ten times bigger than our equally annoying ones at home that plague my own garden.

Children playing outside the Millennium School wave as we pass – the school was built with proceeds from the tour. Started in 2000 (hence the name), the operators of the Millennium tour, we are told, didn't share the proceeds fairly. Now the community runs the tour and keeps the proceeds, so the school and a kindergarten have been built, and the income also helps to pay school fees which are a real burden on families in this country.

Philip and the bus leave us in a village, and we follow our guide, who is called Peter, to join other visitors at the cave, scrambling through it and then down the canyon, part bouldering, part swimming in the river. As we walk back to where the bus will collect us, past plantations and much weed-covered bush, I ask Peter about the giant bindweed which covers the ground and climbs up the trees. He says it came in 1942 with the Americans. The American legacy: the abandoned airstrip, the metal rubbish of million-dollar point, and the weed engulfing the forest. I suppose it could have been worse – they didn't get picked for nuclear bomb testing, as did other Pacific islands.

My perspective has been sharpened by the book I am now reading, *Oceania: Neocolonialism, nukes and bones*, deepening my understanding of what profound and damaging impact colonialism and neo-colonialism have had on this part of the world. Tourism is part of that too. As the author, Andre Vltchek says – come here to feel rich for once in your life. He recounts a conversation with Epeli Hau'ofa, one of Oceania's most eminent writers:

> *I asked Epeli Hau'ofa whether it was too arrogant for me to write a long book on Oceania as a traveler from afar. He stared at me for a while, kindly but ironically. 'How many years have you worked in Oceania?' he asked. 'Five,' I replied. 'Do you care about this part of the world' 'A lot,' I said. 'That qualifies you as one of us,' he said. 'You are from Oceania. And as such, you can; you are actually obliged to write what is happening here.'*

These words hearten me greatly, and much later, when I am home again, I get a copy of Hau'ofa's book, *We Are The Ocean*. He writes:

> *Conquerors come, conquerors go, the ocean remains, mother only to her children. This mother has a big heart though; she adopts anyone who loves her.*

MALEKULA

Sad news comes this morning with an email from my mother to say that Granny is deteriorating. The doctors are speaking about end-of-life care. My mother cuts short the girls' outing she'd organised with Nera to visit Bath Spa for some pampering.

Michael loves an early start. He weighs the anchor, breaking our binding to the land, and off we go at a smart pace, leaving the *No Regrets* crew still fast asleep. Small boats are heading across the channel to Santo, on the early morning commute, while we sail in the opposite direction towards the island of Malekula, whose outline on a map looks much like the head of a dog. The coastline is thick with forest and seems deserted until you glimpse a house between the trees, or a wisp of smoke rising. These days, the forests are a carbon sink to treasure. Deep in the bush, are hidden old cannibal sites, but this is long ago, tales to titivate tourists now.

We anchor in a bay off Malekula's northern coast. A man in an outrigger canoe comes by.

'My wife sent me for news,' he said. 'Have you a rope for my cow?'

Michael finds a short bit of rope. Another younger man visits us who is called Tilden (I think), he offers to take us to the blue hole for swimming. He ferries Dan and I ashore in turn. The canoe is small but sure. It is very old, Tilden says. It has a modern component: a rubber rim around it to protect against bumping yachts. Tilden tells me he has sailed to China working on fishing boats, and he would like to marry a white girl because Vanuatu girls are 'too black'.

We land on the stony beach and head inland, across a river, passing a pile of germinating coconuts' green shoots bursting from the grey shrivelled husks. Dan observes he has now seen the full cycle.

A friend of Tilden's joins us and they both carry huge bush knives. Oh well they seem friendly enough… We pass a few cows tethered to the trees, which is why the man needed a rope. The young men move Tilden's cow to a different tree; it is brown with a crooked horn. He takes a stone, loads his slingshot, aims at a bird and misses.

The blue pool is lovely, Dan and I swim there and jump off the coconut tree perched above the water while the young men wait for us. Bearing in mind Tilden's earlier comments, I feel that my skin is very pale.

'Can we buy any fruit?' I ask, 'like pampelmousse?'

'I'll get some,' Tilden says.

'Have you any coconuts?' asks Dan, which he likes best.

On the way back they draw on the bounty of the tropical forest. The reason for the Pacific islands long-time self-sufficiency was already clear in Tuvalu, where sweet fruits like papaya grow easily, alongside the versatile coconut and starchy staples of taro and breadfruit. Tilden gathers some oranges and his friend climbs an old pampelmousse tree to reach a few for us. With a very long bamboo they knock down some green coconuts and adroitly chop the ends off for us to drink.

'You want to eat it?' Tilden asks Dan. He cuts off a wedge of the outer shell which Dan looks at, puzzled and then throws away. Tilden hands him half a nut and asks, 'where's your scoop?' He laughs and Dan laughs because he hadn't understood what the wedge was for. The young flesh is soft and tasty. Dan keeps the wedge as a souvenir.

With our forest 'shopping' we head back to the beach. A woman with two children is gathering small round stones for the slingshot. Her little boy, no more than two or three, carries a knife half as big as him. I smile to think of over-protective European parents not letting their children play with anything sharp. The little boy struts his stuff until Tilden's friend grabs him and puts a pair of red shorts on him. The little girl stays close to her mother.

'How much you would like for the fruit?' I ask.

'Whatever you like.'

He ferries us back to the boat.

'Have you any clothes?' he asks.

Dan finds a shirt for him that someone had given us in Apia.

As he paddles away, playing music on his mobile phone, I think how that canoe is such a simple and effective piece of technology. The outrigger can be found all over the Pacific, shared despite the wide variety of people, cultures and languages. It is believed to be an invention of the ancient Lapita people, who were also proficient in the skills of open ocean navigation, and no doubt the outrigger spread from island to island because it was so useful, and easily made from available materials. The Lapita settled Vanuatu some 3,000 years ago, though there were further waves of migration after that. Although volcanic eruptions and other factors have made it hard to ascertain its prehistory, Vanuatu is a place of incredibly diverse and rich culture, self-sufficient communities separated by a challenging geography, which perhaps explains the existence of some 100 distinct languages. Languages, not dialects. There are 30 on Malekula alone.

❄ ❄ ❄

An email from my mother, which maybe came last night, I don't know exactly. The time difference is confusing and makes it hard to work out when things are happening back at home. We are all existing in the same planetary time and space, just these human time zones are laid on top.

Granny has passed away. I call my mother. At the end, she was only sleeping, not eating or drinking, so my mother stayed for a while and then decided to go. 'Goodbye mother,' she said and kissed her. Only ten minutes after she had left, the call from the care home came to say: she's gone.

I cry a bit when I speak to my mother. I like that they tucked up her toy dog Cuddles beside her. It was peaceful, which is the best way.

The funeral will be postponed until 1 September so we can all be there, that at least.

Irene: 23 March 1917 to 12 August 2015. Rest in peace dearest Granny.

I find these lines in the book of Vailima prayers.

To our absent mother,
give my armfuls,
the last gleanings
of the harvest of her life
so that she may go down there
where she must go
in the beauty of a serene evening,
not without its songs.

I am a long way from home.

Four generations of women: Irene, Gwenda, Doina, Nera

SOUTHWEST BAY

We head south, to meet Luc and the other Odyssey boats. Michael tries fishing as we sail close along the coast; he catches a barracuda.

'I don't like to eat these,' he says. 'I'll give it to the village when we arrive.' The fish is long and silver like a blade. Laid on the aft deck, it flops ineffectually, gasping its last breath, hoping in vain for respite from the thin and killing air.

In the early afternoon we come to Southwest Bay; no other boats have arrived yet. Michael hails a passing local boat and gives them the fish.

The Odyssey fleet arrives at last: *No Regrets, Tahawus, Chapter 2, Blue Wind* and *Maggie*. It is good to meet all the crews again.

Luc has brought us to this bay as he has spent time here before and he is officially 'brothers' with one of the elders of the small village, Bulbul, near where we are anchored. We visit the village and meet Chief Esrom who always wears dark glasses and looks very cool; only later do I realise he wears them because he has lost an eye.

Behind its protective veil of trees, Bulbul is surprisingly large, hidden from the shore, and cupped defensively by high cliffs all about clothed in green. The villagers cultivate pineapple and cocoa for cash, as well as copra which they dry in small huts. It is a subsistence life; a little income also comes from what visitors like us pay to visit. Many of the houses are built in the traditional way: woven pandanus panelled walls and bamboo, while others are now made of breeze blocks – which withstands cyclones better although at least Malekula was one of the islands not so badly affected by Pam. They gather dead coral pieces from the seabed and mix them with sand for cement for building. There is no electricity other than small solar panels fixed into the thatched roofs, and little solar chargers left outside the huts which charge their mobile phones. There is a store and a post office, and larger, grander houses are now being built. A saltwater lagoon lies behind the village, flanked by the hills. The hills are divided in ownership between families that can trace their tenure back through generations. Borders between one family's land and the next are made by the natural folds in the land formed by creeks or streams. Each plot is accessed by an opening in the thick mangroves which form a great protective barrier to the land all about the lagoon, and can be reached by each family by canoe.

Luc and his partner Jackie were given a garden a long time ago and a bungalow up in the hills, a rare gift and a mark of their longstanding friendship with the village. The bungalow is falling down now but there is still produce to be gathered

Luke and his village with Blue Planet Odyssey sailors

from the garden. That evening as we sailors gather on one of the boats, to socialise and exchange stories, Luc explains the difficulty of Europeans attempting to buy land here. Land rights in Vanuatu are a big political issue.

I finish reading *Oceania*. What a mess we Westerners, we Europeans, have made of the world with plenty of the worst examples here in the Pacific. In the balance does so-called civilisation and its benefits weigh well enough against disease, exploitation, corruption, enslavement? (In fact China, and Taiwan, and Japan, also have helped mess up Oceania too, and they are not done yet). Oceania was free and self-sufficient once, before we came along. Wouldn't the world have been better off if we had left well alone, stayed on our own lands instead of pestering the world?

❄ ❄ ❄

A local man takes us in his motorboat for a small fee across the bay to the village where Luc has arranged for us to see a festival. As we zip across the bay I talk to a French woman from another boat here, not taking part in the Odyssey. She lives in Tahiti, where she is a researcher into ciguatera fish poisoning; she tells me due to the warming oceans they are seeing this toxin, which can be fatal to humans and was once confined to the tropics, spreading now even to the Mediterranean and the Canaries.

At Fire Beach, named for the stones which can be struck together to make fires, the villagers have gathered and we sailors are welcomed with flowers. We sit on benches before a beautiful natural theatre, a green backdrop of a huge banyan tree, red flowers encircling its roots and rising cliffs behind covered in vegetation. Musicians sit surrounded by leafy screens embellished with flowers, playing drums, smaller ones upon the ground and a larger drum, the size of a man, with a face carved into it, propped upright. The drumming is compelling, a clear, pure rhythm, now fast, now slow.

The dancers are hiding somewhere; before revealing themselves, they call and respond with curious birdlike cries, and then we see them coming down the beach, slow and colourful. Only men, they wear waistbands of bark into which leaves are tucked and more of those red flowers, while their dark hair is coloured bright pink and yellow from pollens or petals. They keep their eyes lowered to the ground, carrying long spiky staffs, while their leader holds a coloured symbol swollen like a giant yam. They tread and shuffle along the beach and into the

arena, winding back and forth, calling and replying. The dancers look incredible, although the dance itself is not wildly exciting, and each of the dances we see is much the same, although for the final one they wear great conical headdresses, as bright pink and orange as the most artificially enhanced colour you could imagine. The men hold these hats upon the heads and peer out.

'What are the hats made from' I ask our guide, a woman from the village named Angela.

'I cannot tell you,' she answers. 'This knowledge isn't shared with women.'

The traditional ways remain – men and women bound by the island customs. No wonder Grace Mere Molisa described her fellow ni-Van women as 'colonised'. As an elected politician myself, I read that it is basically impossible for women here to be permitted by their communities to stand for election. There are no female MPs.

We eat a lunch of 'island food' while the women who have prepared it sit on the shore talking, watching, politely from a distance. After, the women show us their water music. This tradition comes from the Bank Islands, the northern part of the Vanuatuan archipelago. With huge crowns of red flowers on their heads, they stand up to their chests in the sea and are a whirlwind of energy as they splash and beat the surface of the water together in unison – in some clever way with their hands and arms, they create a wonderful music of big and small sounds out of the sea.

There is a large banyan near the beach; I've heard they are sacred trees. I pass through it and make a wish.

❄ ❄ ❄

On our final day at Malekula all of us go ashore to Bulbul. We are officially welcomed with green garlands, hibiscus flowers and drinking coconuts. Chief Esrom grabs a guitar, adding to his coolness, and the women sing. Afterwards we gather in the church and the sailors set to work. As part of the Blue Planet Odyssey community programme, some of our yachts have been trained up to offer basic sight tests, above all for children; the data is sent back to the organisation we have partnered with in Germany, and later, glasses will be sent out for those children who need them. We have a supply of reading glasses also for older people. Esrom tries a pair and is delighted to be able to read again. We finish our day with a group photo, sailors and villagers, some of them wearing their new glasses.

Sailors are sometimes best placed to help. In 2010 when the terrible earthquake hit Haiti, with great loss of life and damage to the country, crews of small yachts located nearby got together to deliver supplies and assist survivors quickly – when larger scale responses were taking their time. In the same way as we found in our partnership with UNESCO in gathering data from remote parts of the ocean, small sailing boats can reach where others cannot, getting to coastal communities where there is no air connection, or even a protected or deep ship anchorage, and many sailors are ready to play their part.

MASKELYNES

Luc's itinerary is taking us next to the island of Ambrym, and en route we have a night's stopover in the Maskelynes, a collection of little islets just off the southeast end of Malekula. The anchorage is tucked behind a protective reef which is now visible at low tide where the small figures of people can be seen wading through the shallow waters. A man in a canoe who has been fishing nearby stops for a chat. He tells us he hasn't caught much; his wife is out on the reef searching for octopus and other sealife. Michael gives him a can of Uruguayan corned beef which has travelled via the Arctic and into the Pacific, thousands of sea miles to finally end up here in the hands of the fisherman who turns it over in his hand as if not sure what to make of it.

Dan has discovered that Bob from *No Regrets* is also keen on snorkelling. Bob says he thinks he has seen a snake which they go to investigate but it turns out to only be a stick. They bother a sea slug which shoots out an impressive set of white tentacles. Other canoes pass by – a sailing canoe with three young men in it who

give Bob and Dan a lift back from the beach. They're on their way to fish also, throwing their nets along the reef. Two women pass with a canoe full of produce they've gathered from their garden, their dog swimming dutifully behind. And then the man we met earlier, passes by again, going home with his family. What if they don't catch anything that day? We exchange a few words. There is only one village on the island, with a population of 15.

By first light a few hardy souls are again already out braving the reef, searching the corals for something to eat, as we leave early in a grey fine rain. Two white birds fly by far away – otherwise I have seen no seabirds around Malekula at all. They are hunted no doubt (I remember Thilden and his slingshot); and also there are less and less fish not only for people but also those sea creatures who depend on the fish. This may perhaps not be the fault of the ni-Vanuatu fisherfolks, as it is out in the open seas that commercial fisheries decimate fish stocks, and the knock-on effect is the fact that scraping away a livelihood in the places the ni-Vanuatu and their ancestors have fished and lived off for some three thousand years is evermore impossible. This scarcity has accelerated in the last two generations. The warming ocean brings another threat, to the health of the coral reefs which are the nurseries and habitats of so much marine life. The right noises are made about conservation, and the knowledge exists to learn how to pause and let fish stocks recover, but it may be too late – the predicted future is coming and could already be here. I see it in the bird-free seas and the good Maskelyne people desperate for a catch to take home after a long day's work working the waters. As I observed on our way to Tuvalu, the ocean is in danger of becoming a desert.

I feel off colour, it is drizzling, I do not want to sit in the cockpit for several hours, so I go below for a little rest. Perhaps this lethargy is because of being a crew on this boat, with no control over where I go and what I eat. (We have consumed a lot of corned beef). Curled up in my bunk, I scribble in my diary. Twelve years old to forty-eight – some thirty-six years of my life, scratching blue and black marks on paper. This is the only thing in the end left me, when my movements, my food is curtailed, when no one will listen to me or give my views any credence, at least the page doesn't answer back or ignore me, and the white unfilled page is like freedom – stretching all the way to the grey-blue horizon, and beyond. Ready to be filled with words.

When finally I peep outside, Ambrym is ahead, dark and looming. No more the small islands of the Maskelynes, busy with fishermen and bright channels of reefs and white-yellow beaches – the grey sinister shape rises out of the mist. Island of black magic and live volcanoes.

But it is another moment of illusion, as the air clears, revealing the green details of the shore, a thin strand of black beach, stark white trunks of fallen trees, and smoke rising.

I am reminded of Bob's comment yesterday when he went to the beach with Dan. 'No one lives there, it isn't anyone's.' But in fact there was a village on the other side of the island, and I'm sure like everywhere else, all this land is spoken for. This is the point at which I am really struck that I myself look at these islands in the same way as the first Europeans did a century or two ago, wanting to see a blank, natural landscape, barely impacted by humans. We do not see the handed-down knowledge, the remembered land tenures, the chief-resolved family disputes. The trees and plants are alien to us, with our visions of tilled fields and hedgerows, and we see wildness not gardens. At least I am now just a fleeting visitor with no power, and a handful of Vatu to spend in the villages, while when they came they grabbed what they could in a frenzy, stabbing the earth with their sharp flagpoles. We have our own lands, but we want yours TOO. In the name of the King, the Queen, la Republique, and God. This was the great European trespass. Remember 'trespasses will be prosecuted', remember 'and forgive us our trespasses, as we forgive those that trespass against us.'

As we motor up the coast the hill that a few minutes ago appeared sinister and conical has lost all its mystery, is now soft and green and crowned by a radio mast. That magic has arrived here also.

BACK TO OUR ROOTS

Black Stone
hard
and obstinate
indelible
solidity.

from Black Stone, by Grace Mera Molisa

The coast is dark brown and black; the rocks of the cliffs are stratified and pushed upwards, and up on the topmost ridges when the clouds move apart they reveal the red-brown bare places which are the start of the ash plains covering part of the interior.

We anchor off a yellow beach, caught between black rocks, a village perched up on the slopes, and a neat steep meadow full of grazing cattle. Luc goes ashore to prepare the way. As darkness falls the active volcano lights the southern sky with a warm glowing but also faintly sinister red.

Luc has organised everything supremely. The festival, named 'Back to my roots', is taking place over three busy days. All the Odyssey sailors are here; we gather on the beach, meet the local Chief Massing, and start to walk around the north end of the island, past villages, plantations and wilder places. There are friendly greetings along the way from the islanders who are walking to and from their gardens, with bush knives and bags of produce. Lea, the chief's wife, accompanies us, on her way to the family's garden. Birds fly and sing high up amongst the tallest coconut palms, no doubt safer from slingshots up there; at dusk we've seen the dark shapes of the flying foxes silently flicking between the trees. A little black pig rummages in the undergrowth and when he spots us, scarpers pretty quick. Later, we will realise why.

It is a long hot walk along the earthen track until at last we leave it for a path into the trees. A coconut falls near us from the heights with a great thump and we see a wooden statue standing before us, a long face with big blank eyes – guarding the site. We enter a forest clearing encircled by more watching statues, a man takes our festival fees and writes our names in the book. They ask for volunteers, six are chosen including Dan. I wonder what for.

This is a sacred spot and we must be welcomed in the proper way. In the distance we hear men's voices, singing.

Now they come, wearing broad waistbands of bark, and a tuft of greenery tucked in at the back, a palm frond, leaves with red flowers, and at the front the penis wrappers known as *namba*, traditional to these islands. Some men have stuck a rooster feather or red flower in their hair, and some have curling white pig's tusks around their necks. The feathers, and especially the tusks, we later learn, are a sign of rank. The women come after, in simple grass skirts, bare-breasted, and no adornments. They place garlands over the heads of the volunteers and shake our hands. Men and women turn and the men start to sing, and stamp their feet, making the earth vibrate. Singing and dancing, they lead us slowly into a larger clearing, the dark earth packed hard and swept clean, with benches for us visitors. Opposite stands a line of wooden figures and large slit drums, with inscrutable faces, some looking very ancient, with bright green ferns sprouting from the porous black wood. Some of the figures are six or seven foot high. I wonder if once all this was tabu to visitors, only now the dollar permits us to enter.

The dancers stand in a group, their backs to us – I can't help but feel it would be more interesting to take part than watch … inside that circle, singing and stamping.

A crowd of villagers gather and watch the dancers also.

Some men have brought wooden carvings to sell and Dan buys a black stick from the father of a man who carved it and who is also called Dan. These used to be carried by men on the forest pathways for personal protection, tucked up the forearm out of sight. Dan is very taken with it. The wood is hard; a formidable weapon.

As well as the dancing, there is a demonstration of sand drawing. Two of the male dancers who are

twins kneel on the ground and quickly and beautifully trace ornate patterns with a finger in the black dirt. The patterns, I gather, are heavy with symbolism. They work fast and with such surety, never faltering, creating complex, entwining patterns, perfect and sure in their lines and circles. When the drawing is done, after a few moments they sweep it away with a quick gesture of the hand and it is gone. This sand drawing, I discover later, is recognised by UNESCO as a 'Masterpiece of the Oral and Intangible Heritage of Humanity.'

'You'll see some black magic now,' says Luc, 'which the island is renowned for.'

Some men kneel in a circle, holding a black protector stick, while others surround them and beat stones upon the bare earth. The stick moves; on its own, so they tell us. Dan is invited to join, he is told to close his eyes and guided towards the stick, shuffling forward on his knees, with his hands held out. He grips the stick alongside the men, and it moves vigorously back and forth. Who knows if it did move by magic, but it certainly makes the arms and hands work as if by an outside force.

Afterwards, some of us women search out a bush toilet. Miriam, the sister of Chief Sektor whose village this is, and who is going to be part of the chief grading ceremony tomorrow (one of the main purposes of the festival, which is not particularly put on for tourists), shows us to a discrete little hut in the bush, where inside the earth has been dug and shaped into a black hole that looked, on reflection, as much like a mother's hole as could be, mother earth who bore us all.

❄ ❄ ❄

On the second festival day, on our way to the clearing, I see a large black pig tied and trussed up to a stake at the entrance to the site, feet bound so it cannot move. Its lively, intelligent eye looks at me full of expression although it cannot know its fate; pigs are valued currency here, and today the chief-grading ceremony will be taking place, with men bringing pigs and yams alongside money, as they seek to move on up through the ranks.

The women and men dance again; during a break we buy snacks from the women sat under the trees – coconuts, mini sweetcorn cobs and *laplap* served on banana leaves, manioc chips (with extra ants who have crawled their way in, unbidden), wrapped in pages torn from French school books. These are a relic of the old colonial days when France and England decided to run the colony jointly, then called New Hebrides – a unique arrangement that was officially called the Condominium, but nick-named the Pandemonium. Independence came in 1980, by which time we'd already sailed through. 1978, Tuvalu; 1979, Kiribati. In those days, after India broke the British resistance to losing colonies, the Empire couldn't wait to be rid of them.

The business of the chief grading begins. The men break up small pieces of bamboo to use for percussion and enter the site in a long line beating the bamboo. Some carry coconuts also. The line curls in like a spiral, tighter and tighter. Each of the three chiefs seeking grading, red hibiscus flowers bright in their black hair, take it in turns to climb onto the top of a bamboo structure which has been raised on one side of the enclosure, and spread their arms wide, yelling defiance it seems to me, and some cast nuts and other things at them, while the singing and rhythm goes on, although it doesn't seem they especially want to hit them.

Up to this point we had enjoyed all this spectacle, the dancing and singing, the drawing and the magic, but now comes the other part, which is hard – the ritual pig killing – and the screaming is the worst. Miriam explains some of this to me and shows me the pile of yams piled on the ground that are also to be offered. Money is handed over and the bamboo structure is adorned with red flowers. The same pig which had looked at me as we arrived has been brought in and tied up on the ground. The chiefs take it in turns to bash it on the head with a ceremonial wooden club. Soon its snout and mouth are red with blood. The screams of agony are terrible, shrill and piercing and almost human. It doesn't seem however that they mean to kill it outright; it is still alive; and yet there is no way out for it, only pain and death.

I'm going to give up eating pork now.

I watch, though really I want it to stop, and I push down at the sickness rising in me. We'd observed the earlier dances and ceremonies with a warm interest, because it was different and picturesque, and maybe it was a bit like a TV documentary – quaint traditions we ourselves don't follow, subject matter for colourful photos to take home…

This summer and last summer, visiting these places, the Arctic, Vanuatu, where traditional ways are still alive – I have seen seal, porpoise, pig, killed for ritual and food – and in both places, the strictly defined roles of men and women.

Now my main thought was – here you go, this is it, this is what it's really about, and you don't like it now do you? In the forest clearing, watching the ritual cruelty performed on a creature whose brain, bones and being are not so very different to us, comes the truth of it, that tradition was and is brutal, and I for one certainly don't want to go back there, to that place, where the men are men, the women are women, defined and confined by the bodies we were born in, and the animals are killed with pain and without mercy – because that is the way it has always been done and will always be done so.

❄ ❄ ❄

At the end of the day's ceremonies, we walk back to the beach where a group of women are gathered; they invite us to join their feast of beef and root veg which is laid on the ground, wrapped in leaves, left over from a wedding down the coast.

The generosity and welcome from them, as in all the other places we have visited this summer, is what I have always known from islanders. Over and over, they welcome us in, and we always feel what we can give in return – thanks, money, friendship – is so inadequate, to balance against all that has come before.

Our afternoon is busy, helping with eye tests at the village of another friend of Luc's, Chief Johnson, a short way along the coast. On the way back we are treated to a proper kava preparation at the village overlooking the anchorage. Kava is the mildly narcotic root that is prepared into a drink in various parts of the Pacific, mainly Melanesia. The preparation and drinking of it is often formalised and ceremonial, and kava is a gift sailors will often take to remote communities when they arrive, asking for permission to anchor, or go ashore.

I try a bowlful of the muddy liquid and feel my mouth and lips going numb and my throat close up. The root of the earth – cleaned, cut, mixed with water, pulped, filtered – made into a potent brew that numbs your mouth and relaxes you, the hand of the earth that holds you.

Dan is invited to join *No Regrets* ashore for 'island night' at the small restaurant along the coast named the 'yacht club'. Michael and I let him go on his own. He tells me afterwards he enjoyed the food on offer, especially the chocolate cake, and the fact that two of his favourite male dancers were there from earlier in the day, quite normal looking now in their regular Western attire. He tries a bowlful of kava – at thirteen he is growing up fast. This visit to Ambrym – the magic, the pig-killing, the chief rituals, the protector stick he is taking home with him – have all marked him deeply.

The following day is the day of the Rom dance. A small motorboat arrives at the same time as we come ashore with our dinghy. A man hands to another a bundle of brown dry leaves, which look rather dead. Later, as we enter the sacred site, I see a man behind us carrying that dead bundle of leaves again. I ask Chief Massing who has accompanied us on our walk, what it is.

'That is part of the Rom costume,' he tells us. The man, who has a round and cheerful face, grins at me, he is also carrying a bulging crop sack which no doubt has the mask concealed inside. How the costumes are made is a secret, the chief explains, and only men who have paid money, cash and pig money, may enter the *nakamal*, the traditional meeting place, and be present at the making.

Before the dance begins we are instructed not to touch the banana leaves or we shall have to pay a price ourselves. There is nothing to be seen at first, but behind the wooden figures and the trees we glimpse movement. Then they come. There's something rather frightening about those tall figures – despite us watching in the morning sunlight which dapples the grove, and despite us knowing there are men beneath the costumes. An occasional glimpse of a bare foot is all you can see. The painted wooden masks with their high crests and serrated edges, the long swaying banana leaf robes and the figures moving slowly forward in a repetitive fluid dance – what does it mean? Are these spirits of the sea or air, the sharks and turtles, the winds and waves?

The six Rom dancers flank a group of men who are dressed as before, simply, with their waistbands and green-leaf adornments. The group dance and sing and move towards us – but it takes a long while, a few steps only at a time. The dance is ancient and its meaning shrouded in mystery. This is the climax of the festival and many more local people have come to watch – the women and children are gathered in their usual place under the trees, the men stand behind us tourists sat on our benches. I glance behind to see the phones held up, taking photos. Same sight here, in an obscure Ambrym village, as every other place in the world. Some of the dancers have mobile phones tucked into their waistbands.

Eventually the dancers draw closer and a complicated stepping to and fro begins back and forth in front of us. Two men play the largest slit drums with a loud and compelling beat – and the dance finishes with a spiralling turn. At the end, the magic is a little broken as we are allowed to take photos with them. Us at a suitable, non-touching distance.

The father of the other Dan, who had carved the protector my Dan bought, greets us and gives us a gift of a bag of grapefruit and then we meet Dan himself who has wounded his finger. We share out some of the grapefruit with the other sailors, we say our goodbyes, and slip away. Michael didn't come today; he stayed behind on *Drina* and he wants to leave promptly... it is time to head back to Santo.

It is very quiet on the road as most people are at the dance. I quite enjoy the walk, even though it is long and we walk fast. A young boy comes towards us with a huge bush knife. He holds out his hand for a high five from Dan and grins and after we have passed on our way, let's out a great joyful shout of a laugh.

Chief Johnson is waiting on the beach to say goodbye. One by one the Odyssey crew return, and the boats raise their anchors and slip away.

On the walk back, I reflect how very different the dancing and the costumes of this festival are from Fire Beach in Southwest Bay. Although much about the world has changed in 30-odd years, the richness of Pacific cultures, their incredible diversity, is still alive, still present. This one place, on one single island, has its own unique dances and customs; a bay away you'll find something quite different, and this has not yet been lost. I'm struck by the relative geographical homogeneity of the Pacific Islands, their flora and fauna, contrasted with the incredibly rich and diverse differences of their cultures. There is no other place on earth with quite so much richness in such small groups of peoples; as many have commented before me.

The festival's name 'Back to my roots' seems very appropriate. However pale and awkward we foreigners are, we share, with ni-Van people, common ancestors, and once upon a time, our own people in our own places sang and danced and chose leaders and thanked the Gods and spirits for the crops, in a Transylvanian valley, a Celtic forest or an American prairie.

So we can come here, as pale and awkward as we are, and taste a little, and remember a little.

Therefore, as the Tuvaluan music tasted of the salt sea – here, the Ambrym men's and women's songs are the voice of the earth, and the deep roots that anchor us to the land. The crops to be thankful for, the animals that live off them and nourish us, the places where we are born and die, and the good soil that blackens our feet.

I have wondered how this Vanuatu visit should be included in the climate change narrative, and it seems to me that the theme is land, here, if anything – while in Tuvalu it was the sea.

All of this matters, because the soil is growing as poor as the sea now, and if we do not declare a jubilee soon, what will feed us in the future?

I don't say we should be like them and not like us; being a woman in this traditional society is pretty dire, and I'm thankful every day for having been born a woman in 1967 not 1867 or 1067, in England and not somewhere else on the globe. We must accept who we are; and yet – when we cut our roots for modern life and make men and women the same and equal, what do we give our young people in exchange? What new and meaningful roles for our young men to sustain them, if they're not to be hunters and fighters? What power for our young women, if they are to contribute fully to our communities and nations, if they are not to be mothers and keepers of the hearth and home? No – all too often we just dig them up, cut them adrift and let them drown.

In the forest glade, the ni-Van children gather on the sidelines and watch their adults and learn. Our children are watching also – but what do they see? Is it us, their living elders, or the little blue screen?

THE SAILOR

At least for once the weather is balmy and the wind is behind us for our sail back to Espirito Santo. This is likely to be my last Pacific sail for a long while. Even Dan upends himself from his bunk and comes out to take a look. Michael sits in his usual place in his camping chair on the aft deck, just enjoying being outside with the wind, the waves, and his beloved boat. Old man of the sea, in his element, wanting for nothing. I saw my father do just the same, faraway in the Arctic.

Over four decades of my sea life I have met a great many sailors, all 57 varieties of salt. The less experienced often fuss and worry, and pile themselves with stress about sailing. Those with a little more knowledge and experience make a great deal of what they know and have learnt, sometimes too much. Others learn from their mistakes, and keep accumulating experience, and as the years pass, become richer, deeper, more solid in what they know. Then eventually, after a long time, maybe only after decades at sea, they shoot beyond that learning place, or drift beyond, or just plain sail over the curve of the horizon, and get into the zen place.

It really is the zen place. A calm place, full of wisdom, and the joy of the moment, just like in all those martial arts films, that's the place where the master is. (Or mistress, if you like).

The old sailor sits on the deck of their boat, keeping one eye on the course laid, how the sails set, and the other eye out far to the horizon. Disciplined and calm, they are at peace and want for nothing. This is the lure of the sea, which captured my father as a tiny boy. After a summer spent with Michael, I've learnt it wasn't just unique to my father, Michael has this too; and the poets had the same insight.

I am a part of all that I have met;
Yet all experience is an arch where through
Gleams that untravell'd world whose margin fades
For ever and for ever when I move.

Here my father, here Michael, belong, sailing on, towards the untravelled horizon, the wind in the sails and blue water beneath the keel.

I've heard it said that cyclists who spend hours of their lives on their bikes end up exchanging enough atoms with their machine that they become half human half bike. We know our bodies are constantly breaking and renewing themselves at the cellular or molecular level, and the atoms that make us up at any time have spun down through the ages to create us for a brief moment. So those old sailors whose beloved boats I shipped on as a willing crew were truly 'old salts', part made up of the salt of the sea. And after all the years I spent at sea, I hope I am partly made of the ocean also.

I wonder, did my own childhood years of travelling bind each place and each person of the world tight inside me? I shared their breath and sweat and skin, shared the salt drops and the fish scales and the flies and dirt and seeds. Travel broadens the mind, the well-worn adage goes, but does it not also reconstruct us on a sub-atomic level so we become true citizens of the world – even if our minds are fierce to resist, our soft and porous bodies cannot.

So therefore let us love and be loved, right down to the atom, and celebrate the dance of the elements that has brought us this far.

❄ ❄ ❄

On 23 August, as we get a 7a.m. taxi to the airport and the end of our stay on *Drina* finally comes, the message comes through from Jimmy; at dawn today *Aventura* crossed the Arctic circle. She and her crew have completed the Northwest Passage, west to east.

I present Michael with a plaque commemorating his part in the Blue Planet Odyssey

AOTEAROA

Seen from high up in the sky, islands like Ambrym are small grey shapes, and the sea is crumpled silver. Over Malekula we go, passing high, right over the Maskelynes, so I can see where we were snugly anchored. The reefs appear like thin lines around the islands, and the breakers are no more than faint spittle on the surface. All is dim and distant, indistinct and far away. No struggle, no difficulty, each wave is only a tiny wrinkle and of no consequence.

I wonder how long it will take for our hearts to be liberated from the bonds of the boat, confined all those weeks onboard, to leave that behind, and the anchor chain let out. I don't feel like I have left *Drina* yet.

Coming to land in Port Vila, the Vanuatu capital, coconut trees like single strands of hair, herds of cows like grains of brown rice. More animals destined for death and slaughter, their beef prized by the Japanese, though at present they graze, their destiny unsuspected. The same for the tiny lambs I see later in New Zealand fields, bouncing and full of the joys of spring. Still, I just ate a plane meal of beef stew. Even Dan though says he will go vegetarian later on in life. This is the Dan who lay on his bunk moaning 'I want fruit' and pounced on any scrap of salad he got as a garnish to any meal we ate out. I think we had too many of Michael's corned beef dinners.

Waiting for our connecting flight to Auckland, it feels strange in the departure lounge to see all these white faces again, a crowd of them surrounding us. Except for the few sailors we met, I had got used to being with Samoans, Tuvaluans, and Ni-Vanuatu.

Green and bright New Zealand appears out of the clouds, and another adventure, the Pacific is not quite finished for us yet. The same Pacific Ocean surrounds this island nation, and it is a Polynesian place also, even if overlaid thickly with white. A lot is made throughout New Zealand of the Māori heritage – myths linked to places, and sacred sites respected – though I wonder how much the Polynesian First Nation is truly reflected in structures of power?

Not that I can tell anything, because although Dan and I are going to travel through a real, living, working country, in fact we are about to make a pilgrimage of sorts through a fictional land, Tolkien's Middle Earth…

The Hobbit, and the *Lord of the Rings* trilogy, cheap paperbacks picked up in the US in the 1970s, were stories I loved as soon as I read them, and I have those books still – when most of my other childhood books are gone, lost somewhere or swapped away for others on our travels.

The film adaptations came in the early years of Nera and Dan's lives, and captured so well the spirit of the books; my love for both books and films passed onto my children. In many ways we were all quite obsessed with that fantastical land and the characters who inhabited it, some brave, some evil. As Nera and Dan grew older, we watched the films together, and so, with our stopover in New Zealand, before we headed home, Dan and I leapt at the unique chance to spend a few days visiting some of the places used as settings in the films which had given us so much pleasure over the years.

❄ ❄ ❄

Some luxury is very acceptable as we check into the hotel a few paces from Auckland's airport terminal. Our luggage and ourselves are pretty bedraggled, plastic bags of salt-soaked clothes from last night's unfortunate dinghy ride back to the boat when a wave swamped us, and dirty clothes from Vanuatu earth and the salt sea. Sleep in a bed is exceptionally delightful. I return to a landlubber's life with no qualms whatsoever.

We collect a camper van we've rented for a week and get supplies. I remember the Tuvaluan shops with a few canned goods, 10kg bags of rice and sugar, and a few apples if you are lucky. Now we eye with glee the rows and rows of different types of apples – right at the source! After all these years buying them in supermarkets on the other side of the world. We gorge ourselves on the fresh bounty of New Zealand farming.

Driving south out of Auckland the countryside pans out into typical agricultural landscapes, green pastures that reminded my English grandmother of home all those years ago when she visited us here in 1978. Livestock, farmhouses and rolling green hills. It is the agricultural method that makes it like England, not the landscape itself, because when we glimpse the native trees and forests, and the birds in the trees, they're unfamiliar and alien. The fact that all this once was ancient forest, now cleared for the sake of milk and meat, is much more apparent than at home where the memory of the earlier landscape is too faded now to recall. Just to emphasise the point, in places the stumps of great trees are left in the fields like a scattering of monuments to what was.

To see spring lambs is disorientating, having travelled through so many time zones, weather systems, climates, tropical, Equatorial, subtropical, squalls, low-pressure systems, intra-convergence zones, Southern hemisphere winter...

Rain sets in but as we enter the film set of Hobbiton the sun pokes out and a lovely afternoon light remains all through our visit, bathing the location in

a warm apply glow, bringing out the colours of the bright painted front doors to hobbit holes, and all the accoutrements, belongings, household goods, fresh produce, kitchen gardens and ornaments, fake and real, joined together to make a delightfully realistic hobbit village, for all the world as if its inhabitants just popped out a moment and will be back very soon.

❄ ❄ ❄

The kiwi bird is sleeping at the Te Puia Māori centre. White steam curls up from all the bubbling mud pools, and we wrinkle our noses at the sulphurous smells of the mud. In the gift shop I buy a greenstone necklace, a spiral which means, among other things, new beginnings, as that is what is coming for me when I go home – waiting just over the horizon at present. Give me strength, green stone, to cope with it. I have a failed marriage to unpick and many years of two lives spent together to be unravelled, while we attempt to keep our children's lives steady and whole.

Dan buys a copy of *The Two Towers*; he has just finished reading *The Fellowship of the Ring*. We park ourselves at the Thermal Holiday Park which is nearly empty and watch Gremlins on the van DVD player and eat ice-cream.

'Dan, stop reading,' I say, 'and eat your ice-cream.'

'What kind of a mother are you?' he responds.

Cue hysterical laughter from both of us.

'Back to Middle Earth please,' says Dan. 'I prefer that to all these stinky pools.'

South to Lake Taupo, the sky is blue and bare of clouds from horizon to horizon except for a little ribbon around the mountain, the perfect volcanic cone that stood in for the evil land of Mordor's Mount Doom, now white with snow though for the film it was brown and bare. We climb the slopes past the holiday skiers, trudging deep into the snow. Dan perches on a rock with a perfect view towards the mountain and sings in a clear and beautiful voice his favourite song from the film, The Last Goodbye, with words that speak to me too: *I turn at last to paths that lead home/though where the road then takes me/I cannot tell.*

At the end of the day we search in vain through the forests, waterfalls and rocky pools for more film locations that the book we'd bought at Hobbiton assures us should be there. We are quite alone. The sun is nearly setting and the woods are illuminated by a wonderful rich light, that in places touches a tree, green branch or fern, and set it alight with a fiery golden light just like in the films, when a touch of light brought a moment of hope out of the darkness.

A one-way bridge crosses a deep gorge and we gaze at the pale blue river below which stood in for the great mythical river Anduin. The bungee jumpers here and skiers the day before make everything rather mundane and detract from our Middle Earth experience. But it is a scenic peaceful spot and I'm glad to see the river. We park by a grassy space for lunch and while Dan rests in the van I have a few precious moments alone in the forest, with peculiar birdsong, interesting trees and leaves, fallen dead trunks, mosses, lichens and ferns, the slow uncurling and turning towards the light and the end of southern winter. I hold a dead fragment of a grey fern leaf in my hand, that is just like the silver fern symbol of this country, and if anywhere is to be an Elfin forest and a moment of peace, it is here for me.

It is time to turn back north, onto the desert road that travels east of the volcanoes. The countryside is wide open and photos could never do it justice. To our eyes the volcanoes are vast, majestic and dominating the skyline, when in a photo it is barely there beneath the giant sky. Dan sleeps through all of this until I wake him at a viewpoint where there is a lovely final view of the national park and mountains, illuminated again by that wonderful warm late afternoon light. In front of us stretch waves and waves of unbroken thick forest.

'Mirkwood,' says Dan, binding mythical places into real ones once again.

Here, as elsewhere all through today, we are on our own.

❄ ❄ ❄

Before we must return the van, we head to the coast to see and touch the Pacific for one last time. We have a few moments spare to walk on the beach which is covered in broken shells and I have one last paddle in the sea. Across the water are islands, and beyond, much further, the other places we visited. Who knows when I will come to the Pacific again and touch these waters. The gulls and terns are on the beach too, standing and watching. It is not really wilderness, a few metres beyond where we are, neat houses overlook the sea, and the grass is manicured and there are car parks, toilets and instructive noticeboards.

Dan reads every moment he can, and he's just read of the elf Legolas and his mention of how the cries of the gulls spark such a yearning in him for the sea. Coming in a final moment to the sea seems a quite fitting way to conclude our pilgrimage to Middle Earth. It is always good to end with the sea.

We are both weary now and long to be home. We're not quite the same people who set off 54 days ago. If nothing else, Dan's feet have grown one or two shoe sizes.

A little less innocent, and knowing a little more of the world. No doubt our home and our village will seem small and plain to us now – but at least they will be ours. For a time we'll be glad to rest there and work, until cabin fever takes us again, and the gulls call us to come away once more. It will happen, I know it, sooner or later. I cannot escape the sea – my past is salty and it flavours my present and my future, always.

Too much salt is bad for humans … and the Tuvaluan breadfruit trees and *pulaka* trying to grow. But without a little salt, the food is very plain.

OUR ISLAND HOME

We return to the news of people trying to reach the sanctuary of Europe by land and sea. In the Pacific, those who had so little, had extended their hospitality to us – and we are so rich compared to them, and above all, we are rich in freedom, but many of us do not want to extend a welcoming hand in our own country, to those fleeing war and persecution.

I give a tribute to my grandmother Irene at her funeral: I said that she was the salt of the earth, and represented what was best about the English soul, its moderation, frugality and tolerance.

We buried her ashes alongside her parents, her brother and sister, in the graveyard by the little church in the Surrey village where she grew up. A handful of black English soil in my hand to sprinkle on the wooden box. The good English earth where she shall lie until the end of time, overlooking the winding river and the green meadow where a white swan is cropping the grass. England is here and will be here until the end of our days. It was a good end, a peaceful end, and my mother laid a single yellow rose beside the hole which I hope the sexton will quickly cover over. The soft rain fell. In these divided days when I hear people say England is under threat, that our land is full up, I see this quiet green land, this river and this meadow where no house will ever be built, I think of the forests without end that I drove through on my way here, from Gloucestershire to Surrey, vast acres of green land, fields, trees.

Back home, I walk the dog through the green field near our house and turn and look – this one English field is almost as big as a single Tuvaluan island, it is given over to nothing but grass, and one tree grows in its midst – a field never grazed, never sown with crops – although the earth is good enough. They say we are 'Full up'. Full Up – they don't know what they're talking about.

If only those distant Tuvaluan islanders could be given a bit of this land – space – and good earth to grow food again.

If we cannot do that, if we will not do that, at least let us change our ways, so they can stay in their country – so that their country will survive and not disappear beneath the waves, so we will not break the hearts of that ancient proud and beautiful nation.

Is England so frail a place that it is under threat, are a thousand years of slow history for nothing? Surely we are stronger than that.

Jimmy arrives back in England but too late for the funeral; *Aventura* sails up the Thames and takes advantage of a vessel's right to sail under Tower Bridge, which is opened for her sole benefit.

THE PACIFIC: DAN'S VIEW

My experience all those years ago is not something I could paint as vividly now as I could back then, and my younger self did not document the voyage in any diary or other form of writing. Yet so many scenes of beauty and fascination remain quite untouched by time; perhaps I could do them a pinch of justice.

The first leg of such journeys perhaps deserves little recognition for its worth, if only for its unworth. It is merely the commercial flying we are all so used to: those long flights with airplane dinners and seat-embedded tellies with films galore; the flights which lull you into a zombie-like state and whisk you thousands of miles across the earth with minimal exertion, with only a brief glance out the window to comprehend the lands sweeping past distantly below. We take this marvel for granted; we are used to it; should we be? And would we still make this flight now, the knowledge of its harmful environmental effects pressing on our minds? Would we still give in to the selfish Western feeling of entitlement we were raised with, that we somehow deserve to see the world; without sweating blood for it, regardless of the damage we may cause? I think now, I would rather set sail from England and take the long route there. But from Paris to Singapore, Singapore to Auckland, and Auckland to Samoa, we arrived at last where the truly meaningful excursions could begin.

The first of these was our venture to the tomb of Robert Louis Stevenson on the summit of Mount Vaea. The trek took us through Samoa's inland tropical forest, along circuitous and exceedingly slippery paths accompanied by heavy bursts of rain, making one wonder whether Stevenson had in his motives to make people rather suffer, or at least earn a view of his final resting place, in addition to enjoying the very beauty of its location. But we made it to the top, and enjoyed a moment with no tourists but ourselves. Such out of the way places have retained those rich atmospheres, still heavy with history, the kind of ambience experienced naturally when one can feel like a discoverer. Visit the Parthenon nowadays and the swathes of tourists almost block out the sun; on Mount Vaea, and throughout our voyage, the immersion was quite effortless.

The voyages at sea, however, were not so much my cup of tea – initially, at least… well, more like for the entirety of the ocean passages. My younger self seems to have completely lacked the ability to acquire what is commonly called the development of sea legs. Little could mum or captain Michael – a man I'll always remember for his illustrious wit, who throughout the journey teased me – do to abate my utter uselessness as a crew member, being so inexorably incapacitated and seasick-pinned to the sofa as I was.

Following such existential throes, however, arriving on shore after weeks at sea was all the more rewarding. I'll never forget the feeling of clambering from the dinghy onto Tuvalu, to feel the world tilting, and after all the anchorage faff was sorted, stumble semi-dehydrated to the bar at Tuvalu's airport, and order what tasted then like the nectar of the Gods: a cool and crisp, Fanta Pineapple. But this was in tough competition with my discovery of fresh coconuts: a glorious treasure I often wish we could produce in England. What you get here on the shelves is nothing in comparison.

Our time in Tuvalu was the warm heart of the journey. The Tinilau family with whom we stayed may forever be the most generous and hospitable people I have ever known. To have only arrived a day or two before, and to be welcomed into their home so warmly, and met with such kindness, to join them at dinner and be permitted to stay there for the night, shows just how deeply the connections we made with them some forty years ago were – long before I was born of course!

The voyage between Tuvalu and Vanuatu was far rockier and longer than the first leg. The storms were endless. A second set of existential pangs struck my poor, useless thirteen year old self. But then, at last, land ho! The beautiful archipelago of Vanuatu emerged from the horizon, and in the course of sailing amongst its islands, my seasickness finally abated.

Of our various expeditions in Vanuatu, the first that springs to mind is one of simple beauty and elegance; something unexpected, rare and most wholesome. We anchored off the coast of a small island with a village near the shore, and shortly afterwards, in a traditional canoe with one small hull for buoyancy and the other for transport, we were approached by a man offering to take us to shore. I went in first, and soon Doina joined me on the island. We were then escorted inland through the forest, guided by two young men with machetes. Should one have had apprehensions? No matter. We were met with the most gorgeous, hidden lagoon, and invited to swim; the water was glorious. On our return, the young men brought us coconuts, and we purchased a ton of fruit from them, for what felt like far too little. I still recall one of their names: Thildan.

When at the age of thirteen I departed my small English countryside town, took flight to the other side of the globe, and set sail across the Pacific ocean without familiar company save for my mother – a mother who did not coddle and spoil me like a child who is not permitted to grow up, but who is herself of an extraordinarily adventurous nature, a true heart and spirit in love with the freeness of the world and its peoples – it should be expected that such a voyage of this calibre might change that young teenager's perspective of the world, in showing him such a powerful glimpse of the beauty of the cultures of the Pacific. If such expectations were had at that time, they did not miss their mark. I only hope I can return there someday, leaving my little Shire-like reef of home far behind me – and this time, taking the long route.

Welcome to
STROUD
DISTRICT
COUNCIL
Ebley Mill
Short Stay &
Disabled Parking

EPILOGUE

A huge climate march takes place in London as the COP21 conference gets underway in Paris in November 2015. Our hopes are riding high; I take the Tokelau flag with me as I march with people from Stroud and from my own town of Dursley, with thousands of others, in solidarity with our island brothers and sisters.

The Prime Minister of Tuvalu delivers a keynote statement to the gathered heads of State:

> *This is the time. We must all stand together and reshape our future. A new, comprehensive treaty on climate change is in our reach. Let's do it now. Let's do it for the future of humanity.*
>
> *Let's do it for Tuvalu. For if we save Tuvalu we save the world.*

I ask for the Tokelau flag to be flown outside our district council offices in solidarity with that small nation, for the duration of the conference. Paula Faiva messages me her thanks.

> *Hold our flag high. It is very sad that while the most vulnerable are fighting climate threats, in Paris the wealthier nations are pushing for an agreement of a 2°C limit only. Tokelau is very humbled to have people and organizations such as yours to advocate for justice.*

As promised, I raise money, to send back to the mothers of the Vaiaku church.

❄ ❄ ❄

In 2017, the Blue Planet Odyssey yachts finally complete their circumnavigation, having crossed the Indian Ocean and sailed round the Cape of Good Hope and north up through the Atlantic.

A scientific paper is published comparing the first four years of data from the Secchi disk observations carried out by sailors around the world. The results show seafarers collected useful measurements of ocean transparency that could help future assessments of climate-induced changes in the phytoplankton when used to extend historical Secchi Disk data. It is one example of the usefulness of the sailor-citizen scientists in expanding knowledge and data on the changes to our world.

❄ ❄ ❄

In 2018 I am elected leader of Stroud District Council, leading a cooperative alliance of Labour, Green and Liberal Democrats. In 2015 we had become the first council in Europe to declare ourselves carbon-neutral; and this year we become the second council in the UK, after Bristol, our near neighbours, to declare a climate emergency. The council adopts a plan to achieve a carbon neutral district by 2030; this is ambitious but at least one way I can show solidarity with the people of the Pacific and Arctic. Our council is recognised nationally for showing leadership in the climate emergency.

❄ ❄ ❄

An exhibition of textiles in Stroud includes bright red fragments of cloth incorporated into Inuit clothing. The cloth of the red coats for which the British army became so well-known, was once woven and dyed in the Stroud valleys; Stroud Scarlet, fuelling the beginnings of the industrial revolution, as nascent Empire began to claw its covetous way across the globe. The Inuit, the Iroquois, and perhaps other First Nation peoples, loved the bright red cloth and traded for it.

These threads connect me, once again, across land and sea. I gather these fragments up.

❄ ❄ ❄

As we live through the global pandemic, I learn that in the early part of European efforts to Christianise the Greenlanders, a 1733 smallpox epidemic saw hundreds of Greenlanders perish. Many viruses came before Covid-19. European first contact was almost always inevitably lethal.

In June 2020, Hans Egede's statue in Nuuk is daubed in red paint and 'decolonise' written on the plinth, some two weeks after the slaver Colston's statue is toppled and thrown into the harbour in Bristol. A vote in Nuuk whether to keep Egede's statue or not results in a majority in favour of keeping it.

I recall the Inuit man brought to Bristol for show, made to paddle his kayak on the river Avon, and the woman, both buried in the cold earth of the city that was built on the wealth of the slave trade. There was no justice for them; but a jury acquits those who were charged with toppling Colston's statue.

❄ ❄ ❄

Remember the black rock of the Arctic, where this story began?

Four hundred years on, what has that hunger for the ancient wealth of the earth done to us? Those of us who are young or frail cough out our lives, poisoned by the dirty air, and all of us, rich and poor, are threatening the fine climactic balance that for thousands of years has been gifted to us by this planet, making it a true garden of Eden where our human kind has flourished: with clean air to breathe and the weather mild, or at least, predictable, for we adapted to the extremes of cold or heat or storms, when we knew each year the bears would grow fat on the ice, or the drought would, eventually, pass, or the hurricanes would only come for half the year. Our welcoming planet let us think fast and run fast, with good water and food to nourish us, and yet, our gratitude to her has been meagre – we now threaten those most basic elements that have allowed us to lead our glorious and terrible lives on this planet, glorious in our creativity, our humility and our altruism, and terrible in our arrogance and greed, and in our destruction.

The soil is poor and exhausted. The air is clogged with toxic particles too small for us to see. The waters are full of heavy metals, plastic and hormones that may one day stop our young boys growing up to be men, and thus our girls never to be mothers. We have penetrated our natural world to the very atomic level and spread our corruption well.

And yet, we deny it.

We deny the very science, even when the facts are tearing our hair from our heads and drowning our loved ones before our very eyes.

The sky, you see, is still gloriously blue. We can still breathe, and walk, and love. We cannot really see any of this, so why worry? Why change anything about our lives?

But this is only our story, and not the planet's. One day she will turn, without us; she will still be turning, when we are all gone.

From the black stone of the Arctic to the black stone of the Pacific – perhaps this is what binds this story together.

Leave the stone alone. Don't break it open in a foolish search for gold, or shatter it deep under the ground in the hope of a miracle gas-filled solution to our huge need for energy.

Let it all alone and let us all rest more lightly on this earth – reap the wind and the water, and the heat of the sun, but gently, step gently, harness the bounty of the earth and the sea, but in a restorative, renewing way, which leaves clean air and temperate climes for our children and our friends' children and the children of faraway places we do not know.

Our prehistoric ages were called stone, iron and bronze – defined from the start by our need and desire to take things out of the earth. Extraction has defined us from our earliest days, and like an addict we cannot now shake that habit.

For Tuvalu, for Vanuatu, for Arctic Bay, these precious places, to survive, for our own small towns and villages of Gloucestershire to remain the mild green heartlands of our own country, not parched, not flooded, not fracked, rich in biodiversity, a little bit wild, with good crops in the fields, abundant hedgerows, and in all these places, that children go to bed at night with food in their bellies, and their mothers can sleep near them, easy, and without stress, that the future has hope, and we are living there, and not in despair.

Hope. In the ancient myth, the first woman, Pandora, was gaslighted into blame for all the troubles of the world – that it was her fault, that she let them all be unleashed due to her curiosity at opening the box and letting them all out to rampage through the world. But the little creature, Hope, did crawl out of the box last. We have her, at least.

Not very long after writing the above, by chance I read in *The Book of Hope* a story recounted by Jane Goodall as an example of the indomitable human spirit – one thing she says still gives her hope in this world. She speaks of the Hobbits making their way into Mordor, the same image which came to me all those years before in the Tuvalu church. We must keep on fighting the good fight against the forces of darkness ranged against us. Even if all we have is a handful of good earth in our fist, ready to scatter and bring nature back to life again. Hope, Pandora, let hope out of the box for us.

❄ ❄ ❄

This is the story of my home, the ocean, and her broken heart.

It took me a very long time to write this. As the years passed and my sea journeys receded into memory, and my life was busy with so many other concerns, I often wondered if I should give up. I questioned my words and thoughts, and whether anyone else would be interested. In the end all I could think of was – I shall do it for my children and for myself. It was a simple and selfish wish, and yet I hope it has given you something also – a few words to make you think, and imagine places you may never visit, and give you a little more familiarity with the wonderful ocean that makes our human life possible, makes it possible, and liveable, and breathable.

She is our mother, let us not break her wild blue heart.

Let us try to mend it.

ACKNOWLEDGEMENTS

The creation of this book owes so much to so many all over the world: I haven't space to name you all but you are in my thoughts with gratitude and love. I am so grateful to the Tinilau family, to Paula Faiva and Enele Sopoaga for your generosity and for giving me an insight into your world. Thank you to all those who supported the Odyssey's scientific programme: Martin Kramp who facilitated our partnership with UNESCO's Intergovernmental Oceanographic Commission and JCOMMOPS; Dr Richard Kirby of Plymouth University's Secchi Disk programme; Diana Doyle of SeaBC Sea Bird Count; and Emily Penn and the 5 Gyres Institute who've done so much to raise awareness of the plastic pollution in our ocean. I'm grateful for the support Nera and Dan received from their school, Rednock in Dursley, and headteacher Dave Alexander for allowing them to undertake this adventure. Thank you to the officers and my fellow alliance councillors at Stroud District Council: together we have done our best to make a difference in the creep towards net zero. A heart-felt thanks to Megan Sheer for your brilliant design of this book. A huge thank you to my comrades, trade unionists and campaigners, in my own town of Dursley, and beyond, for your fierce politics and principles, and for all your support. Of all the many people who have raised my awareness of climate change and environmental issues, I'd like to thank two who have been especially inspiring in my life, Paul Denney and Julie Douglass. And of course, my beloved children Nera and Dan, such bright sparks of light in the world – what more could a mother wish for? My parents Gwenda and Jimmy, who made all this possible: I don't have enough words to express my love and gratitude to you both. And above all, thank you Tim, for your support, love and companionship these last few years.

ILLUSTRATION CREDITS

All photos by Doina and Jimmy Cornell unless otherwise stated. Thank you to the following for use of their photographs: the yacht Suilven (84), Emily Penn (131), sailing yacht *Fleur de Sel* (144-45), crew of the sailing yacht *Om* (151), sailing yacht *Libby* (152), Zeke Holland (218), Klaudia Zayonc (246). Credits for other images are as follows: by permission of the British Library Board G.7399 plate opposite page 46 (48); Sir William Parry's *Journal of a second voyage for the discovery of a north-west passage from the Atlantic to the Pacific;* accessed online on the Internet Archive (51); National Snow and Ice Data Center (54); Canadian Ice Service (56); Secchi Disk study (71 and 73); *Ulysses and Diomed swathed in the same Flame* (1824-1827), William Blake, by permission of the National Gallery of Victoria, Melbourne, Felton Bequest, 1920 (116); *Seated Figure*, Rockwell Kent. Purchased with the Lola Downin Peck Fund from the Carl and Laura Zigrosser Collection, 1971, 1971-2-421, Philadelphia Museum of Art (141); the Atlantic Oceanographic and Meteorological Laboratory (150 and 151); NOAA, accessed at https://twitter.com/NOAASatellites/status/576435085773303808 (156); material from Tuvaluan government TC Pam exhibition and High Level Dialogue (211 and 212); *World Cruising Routes* by Jimmy Cornell (220); Black Stone by Grace Mera Molisa, accessed online (224).

FURTHER READING

CLIMATE CRISIS / OCEAN

Being Ecological – Timothy Morton
Learning to Die: Wisdom in the Age of Climate Crisis – Robert Bringhurst and Jan Zwicky
Ocean of Life – Callum Roberts
Our Threatened Oceans – Stefan Rahmstorf and Katherine Richardson
The Sea Around Us – Rachel Carson

ARCTIC

A Naturalist's Guide to the Arctic – E.C. Pielou
Arctic Labyrinth – Glyn Williams
Arctic Voices: Resistance at the tipping point – edited by Subhankar Banerjee
Encounters on the passage: Inuit meet the explorers – Dorothy Harley Eber
N by E – Rockwell Kent
The Search for the Northwest Passage – Ann Savours
The New Northwest Passage – Cameron Dueck

PACIFIC

A History of the Pacific Islands – Steven Roger Fischer
Oceania: Neocolonialism, Nukes and Bones – André Vltchek
Pacific Odyssey – Gwenda Cornell
Pacific Worlds – Matt K. Matsuda
Prayers Written at Vailima – Robert Louis Stevenson
We are the Ocean – Epeli Hau'ofa

PLAYLIST (ON SPOTIFY)

Black Butterfly – Tio
The Ocean – Against Me
Ocean – Anna von Hausswolf
How Big, How Blue, How Beautiful – Florence + The Machine
Into the West – Annie Lennox
Manta Ray – J Ralph, Anohni
The Blue Sea Says Yes – Robb Johnson & The Irregulars
Storm to Weather – Grace Petrie
The Stolen Child – The Waterboys
Where I Go – Gale Mead
Mai Anamua – Olivia Foa'i
Iceberg – Lemur
Sea Ice – Stormfield